RENEWALS 458-4574
DATE DUE

DE[

WITHDRAWN
UTSA LIBRARIES

Metropolitan Communities

TRADE GUILDS, IDENTITY, AND
CHANGE IN EARLY MODERN LONDON

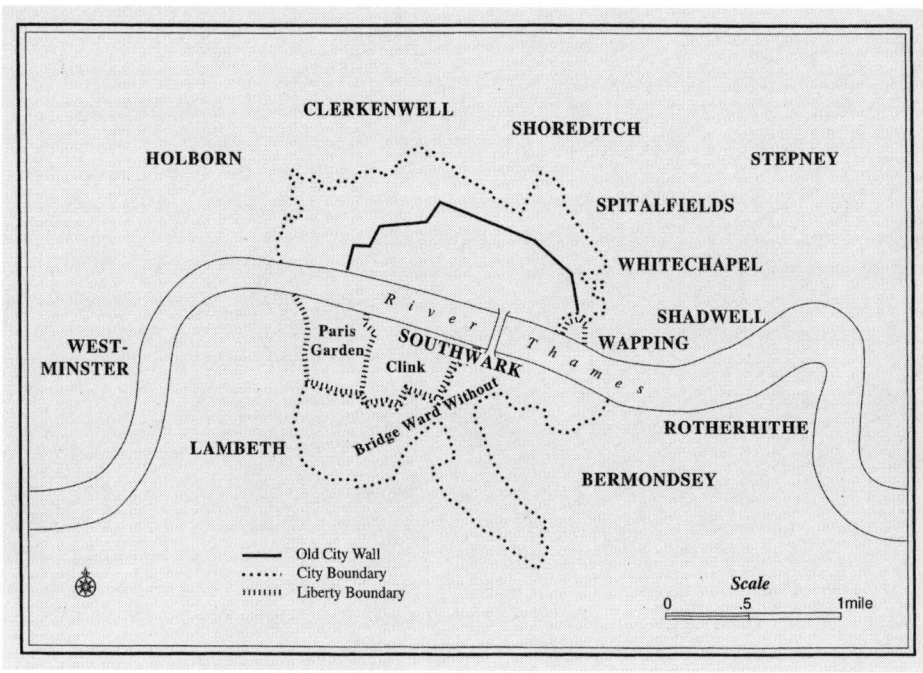

Principal features of seventeenth-century London.
Cartography by Douglas Towns.

JOSEPH P. WARD

Metropolitan Communities

TRADE GUILDS,
IDENTITY, AND
CHANGE IN
EARLY MODERN
LONDON

STANFORD UNIVERSITY PRESS
STANFORD, CALIFORNIA
1997

Published with the assistance of Wayne State University

Stanford University Press
Stanford, California
© 1997 by the Board of Trustees of the
Leland Stanford Junior University
Printed in the United States of America

CIP data are at the back of the book

Preface

During the past decade, I have had the good fortune to live in or near Chicago, San Francisco, London, and Detroit. With each move I had to find my place in a new setting, striving—and sometimes failing—to make the transition from "stranger" to "local." This experience doubtless accounts for much of my interest in the relationship between identity and community in urban settings. While analyzing the consequences of metropolitan London's early modern development, I have been reminded constantly that they are accessible to us only through archival records produced in a distinctive historical context. Still, I hope my findings will be useful to those addressing similar problems in different places and time periods than the one I have studied, for I would like this book to contribute to the multidisciplinary investigation of the cultural consequences of social and economic change.

My bibliography lists those works that have had the greatest influence on my current thinking. Academic publishing is not always the most efficient means for sharing one's ideas with others. The latest available work related to my topic is Richard Grassby's *The Business Community of Seventeenth-Century England*, which I acquired just as I was completing final revisions. I have incorporated its findings as best I could.

I would like to thank those organizations and individuals who offered the most assistance to this project. The Mellon Fellowships in the Humanities, Stanford University, and Wayne State University provided the financial resources to carry this project from inception to publication, and I am grateful to their respective administrators. Everyone at the Guildhall Library in London, where I carried out most of my research for this book, provided me with far more than a steady stream of manuscripts and books; I will always be in their debt. I also wish to thank the staffs of the Corporation of London Record Office, the Public Record Office, the British Library, the Clothworkers' Company, the Drapers' Company, the Goldsmiths' Company, the Mercers' Company, the Salters' Company, the Skinners' Company, the Institute of Historical Research, the Stanford University Libraries, the Wayne State University Libraries, and the libraries of the University of Michigan, Ann Arbor. The staff at Stanford University Press—especially Norris Pope, Laura Bloch, and Barbara Phillips—has also assisted me greatly.

Over the past few years I have benefited from the kindness of many friends and colleagues. Mark Kishlansky encouraged my nascent interest in early modern British history. He also introduced me to Paul Seaver, who has offered counsel at every stage of this project; no apprentice could have a more patient master. Vanessa Harding, Bob Tittler, and Muriel McClendon read earlier drafts of the manuscript and provided many insightful suggestions for revision. I have learned a great deal from conversations with many scholars, and here I wish principally to thank Bob Shoemaker, Wendy Bracewell, and Tim Meldrum, as well as Ian Archer, Caroline Barron, Mike Berlin, Clive Burgess, Monica Chojnacka, Trish Crawford, Jim Epstein, Jeff Fear, Tim Hitchcock, Mark Jenner, Derek Keene, Julia Merritt, James Robertson, Lyndal Roper, Kirsten Seaver, and Tim Wales. The faculty, staff, and students of Wayne State University have supported me and my work, and I want to thank particularly Chris Johnson, Marc Kruman, Sam Scott, Sandra VanBurkleo, Donna Landry, and Gerald MacLean for their advice, and Douglas Towns for drawing the map of greater London.

I am also grateful to the members of my family for all of their help. My parents—Aline Ward and the late Charles Ward—and my siblings indulged my interest in cities great and small for many years. My principal debt is to Sue Grayzel, colleague for better and for worse, who has helped me in countless ways while I completed this project. I look forward to returning the favor, and I dedicate this book to her.

Contents

INTRODUCTION.	Situating Identity	1
1.	Imagining a Metropolitan Community	7
2.	Livery Companies and the Metropolis	27
3.	Companies and Callings: The Diversity of Experience	45
4.	Communication and Company Politics	73
5.	Religion, Economics, and Tolerance in the Grocers' Company	99
6.	Economic Competition and Politics in the Weavers' Company	125
CONCLUSION.	Metropolitan Communities	144
	NOTES	149
	BIBLIOGRAPHY	177
	INDEX	195

I am a handicraftsman, yet my heart is without craft.
—Dekker, *The Shoemaker's Holiday*

Metropolitan Communities

TRADE GUILDS, IDENTITY, AND
CHANGE IN EARLY MODERN LONDON

INTRODUCTION

Situating Identity

Modern attempts to classify forms of human affiliation have ancient roots. Such disparate thinkers as Confucius, Plato, and Augustine devised models that presaged the work of social scientists during the final decades of the nineteenth century. Writing when industrialism and nationalism appeared to threaten communities—localized associations such as trade guilds, neighborhoods, and parishes—modern theorists like Ferdinand Tönnies traced the characteristics of affiliations since the medieval period in order to better chart their future course. Tönnies employed two heuristic types of association, translated loosely as "community" (*Gemeinschaft*) and "society" (*Gesellschaft*), to facilitate his analysis of change over time. For Tönnies, an important difference between the types of association was the degree of personal interaction among their members, with communities requiring significant amounts of face-to-face contact among participants while societies could contain members who were largely unknown to one another. Although his model implied that the ties of community were generally stronger in medieval than in modern times, when society became the dominant form of association, Tönnies insisted that the two types of association could coexist. More recently, scholars have decreased the significance of locality in their models by viewing communities as flexible groups marked by ties of allegiance and affection rather than physical proxim-

---

Throughout this book, spellings have been altered in most quotations to make their meanings more apparent to a modern reader, but the titles of texts have been left in their original form. Dates are given according to the old-style calendar, except that the year has been taken to begin on January 1 instead of March 25.

ity, a trend that has minimized further the distinctions between the premodern and modern eras.[1]

London and its trade guilds from the sixteenth to the eighteenth century provide a useful setting for analyzing developments often considered disruptive for communities. During this "early modern" period, the population of greater London nearly quintupled, surpassing 500,000 by the year 1700, by which time it was the largest metropolis in Europe.[2] Although such expansion reflected London's relative economic prosperity, it was accompanied by disease, poverty, and fluctuating food supplies. Contemporary critics often attributed the consequences of rapid growth to inadequate government immigration policies. In particular, they accused the City's trade guilds—known as "livery companies"—of failing to restrict participation in London's economy to those who contributed to the costs of its government. In their own defense, companies complained of their limited authority over the suburbs and liberties that were outside the lord mayor's jurisdiction, areas that experienced especially rapid development in the early modern period.[3] They also criticized the Crown's policy of encouraging Huguenots and other immigrant groups to live and work in London. As a result, many early modern Londoners believed that their governors were either unwilling or unable to protect their values and interests.[4]

Recent research on early modern London also has emphasized the distinctions between the City of London and its suburbs and liberties while highlighting the clash of values between company members and immigrants. Historians such as Steve Rappaport and Valerie Pearl who have analyzed London's political stability have contrasted the unruly suburbs and liberties with the well-governed City. Rappaport and Pearl have each argued that up to three-fourths of adult men in the City belonged to companies, and thereby were citizens—or "freemen"—of London, who participated in a variety of ways in the management of the City's economic, religious, and civic affairs. Such company members felt threatened by noncitizens, such as native English "foreigners" and "strangers" from other nations, who lived and worked in greater London but avoided responsibility for its government.[5]

Similarly, historians of Renaissance drama have stressed the cultural differences between the City and its suburbs and liberties. Literary critics have often held that the late sixteenth and early seventeenth centuries, the first era of great public theater in metropolitan London, was a period of profound economic and social dislocation.[6] Jean-Christophe Agnew and Steven Mullaney each assumed that, because the City's governors dissented from the Crown's support of theater, dramatists were forced to join noncitizens in seeking refuge beyond the lord mayor's reach in the suburbs and liberties. The combined economic and cultural freedoms of the suburbs and liberties in turn enriched the context of Renaissance drama. As Londoners struggled to adjust to the decline of traditional economic institutions, such as trade guilds, theater offered them a way to experiment with new forms of representation appropriate to emerging market relations.[7]

All these arguments support the notion that economic and social expansion divided the metropolis into two camps: the traditional City of London and its relatively novel suburbs and liberties. In their assumption that the influence of the City's trade guilds was confined largely to the City itself, such views are consistent with the notion that, in Tönnies's terms, guilds and their members were the defenders of traditional ideas of community in London, but the immigrants who flocked to the suburbs and liberties were the vanguard of a more modern society. It seems, then, that the civic boundary of sixteenth- and seventeenth-century London marked the front in the struggle between the premodern and modern worlds.[8]

This book reconsiders that view of early modern London. It focuses on London's trade guilds because their presumed inflexibility has been an essential ingredient in many recent interpretations of early modern metropolitan expansion. Taking a cue from research on continental European towns, this book reveals the ability of London's livery companies to evolve in response to economic and social change.[9] Rather than being swept aside by developments, the companies adapted to them and, to a great extent, helped to shape their courses. As contemporaries noted, the rapid growth of the metropolis seemed to encourage the propagation of new attitudes and behaviors that had important consequences for trade guilds. Although Ian Archer has displayed the limited cohesiveness of guilds in Elizabethan London, interpretations of early modern London's companies generally have evaluated them according to the degree to which their members maintained a common ethos.[10] Here, greater weight will be placed on the acceptance by livery company officers of the diversity of their members' goals and values throughout the sixteenth and seventeenth centuries. Guilds, like other types of community, could not simply provide an ethos to their members. Instead, members continually had to determine how strongly they would adhere to their officers' visions of their common goals. At the same time, guild members could also have belonged to other communities—such as parishes and neighborhoods—whose values may have differed from those of livery companies.[11] This process of selectively giving and withholding allegiance was essential to the formation of an individual's identity.[12]

The analysis of the construction of identity in early modern London's trade guilds begins in the first chapter, with an examination of the ideological significance of territory in the metropolis. Moralists assumed that ministers and magistrates would cooperate in maintaining godly discipline throughout their community. The overlapping civic and ecclesiastical jurisdictions in metropolitan London may have impeded such cooperation, but they prevented any areas of the metropolis from being ungoverned. Furthermore, even those who criticized the relative licentiousness of the suburbs and liberties understood that, along with the City, they were integral parts of the metropolis. As greater London's population steadily increased, those who sought to reform its government were forced to develop metropolitan-wide solutions.

Most significantly, livery companies were metropolitan by nature. Historians have often noted that guild charters empowered their officers to regulate their respective trades throughout the metropolis, but they have downplayed company activities beyond the City's borders. The second chapter therefore draws upon the records of guilds in the retailing, manufacturing, and building trades in order to demonstrate that companies often exercised their metropolitan-wide mandates. These sources also indicate that company members, including some officers, lived and worked in suburban areas as well as in the City itself. Rather than symbolizing the disintegration of metropolitan society, the administration of livery company government provided Londoners with a way of imagining, and realizing, that they could be members of communities that were metropolitan in nature. This also suggests that, contrary to much historiography of early modern English trade guilds, economic development did not necessarily threaten company members.[13]

Nevertheless, as metropolitan institutions livery companies had to cope with the problems that accompanied London's growth and attracted the criticism of contemporaries. Companies often cited their efforts to protect the "honest callings" of their members against the encroachment of noncitizens by restricting participation in their trades to those who were skillful in them. Nevertheless, Chapter 3 argues that guild members did not always exercise the trades associated with their companies, and they were as capable as anyone of incompetence and deceit. In addition to taking advantage of the custom whereby a member of a livery company could work in any trade in the City, the willingness of poorer company members to occupy menial posts such as porters for their former colleagues displayed the complexity of ideas of vocation circulating within the livery companies.

The diversity of company members' attitudes toward their crafts may have indicated their lack of consensus, but this was only one potential source of division within guilds. Historians have often characterized the company governments as oligarchies of wealthy merchants who were out of touch with the interests of most members. However, the fourth chapter here demonstrates that company officers were not always unified. On some occasions, factions within the elite would side with the broader membership, complicating assumptions about the connection of rank and identity within guilds. The high turnover rate among officers also disrupted the continuity of policy. Because much of the communication among members was carried out in writing, companies had permanent staffs of clerks and beadles to manage their information. In addition to formalizing the interaction of members across company ranks, such bureaucratization of company affairs encouraged some staff members to promote their own private interests above those of their companies.

The remaining two chapters each interpret the ways in which members of individual livery companies dealt with the problems posed by their diverse attitudes, interests, and experiences. The first analyzes the construction of loyalty in the Grocers' Company, a wealthy and politically powerful guild, from the Reformation to the Restoration. The company's records reveal that religion and economics were both sources of tension among grocers, and that the most important causes of conflict were controversies among company members rather than between members and nonmembers. In response, the company's officers appealed to their members' sense of loyalty and tradition, often employing the language of the family to remind them that their common heritage could not be taken for granted. The company's commemorative rituals indicated that there was more to the officers' appeal than custom. The challenge here is to determine the extent to which the image of the company that appears in its records reflected the views of its members more generally.

The next chapter focuses on the Weavers' Company, a guild quite unlike the Grocers' Company, from the late sixteenth to the early eighteenth century. From the arrival of the Huguenots to the revocation of the Edict of Nantes, religion, work, and identity were the major issues driving the company's affairs. Contemporaries and historians have generally concluded that the early modern Weavers' Company was an especially troubled organization flooded by refugees during Elizabeth's reign and subsequently divided by the battles between artisan freemen and their retailing governors. However, instead of emphasizing economic conflict, the chapter explores the motivations of those who joined an apparently poorly run company. Surely, everyone in London must have known that the company's officers took bribes from strangers and from apprentices who were eager to be freed before their time. Why, then, did company members continually fight to uphold their regulations?

Many Londoners defended companies because they lent stability to their lives, and to the lives of their spouses and children, during a period of considerable economic, social, and cultural change. The extent to which Londoners considered companies to be meaningful associations—and therefore sources of community—depended largely on how closely they chose to identify themselves and their interests with their guild's. Such choices were constrained by many factors, including age, class, and gender, but none of these was strictly determinative. Officers often had to contribute large amounts of their time and money to support their companies, though not everyone who had such resources agreed to hold company office. And although women were discouraged from participating in company affairs, some nonetheless served apprenticeships with company members, gained their freedom, and paid their dues throughout their careers.[14]

For these reasons, despite the emphasis of both contemporary commentary and modern historiography on the divisions between groups in early modern London, this book relocates the site of contention within individuals. Most Londoners belonged to a variety of associations, but the extent to which they identified *with* these groups, as opposed to being merely identified *by* them, remained largely a matter of individual choice. It would be impossible to reach any precise conclusions about Londoners' loyalty or ambivalence toward their guilds. This book instead exposes the range of ideas of community within the guilds in order to argue that while some citizens considered immigrant settlers in the suburbs and liberties a threat to their values and livelihoods, their more pressing challenge was the diversity of attitudes within their guilds and within themselves.

CHAPTER I

Imagining a Metropolitan Community

Historians have long assumed that territorial expansion undermined ideas of community in early modern London. The metropolis grew steadily during the sixteenth and seventeenth centuries, forming a conurbation along both banks of the Thames and enhancing the complexity and interrelation of areas both within and beyond the lord mayor's control. While some neighborhoods were wealthier than others, every section of the metropolis contained a blend of rich and poor.[1] Nevertheless, historians such as Valerie Pearl and A. L. Beier have emphasized the social differentiation of the City of London from its suburbs and liberties. Pearl found that the "expanding, turbulent liberties and suburbs" were "often radical and socially inferior" to the City of London, and Beier asserted that suburban London was "another world" that "presented a sharp contrast to the well-ordered world of merchants and professional men within" the City.[2]

Historians of drama in Renaissance London have embraced such findings. In her study of Ben Jonson's plays, Susan Wells concluded the City's ideology was "visibly at odds with its real structure" because the growth of suburbs and liberties "placed most of the new crafts and industry in the city outside the purview of traditional regulation." And in his analysis of the market and the theater in Anglo-American thought, Jean-Christophe Agnew observed that playhouses were located in the suburbs and liberties of London, places that constituted a "new extraterritorial zone of production and exchange . . . outside London's ancient marketplaces and thus out of reach of their juridical, ceremonial, and talismanic protection—and restrictions." Following Agnew's lead, Steven Mullaney's interpretation of Elizabethan and Jacobean drama relied on the assumption that London's ministers and magistrates considered the suburbs and liberties a "discomfiting and anamorphic scene," an area suitable for leprosariums, cemeteries, places of execution, and playhouses. In contrast to the City, London's liberties fostered cultural change because they were "privileged or exempt arenas where the anxieties and insecurities of life in a rigidly organized hierarchical society could be given relatively free reign." Recent works by Jean Howard and Lawrence Manley have endorsed this approach to the relationship between the City of London and the rest of the metropolis.[3]

Religious controversy amplified the divisive influence of social and economic change on ideas of community in London. Patrick Collinson has argued that although the Reformation had the potential to transform England into a godly nation under the direction of a godly prince, the short-term effect was "separation and confusion." Susan Brigden's research on London supports Collinson's view. She recently suggested that Londoners' common beliefs and practices had enhanced their sense of community prior to the Reformation, but by the outset of Queen Elizabeth's reign their "world of shared faith was broken . . . and the Christian community divided."[4]

Although religious change sparked controversy among Londoners, reformers continued to encourage them to consider the metropolis an integrated moral community. After discussing the working relationships among the various governments of greater London, this chapter analyzes the variety of ideas of community in London by interpreting sermons and pamphlets that addressed the moral condition of the early modern metropolis. Many authors were concerned about the playhouses and other alleged sources of immorality in the suburbs and liberties, but they also addressed the theological implications of a broader range of activities within and without the lord mayor's jurisdiction. In particular, as Londoners searched for the causes of metropolitan expansion, they became increasingly aware of the relationship between economic and demographic changes. While moralists hoped that the reformation of behavior would improve the material conditions of life in the metropolis, politicians claimed that regulating the metropolitan population would ensure the prosperity of Londoners. Such attempts at reform forced early modern Londoners to acknowledge the suburbs and liberties as integral parts of their communities.

The Jurisdiction of Providence

The City of London was the largest corporate entity in the metropolis. Livery companies conveyed London citizenship—as well as the "freedom" to work in the City—to their members, who joined the guilds through apprenticeship, patrimony, or purchase. Citizens participated in City politics through their wards, the 26 territorial subdivisions of the City. In their wards, citizens selected representatives to the Court of Common Council, the City's main legislative body, and to the Court of Aldermen, the City's executive. London's members of Parliament and the lord mayor were chosen in the Court of Common Hall by liverymen, who typically were among the more senior members of companies. The lord mayor and senior aldermen were justices of the peace in the City, and after 1638, four aldermen also served as J.P.s in the neighboring counties of Middlesex and Surrey.[5]

The lord mayor's jurisdiction covered an area that extended beyond the City's ancient wall. The expression "suburbs of London" sometimes referred to those areas between the walls but within the bars that marked the civic boundary. In 1608, a Court of Chancery suit concerning a playhouse in Whitefriars described Fleet Street as being "in the suburbs of London," although Fleet Street was within Temple Bar.[6] To avoid confusion, in this discussion such areas will be referred to either as "London between the wall and the bars" or "the extramural parts of the City"; "suburbs" will refer to those areas adjacent to the City's outer perimeter and beyond the lord mayor's jurisdiction.

London's suburbs fell within a variety of jurisdictions. To the north of Moorgate lay Moorfields and Finsbury, two manors that the City purchased and that its officers continued to regulate as manors.[7] Other areas north of the River Thames fell within the County of Middlesex. After 1585, Westminster was a borough under the direction of a high steward who was appointed by the Dean and Chapter of Westminster. The steward chose twelve burgesses and twelve assistants to oversee the borough's twelve wards. Nevertheless, Middlesex J.P.s continued to have jurisdiction over Westminster.[8] Along the south bank of the Thames lay Southwark. The City government had long controlled the area immediately beyond London Bridge, but it acquired additional Southwark manors in 1557, which it incorporated into Bridge Ward Without. London's remaining southern suburbs fell under the purview of the Surrey J.P.s.[9]

The metropolis also contained a variety of "liberties," administrative units whose relationship to the Crown was distinct from that of boroughs or counties. They included former monastic lands—such as Blackfriars, Whitefriars, Holywell Priory, and Paris Garden—and the Inns of Court and Chancery. The Crown was the source of the liberties' privileges, and what it could give, it could take away. The City's charter of 1608, which extended its officers' influence by appointing several

City officials to serve as J.P.s in six of London's liberties, was an important indication of the constraints on the alleged licentiousness of liberties.[10]

In more routine matters, residents of liberties were the subjects of governors who cooperated with the Crown in maintaining order within their precincts. In 1593, the constable and headboroughs of the liberty of St. Martin le Grand requested that the Privy Council enhance their ability to enforce law. They reported that some of those whom they arrested claimed to be immune from punishments enacted outside the liberty, and so they requested permission to build their own jail. This case suggested that there were limits to the effectiveness of law enforcement in liberties, but it also revealed that the residents of such places could themselves take steps to improve the situation. Further, the precinct's officers acknowledged the right of the lord mayor and his officers to inspect economic activity within their jurisdiction, although they pointed out that all goods confiscated in such searches should go to the benefit of the liberty.[11]

The administration of ecclesiastical law in the metropolis was similarly complex. The residents of greater London north of the Thames lived in the Diocese of London and were subject to the discipline of their bishop's many courts. Although the bishop's consistory court supervised the activities of all the other courts in the diocese, the jurisdictions of the inferior courts—such as the archdeaconries of London and Middlesex—encroached upon one another. Nevertheless, Richard Wunderli's study of London's ecclesiastical courts prior to the Reformation indicated that their case loads were all too heavy to justify jurisdictional squabbles. Although his court officers may have struggled to cope with metropolitan growth, Bishop John King took a holistic view of greater London. In an effort to encourage James I to renovate St. Paul's Cathedral in 1620, the bishop asked the king to consider several buildings and institutions throughout the City and its liberties—such as the Royal Exchange, livery company halls, and hospitals for the poor—proof that London was an "Augustious and majestical city" fit for a great cathedral.[12] London's southern suburbs fell within the Diocese of Winchester. The ownership of the Clink Liberty, home of some of London's more notorious brothels, by the bishops of Winchester was a source of frequent controversy for moralists.[13]

However, for London to have coalesced as a metropolis, its many governors had to cooperate. Crime was one key test of such cooperation because the existence of an exempt area in the metropolis would have undermined law enforcement throughout the whole region. In practice as well as in theory, the suburbs and liberties of London proved not to have been lawless. City J.P.s had the right to pursue felons into London's liberties, and while the enforcement of statutes in the counties around London may not have been as efficient as it was in the City, there is considerable evidence that suburban J.P.s enforced laws concerning activities as varied as apprenticeship and prostitution.[14] And although riots, in their complexity and mobility, posed a particular threat to magistrates, Keith Lindley has shown that metropolitan governors had the potential to cope with them.[15]

Social problems also demanded metropolitan-wide solutions. The City government played a role in this effort by redistributing the proceeds of the poor rates of wealthy City parishes to poorer ones, many of which were outside the City wall.[16] London's hospitals had an even longer reach. Christ's Hospital accepted orphans, sent them to nurse, and assigned them to serve apprenticeships throughout greater London.[17] Individual charitable bequests buttressed this approach. For instance, in 1584, Steven Skidmore established a poor relief fund in the Vintners' Company that offered charity to parishes across the metropolis, from Clerkenwell in the north to Bermondsey in the south.[18] Like poverty, disease solidified the contemporary understanding of the interrelation of the City of London and its suburbs and liberties.[19] In particular, the weekly Bills of Mortality employed parish officers from across the metropolis to track the progress of disease. By the early seventeenth century, the Bills covered an area that included sixteen parishes that lay between the City's wall and its bars, as well as eight parishes in the suburbs.[20]

For early modern Londoners, disasters such as plagues were warnings of divine displeasure.[21] In 1577, John Northbrooke warned his readers that their immorality would bring upon England the sort of divine punishment that had destroyed Sodom and other biblical lands. He therefore urged ministers and magistrates to cooperate in leading their dissolute subjects back to godliness. "I doubt not," Northbrooke asserted, "but God will so move the hearts of magistrates, and loose the tongues of preachers in such godly sort ... that both with the sword and the word such unfruitful and barren trees should be cut down."[22] Elizabethan moralists frequently complained of plays and other forms of popular entertainment in metropolitan London.[23] In 1577, in a sermon delivered at Paul's Cross, Thomas White argued that "the cause of plagues is sin, if you look to it well, and the cause of sin are plays; therefore the cause of plagues are plays." White warned the City magistrates that unless God "should rent asunder the very heavens, and break the clouds, and come down himself to visit, I think we are at a point for all other visitations." He concluded by challenging London's governors to "thrust diligently your sword of justice in, to lance out all corruptions and baggage which is gathered in the bowels. . . . God has a work to do by you, do not the Lord's work negligently, for fear of a curse."[24]

Two years later, Stephen Gossen directed his attack on poets, pipers, players, and jesters at the young men of the Inns of Court and Chancery, which were located in liberties between the walls and bars of the City. He dedicated his book to Sir Richard Pipes, the lord mayor of London. Gossen based much of his argument on classical sources, and sought to persuade his readers that plays, gambling, and other forms of entertainment would bring ruin upon them. Despite his appeal to individual interest, Gossen expected governors to lead their subjects to reform. In a postscript, he asserted that "I doubt not but the governors of London will vex me for speaking my mind, when they are out of their wits, and banish their players when they are best advised." In conclusion, he said, if Lord Mayor Pipes wished the City to be well governed, he personally had to "thrust out abuses" and not merely allow others to pursue reform.[25]

This critical view of governors inspired George Whetstone's *Mirour for Magistrates*. Dedicated to Lord Mayor Osborne, Recorder Fleetwood, and the aldermen of London, Whetstone's *Mirour* reminded the City's elite that while scriptural authority gave magistrates "the names and places of gods," other citizens could "discover the mischief the magistrate sees not, but the magistrates alone must remedy the same." Whetstone then appealed to the City governors to be more diligent in stamping out vice and corruption, suggesting it was miraculous "that this city is not always grievously afflicted with the plague, when sacred is the authority that says, 'the plague shall not depart the house of the swearer.'"[26]

Some writers identified the suburbs as the cause of God's displeasure with London. Thomas Dekker's *The Wonderful Year*, a discussion of the plague of 1603, compared death to "a Spanish Leaguer, or rather like stalking Tamberlain" who pitched his tents in the "sinfully polluted suburbs" of London. According to Dekker, as the plague progressed across the suburbs "the skirts of London were pitifully pared off, by little and little." In another response to that same outbreak, Richard Milton argued that God introduced the plague into the suburbs so "that the City itself seeing the rod so near, should fear betimes." He argued that God may have sent the plague to the suburbs as a warning to City residents, but God's action was prompted by "the excessive abominations of filthiness practiced in those places, more than the rest of the City." Milton suggested that the metropolis was an integrated system in which "all the superfluity of extremities, are by the power of a vegetative heat, wrought to the extremity of the body." As a result of the good government of the City, the "filthy froth of sensual beastliness" was "expelled from the inner part, and as I may say, the heart of the City" and into "the utmost skirts and appendant members thereunto." For Milton, the City was not without its problems, but the direction of the plague's progress made it evident that the suburbs were "a fit matter for the first burning of God's revengeful wrath."[27] In that way, the City would continue to suffer until the suburbs were reformed.

Despite such admonitions, other Londoners were hesitant to blame the suburbs for provoking God's wrath. In a series of pamphlets inspired by the plague of 1603, Henoch Clapham warned Londoners of the epidemic's spiritual causes, and counseled them that fleeing into the countryside would do them little good because God would find the sinners wherever they ran. Unlike Dekker and Milton, Clapham refused to attribute the plague to the corruption of any specific area within the metropolis, choosing instead to argue that "we have sinned together, and the hand of God hath come upon us together: let us therefore humble ourselves together before our Lord in fasting and prayer.... It is not a change of place, but [a] change of life that must help us."[28] In a Paul's Cross sermon responding to a plague outbreak in 1636, John Squire—the vicar of St. Leonard Shoreditch, a Middlesex parish adjacent to the City's boundaries—spoke favorably of the theological integrity of metropolitan London. Squire, who referred to the Bills of Mortality in his presentation, noted that during the epidemic more than a thousand people died each week in greater London, but he added that the cause of the plague's retreat had been the prayer and fasting of "all the assemblies in the city and suburbs."[29]

Another tract motivated by the plague of 1636, Henry Burton's *A Divine Tragedy Lately Acted*, also blurred the distinction between the City and the suburbs.[30] The *Tragedy* contained more than 50 tales of divine punishment for Sabbath-breaking from across England. Although several examples included Londoners, Burton did not distinguish between those who lived in the City of London and those who lived in its suburbs and liberties. One telling case involved a maid of St. Giles Cripplegate who was married to a widower on a Sunday in 1636. Burton reported that the couple spent the entire afternoon dancing, and one week later the plague appeared in their house, mortally infecting the couple as well as the groom's two children from his previous marriage, and soon spread throughout the parish.[31] Although St. Giles was a parish that straddled the City's boundary, the *Tragedy* did not bother to comment on the ethical significance of terrain in metropolitan London.

Some authors warned that divine punishment could target the City itself. In *Christs Teares over Jerusalem* (1593), Thomas Nashe advised Londoners that they risked a destruction of biblical proportions for their sins. Proclaiming, "London, what are thy suburbs but licensed stewes," Nashe was also quick to implicate all Londoners in the selfishness, pursuit of fashion, and deceit that tempted God's displeasure. When he called London "the Sea that sucks in all the scummy channels of the Realm" and warned that unless London altered its ways it would share the fate of Jerusalem and Sodom, Nashe referred to the entire metropolis, not just the suburbs.[32] Londoners' general awareness of the City's sinfulness is apparent in the writings of turner Nehemiah Wallington in the early seventeenth century. From his home in the City, he had an excellent view of the efforts to extinguish a fire that destroyed much of London Bridge in February 1633. According to Wallington, the fire was "the will of God" reminding Londoners of the punishment Jerusalem received for violating the Sabbath.[33] Later, the author of a tract inspired by the plague outbreak of 1641 warned Londoners that the pestilence was the product of "the multitude of our sins." The author suggested that in response London should "put on thy mourning garment, that thy neighbors round about thee may . . . commiserate thee in this thy affliction." While unclear about the identity of London's "neighbors," he suggested the metropolis was united by sin and affliction and looked to the rest of the country for help.[34]

Interpretations of disasters later in the century continued to downplay any moral differences between the City and its suburbs and liberties. In 1665, astrologer John Gadbury attributed that year's plague outbreak to God's displeasure with the sins of Londoners, and he warned them that there could be no escape from God's hand: "I believe that the Plague is sent, not so much to afflict the City, as the citizens; the Houses, as the owners of them." The author E.N. concurred in two poems published that year. One offered counsel to "the willful, wicked, and woeful City of London," and the other cautioned those who planned to escape the plague by fleeing into the country:

> Now therefore hark, ye Gallants of the time,
> You that have counted Godliness a Crime,
> What do you think, or where do y' mean to stay,
> That you from London make such haste away?
> Hear this from me; If you take along
> Your sins with you, you do yourselves but wrong
> To flee away, for you had better be
> Punish'd at first, than to go longer free.

Like Gadbury, E.N. considered the sins of Londoners in general, and not those of any particular part of the metropolis, the cause of God's anger.[35]

Imagining a Metropolitan Community

In a more forceful manner, the Great Fire of 1666 called attention to the character of the City itself. The Fire consumed most of London within the City wall, and much of the area to the west as well, destroying several liberties along the way. In his post-Fire sermon, William Sandcroft, Dean of St. Paul's, began by discussing the destruction of biblical cities and comparing London's experience to "the burning of Jerusalem by Nebuchadnezzar or Titus or (as some will have it) by both." Fearing the violence of scapegoat-seeking Fire victims, Sandcroft counseled that although some might wish to determine the "particular sins" that had provoked divine punishment, it was evident that God had passed judgment "upon us All, as an Evidence of his Displeasure for our Sins in general." Robert Elborough supported Sandcroft's argument regarding the nature of the disaster, but went farther than Sandcroft in pointing to the City as the target of God's anger: "Now this and such Fire God threatens to kindle, and that in thee, not about thee, but in thee; not in the skirts, but in the heart." Elborough's metaphors were similar to those employed throughout the discourse of territory and morality in early modern London; his use of "skirts" for the suburbs and "heart" for the City echoed the works of Thomas Dekker and Richard Milton from more than 60 years earlier. But by utilizing that familiar language to isolate the City as the source of "abomination," Elborough brought the discourse full circle.[36] For many Londoners, the Great Fire ended any assurance that the City was immune to the consequences of immorality that, they may have hoped, were confined to the suburbs.

London's magistrates had often heeded such warnings. In 1574, shortly after a plague outbreak had subsided, the lord mayor and aldermen outlawed the production of plays containing "any words, examples, or doings or any unchastity, sedition, nor such like unfit, and any uncomely matter" in order to keep "the people, especially the meaner and most unruly sort" from forgetting "the fear of God's wrath."[37] By adopting this policy, London's governors may have been offering their own interpretation of a royal proclamation of 1559, which commanded all magistrates to prohibit the performance of plays dealing with religion or politics because such subjects were fit only for "men of authority, learning, and wisdom."[38]

Local governors may have taken the queen's order as an invitation to discourage the public performance of a wide variety of plays, but her actions spoke louder than her words. Privately, Elizabeth considered all but politically indiscreet plays to be proper entertainment, so long as they were not performed on the Sabbath or at other times of prayer, and did not draw together crowds during outbreaks of contagion. As a result, Elizabeth's patronage—either direct or indirect—was instrumental to the dramatic theater during her reign. The first public playhouse in the metropolis opened in 1576 in London's northern suburbs, where its sponsors expected a reception consistent with Elizabeth's personal views.[39]

City magistrates maintained their criticism of public playhouses despite the Crown's continued support of them. In 1580, the lord mayor asked the Privy Council to suppress playhouses located throughout the metropolis because they attracted citizens and their families over whom he held authority.[40] Two years later, the City government passed a law that was more restrictive than its ordinance of 1574 had been, and in 1584 the aldermen complained that the Crown's continued toleration of theater had led to "the preachers daily crying against the lord mayor and his brethren."[41] This controversy intensified in the 1590s. On 22 February 1592, the aldermen, frustrated by the Crown's failure to act on their warnings about unruly playhouses in the metropolis, appealed to Archbishop Whitgift to advise Elizabeth of the seriousness of the situation. The City magistrates complained of those plays that corrupted City youths "by reason of the wanton and profane devices represented on the stages." They acknowledged that the queen "must be served at certain times by this sort of people," but they hoped that such might be accomplished by private performances of Elizabeth's own players, which would rid the City of further controversy.[42]

Nevertheless, the queen continued to support public playhouses, closing them only during the plague outbreak of 1592–93. For those City governors who had counseled the queen that her continued patronage of plays risked divine retribution, her action must have seemed too little and too late. Elizabeth's harsh reaction to the spreading epidemic indicated the severity of the breakdown of policy. In January, the Privy Council informed the lord mayor and aldermen of the queen's displeasure with their carelessness in governing "not only of that place, being the capital city of the realm, and near to which her Majesty makes her continual residence, but of the preservation and welfare of her Majesty's subjects committed to your charge within the same." It concluded the rebuff by asserting that the citizens of London in general and "the poorer and meaner sort of the artificers" in particular could "justly ascribe their present mischief, poverty, and misery" to their magistrates.[43]

Elizabeth's policies confused her contemporaries. Her support for suburban theater drew condemnation from London's preachers and pamphleteers, particularly during times of plague. However, Londoners' attitudes toward the suburbs were not inflexible. Over time, residents of the City who believed God would destroy sinners came to realize that they were not immune to similar punishment. The responses of

Wallington to the London Bridge fire, of Gadbury and E.N. to the plague of 1665, and of Sandcroft and Elborough to the Great Fire signaled their belief that City dwellers were as capable as suburbanites of provoking divine wrath. Among some Londoners, the suburbs and liberties may have had a greater reputation for licentiousness than the City did, but whenever disaster struck London, many realized the futility of displacing the City's immorality onto its outskirts.

Responses to Population Change

In addition to condemning sin, Londoners often blamed rapid population growth for metropolitan social problems. In his *Survey of London* (1598), John Stow criticized the development of rural spaces in the metropolis, such as the common field to the west of the City wall, which were "encroached upon by building of filthy cottages"; it was a "blemish to so famous a city, to have so unsavory and unseemly an entry or passage thereunto."[44] Efforts to check London's physical expansion began with an Elizabethan proclamation in 1580 banning the construction of new houses or tenements within three miles of the City's gates. Those apprehended erecting such buildings would be arrested and released only after they had secured a bond against any future illegal development, the proceeds of which would be turned over to the royal hospitals. The queen justified her action by asserting that she had "principal care under Almighty God" to ensure that the people of London were well governed and able to acquire the necessities of life.[45]

In practice, housing developers and Elizabeth's Exchequer appear to have been the chief beneficiaries of the queen's building policy. At first, the Crown indicated that it expected local magistrates to enforce its policies rigorously. In June 1583, the Privy Council wrote to the lord mayor complaining of the continued construction of new houses and the division of tenements within the City and suburbs, contrary to the queen's proclamation, and it ordered him to proceed against all offenders.[46] However, it seems that the Crown made little attempt to enforce the restrictions until the 1590s, and then its main objective was to recover financial penalties from developers rather than to prevent new building.[47]

The Crown's shifting policy confounded local magistrates. On 25 May 1591, the Privy Council instructed the lord mayor to allow William Kirwin to build four houses in the City because he had already invested heavily in his project and because his development would "not annoy his neighbors, but rather beautify and enlarge the street." The Council simply required Kirwin to take out a bond against the construction of any small tenements or alleys for poor residents instead of houses "fit for the inhabitation of persons of account."[48] Six months later, the Privy Council approved the lord mayor's actions to restrain another man from building new houses, but it soon reversed itself after the defendant complained that, like Kirwin, he would lose a considerable investment in timber if he were not allowed to complete his project.[49] The Council's actions in these cases help to explain the continued growth of the metropolis in the decades following Elizabeth's ban on new housing, and they reminded local governors of their limited authority in their jurisdictions. Nevertheless, the Privy Council continued to badger local officials about their ineffectiveness. In April 1598 the Council scolded the Middlesex J.P.s for allowing landlords to rent tenements to "lewd persons" who "harbor thieves, rogues, and vagabonds, by reason whereof . . . all wickedness is maintained," an indication, in the Council's view, of the lack of Christian government.[50]

King James I renewed Elizabeth's efforts to control development and extended the Crown's reach to encompass new building on old foundations as well. The royal commission on buildings undertook an active enforcement campaign, and research by Malcolm Smuts suggests that Jacobean efforts to regulate building reached their peak around 1618.[51] While trying to curb physical development, the Crown considered a new approach to the problem of metropolitan expansion. Four proposals to check London's growth are extant among the papers of Sir Julius Caesar, James's Chancellor of the Exchequer. Two were unsigned and undated, one was undated but from a group calling itself "the foreign tradesmen," and the fourth was from a group of seven Londoners, including aldermen and common councilors, which was dated 30 April 1610. The precise relationship of these sources cannot be reconstructed, but they appear to be contemporary and part of a debate about the causes and consequences of London's growth. The City magistrates' text was a response to a "petition complained of," and the letter from the foreign tradesmen presented itself as a reply to those who opposed an earlier proposal.

The plans agreed that unchecked immigration was the main cause of London's problems. The City magistrates' proposal, like the others, complained of the constant arrival of men from across England who were unskilled because they had not completed apprenticeships. Nevertheless, the magistrates asserted, these immigrants were able to find employment in the suburbs.[52] This lack of suburban economic regulation, one of the anonymous petitions claimed, allowed those who had not served their full apprenticeships to hire and attempt to train other laborers, including apprentices who had left their masters, all of whom "taking wives must of necessity have houses." This implied that ineffective economic regulation in areas beyond the lord mayor's jurisdiction undermined the traditional balance between London's economy and its population. And the suburban chaos created a cover for criminals. The anonymous petitioners asserted that although some immigrants worked as porters and laborers, others rejected legal employment and supported themselves through crime. They argued that the flood of immigrants to the overcrowded suburbs enabled criminals to hide from the authorities more easily than they could have elsewhere; in addition, criminals found there a steady supply of victims, for they employed bawdy women to trap unsuspecting young gentlemen and apprentices. The petitioners claimed that the criminals' success was evident: they paid higher rents than honest people could.[53]

This suggested that some gained from the misfortunes of others. According to the foreign tradesmen's proposal, suburban landlords benefited from immigration by erecting sheds on vacant lots, subdividing existing buildings to accommodate immigrants, and increasing rents whenever they could without regard to the character or condition of their tenants.[54] One of the anonymous petitions noted that builders also profited from suburban overcrowding, and so it proposed that the king limit the ability of carpenters and bricklayers to erect or divide houses in the metropolis.[55] The gains of landlords and builders came at the expense of everyone else. The anonymous petitioners and the magistrates all asserted that the suburbs attracted those seeking to produce counterfeit goods for sale at lower prices than those produced by honest artisans. Pressured by the combination of unfair economic competition and artificially inflated rents, honest craftsmen were forced to turn to crime and deceit in order to support their families.[56]

The impoverishment of artisans and laborers combined with the immigration of paupers to strain the poor relief system in suburban parishes. According to one reform proposal, the metropolis attracted sophisticated beggars who disfigured themselves in order to deceive the charitably inclined. Others allegedly sought poor relief from suburban parishes, many of which were territorially larger and more populous than those of the City and yet lacked sufficient resources to cope with the problem. As a way of alleviating the situation, the petitioners suggested that the king force profiteering landholders to evict their tenants or at least donate a portion of their rents to their parishes for poor relief.[57] They also proposed limiting employment opportunities in greater London by tightening the regulation of suburban trade and industry. Each proposal contained provisions allowing those already living in the suburbs to remain if they followed the same guidelines as honest artisans, but they also expressed hope that in the future any immigrant to greater London who had not served an apprenticeship or was otherwise unskilled would be forced to return to his place of origin.[58] As a further obstacle to immigration, one anonymous proposal suggested that immigrants be hired as casual laborers in the metropolis only after the supply of native laborers was depleted.[59]

Despite their consensus on general policy, the reformers disagreed over the form of government best suited to economic reform. The City magistrates suggested that King James order those who lived and worked in areas adjoining the City to join the City livery companies associated most closely with their trades and to follow the same rules as freemen regarding the inspection of their work and the training of their apprentices. The other plans outlined the creation of similar yet separate companies in the suburbs. Although they remained vague about enforcing trade regulations outside the City, they did not call for the extension of livery company jurisdictions. Instead, one anonymous proposal asked the Crown to force artisans and traders working as far as ten miles from the City border to join new suburban guilds.[60]

The Crown and the City magistrates continued to discuss the reform of suburban government periodically until 1636, when Charles I created the New Corporation of the Suburbs of London. The Corporation was designed to regulate the activities of all traders and artisans who worked in areas outside the lord mayor's jurisdiction up to three miles from the City, regardless of whether they already were members of City livery companies. The king placed the Corporation under the rule of a warden and ten assistants for each of four wards, and he promised to alleviate many of the long-standing complaints against suburban interlopers. Those who wished to work in suburban London had to pay an entrance fee to the New Corporation that would then go to the Crown's use. This, along with the need for economic reform, likely explains the timing of the king's initiative.[61]

As the authors of the proposals of 1610 could have predicted, the New Corporation faced considerable opposition. In July 1637, its officers reported to King Charles that "thousands" who would have approved of their government pretended instead to be poor in order to avoid paying their entrance fees. They therefore sought further powers to press their subjects to obedience, and the king granted their request a year later.[62] The City governors were also hostile to the Corporation. In the early 1630s, Charles had sought their assistance in governing the suburbs. Their refusal at that time—a period of tension between the City magistrates and the Crown—likely had several motivations, but their reaction to the Corporation was consistent with their predecessors' claim in 1610 that the City companies could have regulated the suburban economy had their powers been increased. As a result, they considered the Corporation "very prejudicial" to the City's privileges.[63] The Corporation's failure to stem immigration did little to enhance its popularity. In 1638, the king ordered a census of all aliens living in metropolitan London because he had learned of an "extraordinary number" of immigrants in greater London who were generally "people of mean condition, and many of them newly come."[64] The New Corporation's records end with Parliament's attack on Crown prerogatives in the early 1640s, and an abortive attempt to revive the scheme in the 1660s had little influence on government policy.[65]

During the late sixteenth and early seventeenth centuries, London's governors sought the means to check metropolitan expansion by regulating the economy of the suburbs and liberties more effectively. These reform efforts drew on the contemporary discourse of suburban licentiousness found in the debate over the link between plays and plagues. Like many of the moralists and preachers who condemned plays, economic reformers tended to assume that suburban society posed a threat to the order of the City. Here, as in the earlier debate, similar assumptions could lead to different conclusions. Although the anonymous petitions to the Crown called for the creation of a new guild system for the suburbs, a plan largely implemented with the New Corporation of the Suburbs, City magistrates called instead for the extension of City guild authority in the suburbs, which suggested that City residents could embrace, rather than shun, their neighbors.

Beyond the New Corporation

The Civil War intensified the relationship between the City and its suburbs. Expansive views of the City received material form in the fortification of London during the war. In addition to refurbishing and strengthening London's ancient wall and placing chains across the City's main thoroughfares, Parliament sanctioned the construction of a series of fortresses that encircled the metropolis from the Tower in the east to Westminster in the west. The forts were connected by a continuous line of trenches that joined the suburbs and liberties to the City, shielding all of them against royalist intrusions.[66] The parliamentary militia expected all those living within the metropolis to support the war effort. A broadside issued by the committees for the City militia in May 1643 called on those in the "City, suburbs, and parts adjacent" to sacrifice one meal per week and contribute the savings to the militia's collection agents to support the defense of Parliament and the metropo-

Metropolitan London's Civil War fortifications. SOURCE: Maitland.

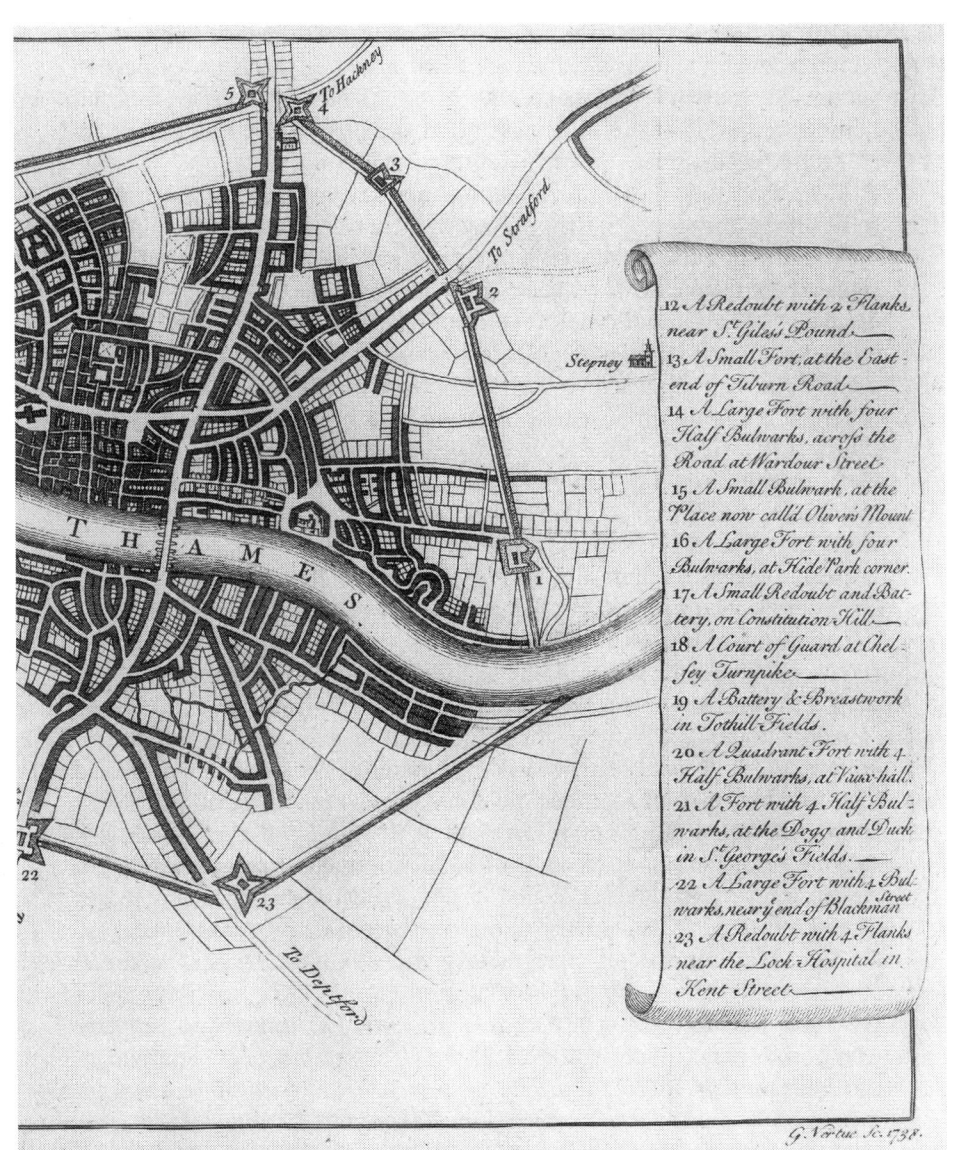

12. A Redoubt with 2 Flanks, near St Giles's Pound.
13. A Small Fort, at the East end of Tiburn Road.
14. A Large Fort with four Half Bulwarks, across the Road at Wardour Street.
15. A Small Bulwark, at the Place now call'd Oliver's Mount.
16. A Large Fort with four Bulwarks, at Hide Park corner.
17. A Small Redoubt and Battery, on Constitution Hill.
18. A Court of Guard at Chelsey Turnpike.
19. A Battery & Breastwork in Tothill-Fields.
20. A Quadrant Fort with 4 Half Bulwarks, at Vaux-hall.
21. A Fort with 4 Half Bulwarks, at the Dogg and Duck in St Georges Fields.
22. A Large Fort with 4 Bulwarks, near ye end of Blackman Street.
23. A Redoubt with 4 Flanks near the Lock Hospital in Kent Street.

G. Vertue Sc. 1738.

ified by Order of PARLIAMENT in the Years 1642 & 1643.

lis.⁶⁷ In 1644, the City's governors petitioned Parliament to give them control over the suburban militia. They also suggested that liberties such as St. Martin le Grand and the Minories be placed under their jurisdiction, and that the lord mayor and the recorder of London be appointed J.P.s for the counties surrounding London.⁶⁸

At mid-century, the problems of poverty and immigration continued to remind Londoners that they lived in a metropolis. Interregnum initiatives for London workhouses included proposals for the suburbs because, as reformer Leonard Lee put it, "in those parts most of the poor do live."⁶⁹ The Great Fire of 1666 intensified the challenges facing unemployed casual laborers. In an attempt to attract provincial workers to rebuild the City, Parliament's Post-Fire Acts removed the requirement of livery company membership for working in the City. Fearing that this would produce a new wave of immigrants, William Ravenhill, the clerk of the Grocers' Company, asserted that while the Crown had through the ages "trained up and disciplined" the City of London, it would be disastrous for "both the City and Suburbs, to increase and multiply with foreigners and natives, trading under no restraint of government . . . and turn all to a receptacle for innumerable vermin."⁷⁰

The influx of those whom Ravenhill considered "vermin" was a metropolitan-wide social problem. Throughout the 1670s, the City aldermen, citing the "great mischief" the renewed building in the suburbs caused the City, attempted to enforce the nearly century-old Elizabethan prohibitions on suburban development.⁷¹ Their efforts produced few tangible results. At the same time, other Londoners continued to pursue metropolitan moral reform. As Stephen Macfarlane has demonstrated, reformers like Josiah Child and Thomas Firmin responded to perceptions of social decay in greater London throughout the remainder of the century. The resulting London Corporation of the Poor was founded on the principle that poverty was a moral as well as a social condition, but if, as the Board of Trade put it in 1697, "the increase of the poor" was the result of "the relaxation of discipline" and "corruption of manners," such would hardly have been a new development in the early modern metropolis. The assumption that such problems were metropolitan-wide was evident in John Dunton's *The Night-Walker: or, Evening Rambles in Search after Lewd Women* (1696–97), which was dedicated to "the Whore-Masters of London and Westminster" and took its reader on a tour of greater London.⁷²

At the end of the century, these concerns inspired the creation of societies for the reformation of manners. Although such groups were formed throughout England, Robert Shoemaker has shown that they were most numerous in the metropolis.⁷³ In 1691, Queen Mary sent a letter to the J.P.s of Middlesex, calling for "all constables, church-wardens, Headboroughs, and all other officers and persons whatsoever to do their part in their several stations" to suppress profanity and debauchery. Seven years later, Josiah Woodward could give an encouraging account of popular participation in efforts in and about the City of London to punish those guilty of an array of activities similar to those that had exercised moralists more than a hundred years earlier. "The prosecution of men for their vices," Woodward argued, "has never been reckoned persecution, it being plainly the duty of the magistrate, from the word of God, which obliges him to execute wrath upon those that do evil." The efforts of these reformers were also metropolitan in nature. Woodward dedicated his pamphlet to the citizens and inhabitants of "the City of London and the parts adjacent," and he noted that members in both Westminster and the City informed against wrongdoers "in all parts, according to their respective places of abode." The City aldermen indicated their support for such efforts by granting a group of "citizens and inhabitants in and about the City of London" who had prosecuted lewd people the right to nominate two individuals to have the freedom of the City.[74]

The work of the societies for the reformation of manners in the late seventeenth and early eighteenth centuries highlighted the willingness of Londoners to advance metropolitan ideas of community despite religious and social change. The relationship between the City and its suburbs and liberties previously had been marked by tension, with reformers not always sure that the metropolis should be viewed holistically. However, the Civil War and the Great Fire combined to blur further the distinctions between territories in greater London.

Early modern ideas of community evolved in ways that gradually encouraged a metropolitan view of London. Although some commentators attributed the trajectory of plague outbreaks to the immorality of the suburbs and liberties, others downplayed the divisions between the City and its outskirts, seeking instead to see divine punishment as a warning to everyone in the metropolis. The Protestant model of godly ministers and magistrates working together to discipline their subjects did not apply neatly to London. Local governors nevertheless tried, albeit with limited results, to coordinate their responses to metropolitan problems such as crime, poverty, and disease, and they expressed their awareness of the complaints of London's preachers when they debated policy matters with the Crown. The Crown played a decisive role in efforts to govern the metropolis. From the regulation of theater and new building to the attempted incorporation of the suburbs, its disagreements with the City's governors indicated the limitations, but not the collapse, of metropolitan government. No place in the metropolis was beyond the reach of governmental authority. If, as some contemporaries believed, certain areas in the metropolis fostered immorality, such as prostitution and theater, they must have had support from at least some of the elite.

Religious and social change therefore did not necessarily overturn ideas of community in early modern London. Recent studies have downplayed the diversity of contemporary views of greater London, choosing instead to highlight the divisions between the City and its suburbs and liberties. This chapter has analyzed several overlooked texts in order to reveal the complexity of discourses of community in early modern London. Like other studies that rely on published texts and governmental policies, it has offered little more than a survey of the ideas available to Londoners. But it has also demonstrated that, ideologically, there was no reason why Londoners could not have embraced the suburbs and liberties as integral parts of the community in which they lived, worked, played, and prayed. The next chapter will examine the extent to which London livery company members acted on this ideological potential.

CHAPTER 2

Livery Companies and the Metropolis

Concurring with the 1610 proposals for a new guild system in London's suburbs and liberties, historians often have suggested that the City's livery companies had little influence in areas outside the lord mayor's jurisdiction.[1] J. R. Kellett, encouraging historians not to overestimate the companies' authority, pointed to the 1610 proposals as well as a series of court cases that curtailed the power of companies to enforce their regulations.[2] Robert Ashton considered the proposals evidence that in certain parts of greater London, City authorities, such as companies, were powerless to do more than complain about the "crime, disorder and squalor" they found.[3] Valerie Pearl acknowledged that some members of livery companies may have lived in London's suburbs, but she asserted that during the seventeenth century up to three-fourths of adult men in the City were members of companies and therefore had an interest in maintaining the City's political stability. By contrast, she found that the companies had little power in the comparatively unruly suburbs and liberties, for although most seventeenth-century company charters enabled their officers to inspect economic activity up to several miles from the City, she doubted that their authority "ever operated very efficiently so far afield."[4]

More recent studies have confirmed Pearl's skepticism. Steve Rappaport extended Pearl's model to cover the entire early modern period when he argued that up to three-fourths of adult men in the sixteenth-century City were company members. Although he suggested that some citizens lived outside the City's limits and that companies had the power to enforce their ordinances in suburban areas, he found a sizable difference between companies' authority and their actions, concluding that suburban residents were "beyond the reach of the mayors' precepts and the companies' orders."[5] A. L. Beier raised similar doubts about guild authority in his study of the political dimensions of London's economic development. He argued that despite their legal powers and expanding memberships, companies were unable to regulate industrial activity outside the City's ancient wall, a finding that held even for those parishes situated between the wall and the civic boundary and therefore within the lord mayor's jurisdiction. In Beier's view, manufacturers who established themselves in those developing areas did so for political as well as economic reasons because they knew they were defying the authority of the livery companies.[6] Like Beier, Jean-Christophe Agnew maintained that London's liberties were economically unregulated places. Agnew found that Renaissance dramatists "sought the same immunities of London's liberties as the alien craftsmen" who built their theaters and stitched their costumes. As a result, masterless artisans and playwrights were "crowded together in the strange, extraterritorial zone outside the walls but inside the 'bars' of the City."[7]

However, guild archives contain data that undermine the all-too-common assumption that livery companies enjoyed greater economic influence in the City of London than they did in the suburbs and liberties. Typically, information regarding enforcement of a guild's ordinances was recorded in the minutes of its court of assistants—a guild's primary governing body—or in the record book the company's officers took with them when inspecting workplaces. Such records often mention the names of individuals charged with violations of company regulations, but they rarely indicate where the accused person lived or where the alleged infraction took place. Additionally, the quality and quantity of records detailing the enforcement of guild ordinances vary greatly among companies and periods, with evidence often accumulating during times of general economic hardship in London.[8] Pearl estimated that there were 79 companies operating in seventeenth-century London, but substantial amounts of archival material are extant for fewer than 50 of them, and most of these records generally contain little information on the geography of company life.[9]

This chapter develops an alternative view of the companies' role in the metropolis by analyzing the activities of more than twenty guilds whose records offer a spatial perspective on their activities. Despite the consensus among scholars that companies were impotent outside the City's walls and borders, many of London's guilds and—perhaps more important—their members exerted influence in the suburbs and liberties. By definition, company members were citizens of London ("freemen") who had the right to live and work anywhere within the lord mayor's jurisdiction. This included the entire area between the walls and the bars that marked the City's limits except for the liberties. However, since at least the mid-sixteenth century, members were allowed to live in areas outside the City for up to a year at a time, and even longer if they could secure aldermanic consent for their move.[10] Moreover, even if company members relocated permanently to the suburbs or liberties in order to avoid the costs and responsibilities of citizenship, they could not be confident that they would evade the ordinances of their companies. The same was true for those who were not members of companies. Therefore, as they influenced the metropolitan economy and maintained ties with members throughout greater London, guilds offered Londoners a model for the metropolis that could adjust to demographic expansion.

Company Authority and Residence Patterns

The following survey of companies' metropolitan activities discusses them in three loose groups—retailers, manufacturers, and builders—because each had a different relationship to metropolitan expansion. Retailers benefited from increased demand resulting from London's growth, and research based on parochial and legal records has shown that they tended to establish shops near their potential customers throughout the metropolis.[11] Manufacturers often needed large amounts of space for their activities and therefore may have been attracted to the relatively undeveloped suburbs. Builders had to go where there was demand for development, and, as discussed earlier, that frequently was in the suburbs. Examples of companies from each group follow in turn, beginning with retailers.

Members of the Grocers' Company lived and worked throughout the metropolis. The company's quarterage records listed members according to neighborhood during a fourteen-year period in the later sixteenth century. The neighborhoods conformed roughly to those of the City of London, but there were potential overlaps with suburban areas, particularly in Southwark, which seems to have included all the areas south of the River Thames.[12] The only sector in the lists that was specifically suburban was Westminster, although it was occasionally grouped with areas of the City such as Ludgate and Fleet Street.[13] Complicating matters further, in some years the records included a category for *extra vagants*; in others, such people were included in a category "Westminster and elsewhere out of London." Although the data contained in the quarterage lists—which are summarized in Table 1—demonstrate that by the late 1570s something on the order of 10 percent of company members lived outside the City, the vagaries of the listings limit an analysis of change over time.[14]

The records also show that some company members lived outside the City for lengthy periods. Of the 28 grocers who paid quarterage in "Westminster and elsewhere out of London" in 1570-71, 13 (46 percent) remained outside the lord mayor's jurisdiction for at least one additional year, and 5 (18 percent) continued there until 1577-78.[15] Furthermore, some company members lived farther from the City than Westminster. In 1573, the Grocers' Court of Assistants assessed freemen for the lord mayor's show, and noted the names of 16 grocers who were overseas and "in the country" and who failed to attend company meetings. A similar list compiled sixteen years later included 46 names.[16] Such cases may account for members recorded in the quarterage lists who paid several years' dues, but they also suggest that the company's quarterage lists can offer only a faint glimpse of the residential patterns of London's citizens.

The efforts of the company's officers to enforce its ordinances provide further evidence of the metropolitan character of the grocery trade. In 1562, the Grocers' Court of Assistants heard Robert Savage's complaint that his fellow grocer Henry Faulk had challenged his lease of a shop that was located outside London. The assistants fined Faulk £5 after deciding that the relevant company ordinance "stretched to the person of any brother of this company as well without the City of London as

TABLE 1
The Grocers' Company ca. 1558–78

Year	Total members	Westm'r (%)	Extra vagants (%)	Westm'r & elsewhere (%)	Southw'k (%)
1558–59	358	3 (.8)	—	—	11 (3.1)
1559–60	370	2 (.5)	—	—	14 (3.8)
1560–65	—	—	—	—	—
1565–66	392	—	—	—	11 (2.8)
1566–67	396	—	—	—	14 (3.5)
1567–68	360	—	—	—	10 (2.8)
1568–69	401	—	28 (6.9)	—	9 (2.2)
1569–70	361	—	16 (4.4)	—	6 (1.7)
1570–71	370	—	—	28 (7.6)	8 (2.2)
1571–72	375	—	—	14 (3.7)	8 (2.1)
1572–73	372	—	—	22 (5.9)	11 (3.0)
1573–74	398	—	—	23 (5.8)	8 (2.0)
1574–75	—	—	—	—	—
1575–76	408	—	—	24 (5.9)	8 (2.0)
1576–77	417	—	—	34 (8.2)	8 (2.0)
1577–78	377	—	—	21 (5.6)	8 (2.1)

SOURCE: GL MS 11571/6.

within the same." Two years later, the company's searchers seized illicit treacle that a company member had put on sale at Bartholomew Fair, and in 1570 the court burned two pounds of tainted ginger and cinnamon belonging to a grocer in Westminster.[17] In 1607, King James bolstered the company's enforcement efforts by empowering its officers to inspect and punish people practicing their trade within the City of London and its suburbs and liberties up to three miles away.[18]

In addition to inspecting grocers' shops, the company's officers hired searchers to regulate street vending across greater London. In 1602, the City's Common Council empowered London's magistrates to control shops and stalls set up in the streets and alleys of the City because traditionally every warehouse, shop, and other place within the City and its liberties that opened onto the street had been considered a public marketplace. Nine years later, the company's officers hired John Mynshall to inspect the sale of grocery wares in all markets, streets, lanes, and "other places" within the City and its suburbs and liberties. They agreed to pay him £5 per year for his services, and the company subsequently employed searchers until at least 1635.[19]

Like the Grocers', the Waxchandlers' Company had authority over a metropolitan trade.[20] Its charter of 1483 empowered the company's officers to inspect the weights, measures, and trade of anyone who produced or sold wax in the City and suburbs of London.[21] The company's surviving search books cover much of the period from 1574 to 1664, but they say relatively little about the geographic range of its officers' activities. Nevertheless, they do contain several instances of company officers' exercising their right to inspect waxchandlers' shops in extramural places such as Holborn Bridge, Smithfield Bars, Shoe Lane, and the Old Bailey.[22] No records of the Waxchandlers' Company membership have survived for a comparable period, but quarterage lists from the early eighteenth century suggest that the company remained metropolitan in nature throughout the early modern period. In 1706, the first year for which residence records survive, the company had 133 members, and the residences of 109 can be identified. Of those, 43 (39 percent) lived in the City within the wall; 25 (23 percent) lived in extramural areas such as Temple Bar, Little Britain, and Without Bishopsgate; and 41 (38 percent) lived outside the City, in places such as Charing Cross, Lambeth Marsh, and Ratcliffe Highway.[23]

The Vintners' Company records allow a much earlier survey of the metropolitan nature of retailing. The company's charter of 1567 empowered its officers to enforce their regulations over anyone who managed a tavern or sold wine within the City of London, its suburbs, and all liberties within three miles of the City.[24] The company's court records seldom mentioned the locations of those who were found in breach of its regulations, but occasional incidents indicated the range of its activities. During the first decade of the seventeenth century, the court punished vintners in liberties and suburban areas such as Gray's Inn Lane, Holborn, the Strand, Whitefriars, and Lambeth.[25] At mid-century, a list of members drawn up by the company's officers for the poll tax of 1641 permits a more detailed analysis of the company's activities.[26] Of the 217 taverns occupied by members of the Vintners' Company in 1641, at least 112 (52 percent) were located outside the City's wall, and 61 (28 percent) were in the suburbs or liberties.[27]

A comparison of this information with the company's court records reveals that vintners who lived beyond the City's wall were not exempt from the company's searches. During the period 1636–46, the company's officers found infractions of its ordinances at 37 taverns included in the 1641 poll tax list. Of that total, 11 (30 percent) were within the City's wall, 10 (27 percent) were between the wall and the civic boundary, and 16 (43 percent) were in areas outside the lord mayor's jurisdiction. Although none of the proprietors of the nine taverns that the poll tax list placed in liberties was fined by the company's searchers during the sample period, officers did inspect shops in other liberties such as St. Martin le Grand, the Minories, and the Savoy.[28]

The Brewers' Company archives are not as complete as those of the Vintners, but they also demonstrate the metropolitan nature of the drinks trade. In 1612, six company members complained to Sir Julius Caesar, the Chancellor of the Exchequer, about encroachments on their right to conduct business in the suburbs and liberties of London. They cited a statute from Henry VIII's reign that authorized the lord mayor and aldermen in London and the J.P.s in surrounding counties to set the price of ale and beer, and then they complained that an officer of the royal household threatened to sue them for charging London prices in areas outside the lord mayor's jurisdiction such as Newington, the Clink, Paris Garden, Whitechapel, and Lambeth. They insisted that freemen of the Brewers' Company who lived and traded outside the City needed to charge London prices to people living in the suburbs and liberties "by reason of the popularity of those places." They therefore requested that the Crown protect them from future accusations of charging excessive prices.[29]

The company's search lists are not extant for the years prior to 1724, but after that date they reveal that many members lived and worked outside the City and that the company's officers monitored the work of nonmembers throughout the metropolis. As Table 2 illustrates, in 1724 the list included 268 brewers, 180 (67 percent) of whom were not members of the company. This list also shows that 90 percent of the company's members worked in breweries situated outside the City's wall, and 67 percent worked in the suburbs. Nevertheless, both members and foreigners paid search fees as well as quarterage.[30] Furthermore, residence outside the City of London was not a bar to membership in the company's livery.[31] The suburban nature of brewing led manufacturers of barrels to work outside the City's wall. The Coopers' Company's earliest surviving search books, which cover the period 1701–30, demonstrate that the spatial distribution of the barrel-making trade closely resembled that of brewing, with most of the company's regulatory activity taking place outside the City's walls and in suburban areas such as Clerkenwell, Holborn, Islington, and Shoreditch.[32]

The members of the Feltmakers' Company also worked primarily in the suburbs. Although James I issued the company a letter patent at the outset of his reign, as late as 1623 the Court of Aldermen of London claimed that the company's 400 members were unfit to live and work in the City, "their trade (in regard of the unsavory things which belong thereto) being noisome to their neighbors."[33] This statement suggested that the suburbs fostered activities that the City's governors found unacceptable, but it represented only one side of the story. The new company's defenders replied to the aldermen by noting that their trade was

TABLE 2
Location of Brewers, 1724

	Thames Street	Goodman's Fields	Shadwell	Spitalfields & Shoreditch
Division total	21	19	22	18
Percent of company	7.8	7.1	8.2	6.7
Free	18	18	15	13
Percent free	85.7	94.7	68.2	72.2
	Cripplegate Parish	Clerkenwell Parish	Borough of Southwark	Tuley St. Southwark
Division total	27	33	14	20
Percent of company	10.1	12.3	5.2	7.5
Free	18	19	8	15
Percent free	66.7	57.6	57.1	75.0
	St. Giles	Westminster	St. James	Whitechapel
Division total	31	20	25	18
Percent of company	11.6	7.5	9.3	6.7
Free	26	13	8	9
Percent free	83.9	65.0	32.0	50.0

SOURCES: GL MSS 5458, fols. 62r–68r, and 5452/1.

no more offensive than other industries in the City, and they reported that because they needed inexpensive housing, easy access to the river, and open land for drying their cloth, "many freemen do live in the suburbs and by-places" instead of in the City.[34]

The willingness of the suburban feltmakers to comply with the regulations of their trade was shared by a group calling itself "the leather-dressers in and about the Borough of Southwark in the County of Surrey." In a petition they sent to the Lord Lieutenant of Surrey during King James's reign, they maintained that although they lived and traded both in areas that were within and beyond the lord mayor's jurisdiction, they expected that the statutes governing their craft would be enforced in all areas of the metropolis. In particular, they complained about several Dutch leather-dressers who, they alleged, violated the Statute of Artificers by employing journeymen who had not served their full apprenticeships, thereby creating unemployment among English leather-dressers.[35]

Like leather dressing, saddle making was a metropolitan-wide activity. The court minutes of the Saddlers' Company survive for the period 1605–65, and though they contain many examples of company officers' enforcement efforts, they only occasionally mention the locations of infractions. However, one case displayed the officers' ability to monitor suburban activity. In 1609, journeyman Thomas Moore resisted and slandered the officers while they conducted a search at a collar-maker's shop in suburban St. Giles in the Field. After obtaining a warrant from a City magistrate, the Saddlers' officers compelled Moore to appear before their court, at which time "in humble manner upon his knees" he admitted his failing and sought their forgiveness. After five of his neighbors guaranteed that Moore would behave himself properly in the future, the officers forgave his offense.[36]

The records of the Blacksmiths' Company contain more plentiful examples of the regulation of suburban manufacturing by a City company. Throughout the seventeenth century, the company's officers swore "English foreigners" who lived and worked in the suburbs—from Lambeth in the southwest to Hampstead in the north and Wapping in the east—to obedience to the company's ordinances.[37] The officers also searched shops and removed goods from those who violated the company's regulations. In 1612, the officers seized items from 27 shops, including 3 in Holborn, 3 in Westminster, and 2 in Wapping. The officers took goods in lieu of search fines from suburban shops at East Smithfield, Drury Lane, Wentworth Street, and Carnaby Street in 1632. In 1649, they acted against a farrier in Westminster who stole the hat of one assistant during a search.[38] At the turn of the century, the officers collected overdue search fines from a retailer of new and used iron wares as well as from a wiresmith, both of whom worked in suburban Shoreditch.[39] The officers' familiarity with the suburban trade may in part be explained by the fact that several leading members of the company lived in those areas. A comparison of a list of the company's livery from 1642 with the roster of company members compiled for the poll tax of 1641 indicates that liverymen lived in suburban areas near the City, such as Whitecross Street and Cow Lane, as well as in areas farther away, such as Wapping.[40]

Like blacksmiths, weavers lived and worked throughout the metropolis. The Weavers' Company officers indicated their attitude toward the geographic distribution of their members in 1617, when they agreed that it was lawful for any company member to apprehend violators of the company's ordinances "wheresoever the same offenders may be found."[41] Although none of the company's search books have survived, the minutes of its Court of Assistants demonstrate that the officers carried out their mandate. In 1616, they warned a foreigner at Charing Cross to stop weaving or be sued, and they required a weaver in Hackney to prove that he had served an apprenticeship to the trade. In 1617, they arrested a stranger of suburban Holywell Street for intermeddling in the trade, and they employed legal counsel to direct an arrest warrant against George Constantine to "all constables, headboroughs, royal officers, and ministers to whom it appertains in London, Middlesex, and Surrey." One year later, the assistants instructed the constables of Stepney to detain a weaver until a future court meeting, and they warned a weaver in Whitechapel to become free or to face prosecution.[42] The Weavers' officers remained active in the suburbs later in the century as well. In 1667, they learned that a draper who lived in suburban Blue Anchor Alley by the Artillery Ground was employing more apprentices in weaving than their ordinances allowed. When the assistants confronted him in their court, he showed them his "affection and respects" by contributing £5 toward the cost of rebuilding Weavers' Hall. The company's searchers were also active in other suburban places such as Spitalfields and the Bankside during the period.[43]

The Weavers' Company officers were well aware that company members lived throughout the metropolis. When it received a new charter from Parliament during the Interregnum, the company's governance was placed in the hands of representatives elected from five districts that traversed the metropolis: Southwark, Cripplegate, Shoreditch, Bishopsgate, and Whitechapel.[44] After 1674, the company's records occasionally mentioned the residence of new members, and these confirmed the persistence of the Interregnum pattern.[45] Furthermore, in 1669, when a weaver donated £200 to establish an almshouse for poor company members and their widows, the assistants decided to place it in suburban Shoreditch, and they subsequently consulted churchwardens from Spitalfields and Shoreditch when allocating its rooms.[46]

Perhaps even more than in the occupations discussed thus far, mobility was essential to members of the building trades, who needed access to work in the rapidly expanding suburbs.[47] The Carpenters' Company officers inspected work in suburbs and liberties such as Whitechapel, the Minories, Blackfriars, and "near the Globe play house."[48] None of the company's quarterage lists have survived, but its court records demonstrate its officers' realization that company members worked throughout the metropolis. In 1613, a committee of London aldermen responded to a complaint brought by the company against the governors of Staple's Inn for their employing a foreign carpenter within the "liberties of London." The aldermen ordered the governors to dismiss the foreigner and to hire a freeman carpenter to complete the project. Although the inn's governors did not concede the legality of the aldermanic ruling, they complied with its intent.[49] In 1628, the company's officers tried to resolve a dispute caused by one carpenter accusing another of supplanting him on a project at extramural Holborn Bridge. The client on this occasion claimed that he had considerable demand for carpenters, and so he simply hired the two carpenters to work on two separate projects.[50]

Similar evidence of suburban connections can be found throughout the records of the Tylers and Bricklayers' Company. According to the company's letters patent of 1568, its officers had the right to inspect the use of tiles and bricks within fifteen miles of London.[51] The company's search books survive for the years after 1605, and a comparison of their data with the company's quarterage books, extant for the period 1605–16, indicates that tile- and bricklaying was a metropolitan-wide trade. A sample of the records for the years 1605–6 and 1615–16 reveals that the company's officers inspected work in extramural places, such as Petticoat Lane, Golden Lane, and Chancery Lane, and areas beyond London's borders, such as the Strand, Westminster, and Islington. Among the 23 identifiable builders mentioned, 13 (57 percent) were working outside the City's wall, including 5 (22 percent) who were outside the lord mayor's jurisdiction.[52] In addition to supervising tile- and bricklaying, a statute from Henry VII's reign empowered the company's officers to inspect the production and sale of tile, bricks, sand, and lime up to fifteen miles beyond the City's limits.[53] The records of their searches demonstrate that their duties took them across the metropolis and throughout the southeastern counties. Their influence was apparent from their ability to collect fines from suppliers as far away from London as Lewisham in Kent, Kentish Town in Middlesex, and the manor of Havering in Essex, as well as from those in extramural places such as Bridewell.[54]

The importance of the suburban trade to members of the Tylers and Bricklayers' Company was evident in the company's response to two developments in 1636. The first was the result of King Charles's creation of a new corporation of brick and tile makers to remedy alleged abuses occurring in the production of bricks and tiles in greater London. The new body, which was based in Westminster, was authorized to supervise production in the cities of London and Westminster as well as in all areas within twenty miles of the City.[55] The officers of the Tylers and Bricklayers' Company responded by claiming that the establishment of the new body only led to the deteriorating quality of bricks and tiles. They charged that brick and tile makers forced tilers and bricklayers to purchase "whatsoever they bring whether good or bad" and also raised their prices.[56] When the tilers and bricklayers complained, the brick and tile makers threatened to call them before the Privy Council, but by 1638, the officers of the City company were ready for such a confrontation. In the event, the Council established a commission to consider their complaints. This commission subsequently reported that unless Charles overturned the new body, "there can be no reformation, but the said bricks and tiles will still be bad and dear," thereby undermining the king's stated purpose for the Westminster-based corporation.[57]

The officers of the Tylers and Bricklayers' Company were also active in efforts to overturn the New Corporation of the Suburbs after 1636. As we have seen, several suburban reform proposals of 1610 had called for the creation of just such a company for all artisans and traders in the suburbs in order to protect London freemen from the unfair competition of immigrants. Contrary to the reformers' assumptions, the members of the Tylers and Bricklayers' Company considered the new suburban guild a threat to their livelihoods. For instance, the company's officers defended the apprentice of one of their freemen who was arrested in Southwark for violating the charter of the New Corporation. Corporation officers justified their actions to the king by claiming that London bricklayers "came and wrought daily in the New Corporation to the great offence of the tradesmen members of this Corporation." However, they also realized that they were stirring up controversy, and so they successfully requested that Charles appoint some of his judges to settle their differences with the freemen. In April 1638, the king postponed the trial of the bricklayers until further efforts had been made to resolve the matter "as shall be reasonable and just."[58]

A petition that ten companies sent to the lord mayor captured the intensity of the controversy surrounding the ejection of London freemen from the suburbs. It reported that "the greatest part" of the employment of London's builders was located outside the City, and it claimed that since they were restrained by the suburban guild from pursuing their work, the families of builders were being impoverished. They therefore requested the restoration of their right to work in the suburbs and liberties of London. The aldermen found that the petition described "a cause much concerning the freedom and privileges" of the City, and ordered their legal counsel to take steps to relieve the petitioners' complaints.[59] The Tylers and Bricklayers' Company was among the sponsors of the petition, and its officers demonstrated their commitment to the cause by spending more than £46 on defending the company's rights during 1638 and 1639.[60] The records do not mention the outcome of this particular dispute—which was resolved ultimately with the effective collapse of the New Corporation by 1640—but they demonstrate that during the mid-seventeenth century, a period of rapid metropolitan expansion, members of London's guilds were quick to assert their right to work in the suburbs.[61]

Companies in the building trades joined together again to defend their rights after the Great Fire. Despite Parliament's liberalization of the building trades in order to attract builders to London, the companies worked with the City government to allow foreigners no more freedom than the law allowed.[62] The companies' efforts had only a limited effect at first, but they informed the foreigners that they intended to reclaim their full powers as soon as the post-Fire regulations expired.[63] The effectiveness of this strategy may be seen in the decision of foreigners who had come to London to help rebuild the City to seek membership in companies in the building trades during the decade following the passage of the post-Fire legislation.[64] The officers of the Tylers and Bricklayers' Company also continued to enforce their ordinances in the metropolis after the Fire. They inspected the production of tiles and bricks across Surrey, Kent, Essex, and Middlesex as they had before the Fire, and they also fined bricklayers for poor workmanship.[65]

The Fire also forced members of companies in other trades to defend their rights across the metropolis. In July 1669, Dyers' Company journeymen complained to the lord mayor and aldermen that the Fire had forced many masters of their company to move their shops to the suburbs. Once there, these masters began ignoring a long-established ordinance against hiring foreign workers without written permission of the company's officers. The company's wardens defended their actions by asserting that they had allowed the ordinance to lapse simply because the Fire had greatly hindered their ability to exercise their authority. Nevertheless, the aldermen ordered the wardens immediately to renew their efforts to limit the employment of foreigners by company members in the suburbs.[66]

The foregoing examples have illustrated the ways companies in the retailing, manufacturing, and building trades became involved in the economy of London's suburbs and liberties. Bearing in mind the limitations that the evidence places on a comprehensive geographic analysis of company enforcement efforts, we can clearly see that the officers of several companies succeeded in exercising considerable influence across the metropolis. It also was apparent to many early modern Londoners that the presence in the suburbs and liberties of noncitizens did not prevent company members from participating in the economy of areas that lay beyond the lord mayor's jurisdiction. Many citizens therefore must have had working relationships with the strangers in their midst.

Suburban Economic Reform Reconsidered

The evidence of London's livery companies influencing their trades throughout the metropolis challenges the claim, made most forcefully in the 1610 reform proposals, that the companies were powerless in the suburbs and liberties. In the face of such conflicting data, it should be recalled that the authorship of the 1610 proposals remains uncertain. Two were anonymous, and one claimed to be from the "foreign tradesmen," suggesting that its authors were not members of livery companies.[67] It is possible that they, like the tile and brick makers of Westminster, sought to break away from the control of City companies, and they used the Crown's concern over suburban expansion—which was evident to contemporaries at least from the 1580s—as a justification for their proposals.[68] For these reasons, rather than indicating the diminishing role of livery companies in the economy of London's suburbs and liberties, the reform proposals of 1610 may be evidence of their continued influence.

As discussed earlier, it was likely in response to such tensions between City companies and foreigners that a group of London magistrates replied to these petitions with a report of their own. The magistrates rehearsed some problems mentioned in the other petitions and proposed that they be rectified by increasing the powers of City companies in the suburbs and liberties. They called for companies to have authority in areas within five miles of the City and for those who traded in such places to be required to join and pay dues to companies.[69] Of course, as we have seen, the City companies already had substantial legal authority outside the City. As leading members of livery companies themselves, the aldermen and common councilors were doubtless aware that their companies possessed considerable influence in the suburbs and liberties.[70] Although dues paid by interlopers and the geographical extension of company powers into largely undeveloped areas would have enhanced the guilds' influence in greater London, the magistrates seemed rather too eager to claim that suburban development, led by aliens and foreigners, was a major threat to the City companies.[71]

By blaming interlopers for the apparently chaotic state of the suburban economy, the City magistrates may have intended their report to deflect criticism from the policies of the companies. Since the only identifiable critics of the livery companies had called themselves "foreign tradesmen," perhaps the City magistrates hoped to defend the status quo, a condition that lent livery company members certain advantages over foreigners in the suburbs and liberties.[72] The activities of the Bakers' Company support this hypothesis. In 1604, the Privy Council included the company among the authorities to regulate bread prices in greater London.[73] In 1631, a dispute arose between the Bakers' Company and the Middlesex J.P.s over the assize of bread that demonstrated the importance of the suburban trade to company members. The company's records indicate that the J.P.s arrested 50 bakers—"being as well free as foreign, and certain other bakers living in London but serving bread in Middlesex"—for violating the assize. The J.P.s lacked the authority to adjudicate such matters, and so they sought the assistance of several privy councilors, but they were surprised by the reaction they received. The Earl of Dorset, for example, corrected one J.P. for his harsh treatment of the bakers, declaring that they were "a company of necessary members and very useful to the commonwealth, and that some of them were men as worthy as himself."[74]

But this was only the beginning of a long controversy. The Middlesex J.P.s soon received the lord mayor's support for a new system that would base the metropolitan assize on bread prices in London. The new scheme would have empowered the J.P.s to enforce the assize, and the mayor subsequently tried to convince King Charles that such reforms were needed for a variety of reasons including the Bakers' Company's ineffectiveness in regulating its members' activities.[75] For their part, the company's officers blamed everyone else for the fluctuating price of bread, and they poured particular scorn on foreign bakers who lived in suburban London. They complained that the foreigners had a considerable advantage over company members who lived in the suburbs—"being the greatest part of the company"—for two reasons. First, they avoided paying quarterage to the company and taxes to the City. Second, they evaded the company's ordinances because the company's officers lacked the authority to punish them.[76]

However, the company's other records contradict the officers' claim of impotence. In 1569, Queen Elizabeth granted a charter to the company that confirmed the power of its officers to regulate the baking of all sorts of bread by anyone in London, its suburbs, and within two miles of the City.[77] Although the charter became entangled in a long-standing dispute between the bakers of white and brown breads, the records of the company's successful actions against interlopers during the period 1631–35 undermined the officers' assertion that the company was completely powerless to respond to challenges from foreign bakers in the suburbs and liberties. Most notably, in 1632 the company took action against one John Whitehorne of Islington who worked as a baker although, as the company alleged, he had "never served as an apprentice." Whitehorne subsequently stopped baking and turned his shop over to a member of the company because "he had heard by diverse the purpose and resolution and the proceedings of the company against such as was in his case."[78] In this light, the officers' claim of ineffectiveness in the suburbs appears part of an attempt to deflect criticism that they had allowed their members to charge excessively high prices in those areas. They doubtless preferred to be seen as victims of unfair competition rather than conspirators against the public interest.

As a result, the reform proposal from the foreign tradesmen—and likely the other 1610 proposals also—indicated the frustration that they felt when competing in the suburbs and liberties against citizens who sometimes bent the rules that noncitizens had to obey. If the petitioners had intended to bolster the position of company members throughout the metropolis, the simplest step would have been to call for the increased powers of the companies themselves. Instead, by encouraging the Crown to create new guilds for the suburbs and liberties, they indicated that their primary purpose was to break free from the influence of the City companies. To enhance their position with a monarch who was concerned about the growth of the metropolis, the foreigners tried to argue that the economy of the suburbs and liberties was out of control when it was merely out of *their* control.

The failure of suburban reform efforts only enhanced the economic advantages that many company members enjoyed over foreigners. Unlike their foreign neighbors, members of London livery companies who lived and worked in the suburbs and liberties also had the legal right to trade in the City itself. As indicated above, company membership would have given a degree of personal mobility to builders or to artisans in the weaving or brewing trades, but it carried advantages in the marketplace as well. The establishment of such advantages was evident in legislation such as the 1603 act of Parliament that ordered leather workers in the suburbs and liberties within three miles of the City to have their leather cured only by members of the Curriers' Company of London.[79] Furthermore, rather than sheltering those seeking to avoid the City's economic regulations, the suburbs and liberties offered economic opportunities to some livery company members. Although company members generally defended their right to live and work throughout the metropolis, they may have had differing attitudes about the employment of noncitizens in the suburbs and liberties. In 1675, the officers of the Clothworkers' Company heard a complaint from journeymen that some company members were employing foreigners in the suburbs and liberties. The officers responded that they could not prevent members from hiring foreigners outside the City, although they could ask such company members to hire freemen instead of foreigners if the freemen were able to work for wages similar to those paid to foreigners.[80]

Members of City companies had economic influence in the suburbs and liberties, but the thoroughness of company regulation remains open to question. However, in a consideration of companies' authority in the suburbs and liberties, the key point is not absolute, but comparative: were the suburbs and liberties more unruly than the City itself? Although the evidence from the Vintners' and the Brewers' companies suggested that company searches and quarterage collections were equally effective throughout the metropolis, there is not sufficient evidence from other companies to make a definitive evaluation. However, two petitions addressed to James I's solicitor, Sir Robert Heath, indicated that rapid growth prevented the City itself from coming completely under the control of some companies. The wardens of the Goldsmiths' Company complained of "sundry grievances" that company members had received from foreigners and strangers who were "disbursed into many lanes and remote places of this city and suburbs," and a petition from freemen of the Clockmakers' Company claimed that their trade was being undermined by "the multiplicity of foreigners using their profession in London."[81]

When read alongside the anonymous proposals of 1610, these petitions challenge the notion that livery company authority was any greater in the City than it was in the suburbs and liberties. But rather than indicating that all the City companies were losing control over their trades, such complaints must also be viewed in the context of other evidence that points to the willingness of company officers to respond leniently when their own members violated company ordinances while still trying to impose them on noncitizens. This suggests that the primary goal of those who sought independent suburban guilds was to free themselves from the supervision of City companies.

The members of livery companies may have had a stake in preserving the relatively unruly condition of the suburbs and liberties, as long as they stood to benefit from it. Attempts at suburban reform therefore were attacks on the discretionary powers of livery company officers, and their failure illustrated the power of companies to defend their privileges. Nevertheless, the suburbs and liberties of London were not places of complete economic license. Royal charters and letters patent as well as acts of Parliament empowered London's livery companies to regulate their trades throughout the metropolis. The records of livery companies are too inconsistent to allow for a detailed study of enforcement, but the foregoing discussion has demonstrated that companies in a variety of trades exercised some authority over the suburbs and liberties during the early modern period. The companies' influence could be seen in the prosecution of violators of company ordinances and in the cases of the feltmakers and the brick and tile makers of Westminster, groups of suburban artisans who sought independence from City companies by starting companies of their own.

Suburban noncitizens may have had some slight economic advantages over citizens. Although they were still the subjects of national legislation such as the Statute of Artificers as well as the ordinances of City companies, those who lived and worked outside the lord mayor's jurisdiction did not need to join London's companies, and thereby could avoid paying company dues. Nevertheless, as the legislation regarding the leather industry indicated, if noncitizens wanted to trade throughout the metropolis, they would have been in a weaker position than company members. Perhaps in order to improve their economic connections, some suburban foreigners, such as several brewers, paid dues to City companies voluntarily. In short, livery companies offered valuable flexibility to their members. The evidence of freemen bakers, brewers, and builders defending their right to live and work in areas beyond the lord mayor's jurisdiction demonstrated that many guild members hoped to profit from suburban development. Living outside the lord mayor's jurisdiction, they potentially could take advantage of lower rents, expanding markets, and noncitizens who wanted to sell their goods and services in the City.

Despite their City origins and ties, early modern livery companies were necessarily metropolitan in outlook and nature. As Londoners debated the causes of social change, they increasingly examined the implications of uncontrolled economic development, which in turn led them to criticize the companies. The failure of the New Corporation of the Suburbs reaffirmed the standing of companies in the metropolitan economy, and the lapse of the Post-Fire Acts positioned them to influence that economy into the eighteenth century. Even if trade regulation was less effective in the suburbs and liberties than in the City, company members stood to benefit from the discretion of their officers on their behalf. As a result, noncitizens who wanted to avoid City guilds by living and working in the suburbs and liberties of London had no choice but to call for the creation of separate companies for those areas. In this way, rather than indicating the decline of guilds, contemporary reports of economic exploitation in areas outside the lord mayor's jurisdiction—as well as the failure of economic reform there—suggested that many members of London's livery companies considered the suburbs and liberties to be sources of opportunity. Building on the observation that freemen could move easily between the City and the suburbs, the next chapter reexamines the assumption that the City and the suburbs represented competing types of societies based on incompatible values.

CHAPTER 3

Companies and Callings

THE DIVERSITY OF EXPERIENCE

Livery company members participated in the metropolitan economy. This meant they encountered the variety of illicit behaviors that contemporaries and historians have often associated with the noncitizens who lived in areas outside the lord mayor's control. Since, as the preceding chapters have argued, the distinctions between the City and its suburbs and liberties have been overstated, it remains to be seen whether the same was also true for the distinctions between citizens and noncitizens. In order to evaluate the relationship between these categories, this chapter maps the diverse ideas about callings circulating within livery companies during a time when freemen often claimed the right to practice any craft, whatever their company affiliation, according to the "custom of London."[1]

This chapter begins by interpreting contemporary responses to deceitful practices by company members. The language company officers used when disciplining members reveals not only the varieties of malpractice citizens employed but also the importance of reputation to freemen. Although strangers and foreigners may have avoided the costs of company membership, they were denied the prestige associated with company discipline, prestige that carried an economic advantage as rapid population change made it difficult for consumers to find trustworthy dealers and artisans.[2] If the livery companies had succeeded in maintaining standards for high quality, consumers would have been assured of an honest deal if they traded with a member of the company associated with the item or service they desired.

However, company officers had dual and often competing concerns, since they sought to support both the employment and the reputation of their members. These aims may have led officers to be lenient when disciplining members for poor-quality work and also to encourage some members to pursue more menial occupations. The suburban reform proposals of 1610 indicated the ambiguous nature of contemporary attitudes toward work. Casual, manual labor was considered to be an appropriate activity for "honest" noncitizens, but it was an unpleasant option for citizens who lost their livelihoods. Livery companies may have sought to defend a craft ideal, but many members expected them also to be sources of secure employment.³

Nonetheless, as this chapter demonstrates, when company members lost the ability to undertake their primary employments, their companies offered them several occupations they could combine with types of charity that were not, by themselves, adequate to meet their needs. Rather than being appropriate only for unskilled immigrants, the casual, waged work the companies provided was accepted gratefully by many freemen. All this challenges further both the necessary connection of a livery company with a specific calling and the essential incompatibility of the values of citizens and noncitizens.

Complicated Callings

The opportunities that social and economic change presented to Londoners shaped the plot of Thomas Dekker's *The Shoemaker's Holiday*, which was first performed publicly at the Rose Theatre on the Bankside as early as 1599. In one scene, the citizen and shoemaker Simon Eyre purchases merchandise from a Dutch ship captain that, once sold in London's markets, will fund his rise to the lord mayor's office. While developing the theme of social mobility, the scene also highlights the role of deceit in commercial relationships because Eyre poses as an alderman to gain the credit he needs to acquire the goods.⁴ That Eyre learns of the shipment from his journeyman—a young noble who deserts the army to return to his lover and disguises himself as a Dutch shoemaker to "clothe his cunning with the Gentle Craft"—underscores the potential for misrepresentation in London's markets. The success of Eyre's ascendance is confirmed when, after discovering his journeyman's true identity, he convinces the king to pardon the man's treason and bless his clandestine marriage. At the outset of his audience with the king, Eyre attempts to establish his credibility by announcing, "I am a handicraftsman, yet my heart is without craft," which only heightened the confusion between craftiness and craftsmanship.⁵

Although deception in the marketplace was a positive force in Dekker's play, it was the subject of more critical comments from ministers who were themselves concerned about competition from interlopers. In 1621, Henry King preached a Paul's Cross sermon in which he complained of those who "never think they have preaching enough but, as exquisite gluttons lay all markets for fare, so do they lay all churches where there is any suspicion of a sermon." As a result, London's pulpits were flooded with those who, although they were not qualified for such service, "teach as boldly as if they were as well able to become journeymen to the pulpit as to their own trades." In response to the risk of deception encouraged by the free play of supply and demand, King suggested that it was "high time that [the] command be reversed: 'Son of man, lift up thy voice like a trumpet,' rather, Son of man, sound a retreat, and be dumb in admiration, to see cobblers and artisans usurp that holy office."[6] Six years later, Stephen Denison advanced King's position by encouraging government regulation in the religious marketplace. After noting the recent case of boxmaker John Hetherington, who had confessed to the High Commission that he had given up his trade in order to pursue a career as a preacher, Denison encouraged magistrates to punish "intruders into that office of teaching [who] have no lawful calling thereunto."[7]

Taken together, Dekker's play and the sermons of King and Denison suggest that early modern artisans were exposed to a variety of often competing ideas about their callings. Other sources confirm that a diversity of attitudes toward work circulated widely in London. For some, a calling may have represented the particular economic niche that determined their identities as well as their fortunes. When one suburban reform proposal of 1610 called for the improvement of economic regulation in suburban London so that "freemen of the City and those who inhabit near the City may live in their calling to the good of the commonwealth," it implicitly connected a calling and an occupation.[8] Other Londoners, such as citizen and turner Nehemiah Wallington, would have taken a different approach to the issue. As Paul Seaver has shown, Wallington's view of life emphasized the Christian's duty to glorify God in whatever activity he or she was undertaking; he certainly would not have expected that diligence in his calling was any guarantee of profitable or secure employment.[9]

Even if one could assume that Wallington's views were not widely shared in London, livery company records reveal that some craftsmen acted like Dekker's characters and used deceitful means to pursue their personal goals. Many early modern Londoners learned to their cost that not all builders who practiced in the metropolis had mastered their crafts. In 1610, the Carpenters' Company officers inspected the work of carpenter John Jerram, who had added one and a half stories to a house near St. Nicholas Shambles. They found "sundry defects there," and their instructions for repairs read like a primer on elementary timber frame construction. Among other changes, they ordered Jerram to replace the support posts he had used because they were "too slender to bear the floor and roof over them," and told him to replace all the beams of the half story because they were also too small.[10] In 1611, the company's officers found that Edward Blyth needed to make several corrections to an upper story and dormer he had installed on a house in Duck Lane. They found that one of the girders was "too short and unworkmanlike," and that the principal rafter in the dormer needed to be supported from the floor "because otherwise it will not contain his burden."[11]

Partly in response to such problems, builders sought to reform the organization of their trades. In 1579, the officers of the Tylers and Bricklayers' Company and the Masons' Company agreed to prevent their members from intermeddling in each other's trade, "to the end that unity, brotherly love, and good will might hereafter grow and continue between the fellowships and companies."[12] However, such agreements proved insufficient to curb the problem. In 1605, the Carpenters' Company sponsored an act of Parliament intended to enhance the ability of livery companies to police their trades. The company hoped to take action not only against strangers who avoided paying company dues by living in areas exempt from the freedom of London but also against citizens who abused the custom of London by joining one company only as a way of evading the regulations of another. It therefore requested that all artisans and apprentices be compelled to join those companies associated with the craft they practiced.[13]

The Carpenters' Company employed a similar argument in a petition to the lord mayor in 1614. It claimed that many noncitizens worked in the building trades in London, implied that some of these pretended to be company members, and asserted that they often would abandon a job before it was completed, thereby hurting the company's reputation. The petition also complained that children of citizens often learned trades other than their fathers' only to join their fathers' companies by patrimony according to the custom of London. It therefore requested that builders be forced to join the companies most closely related to their trades.[14] Such proposals assumed that builders who belonged to the companies most appropriate to their trades were honest and skillful practitioners. However, the company's own records contain evidence that undermines this assumption. In 1611, its officers inspected the work of carpenters William Copeland and John Hand, both of whom were company members, and found that the braces in the house they were building had been nailed rather than mortised and that several joists were secured insufficiently.[15]

The officers of the Tylers and Bricklayers' Company faced similar difficulties. A comparison of the company's early-seventeenth-century search and quarterage lists reveals that members' workmanship was sometimes poor. Of the 23 tilers and bricklayers fined in the sample discussed in the last chapter, at least 17 (74 percent) were quarterage-paying members of the company.[16] An especially embarrassing case took place in October 1606, when the officers fined three company members who had built a wall near Billingsgate that company officers found "to be very insufficiently done to the discredit of the company which was scoffed at by the plasterers and therefore worthy of a great fine."[17] Malpractice could endanger clients as well as embarrass builders and their companies. In February 1606, the company's officers found that freeman Henry Iffe had built several chimneys in Gray's Inn Lane that appeared to be in danger of falling down. Subsequent inspections indicated that Iffe continued his careless ways: the following April he built a chimney in Chancery Lane that was "likely to endanger the house and would not carry smoke," and a month later he was found to have installed at a doctor's house in Smithfield several portlets that were "insufficiently wrought."[18]

The quarterage book of the Tylers and Bricklayers' Company does not survive after 1616, but the company's search records occasionally specified that a bricklayer charged with carelessness was a member of the company. In 1639, the officers inspected a piece of poor workmanship in suburban Holywell Street carried out by two men, each of whom was described as a company member.[19] In December 1650, they found that Michael Carwarthen, a freeman of their company, had used mortar "made of black earth and bad and insufficient" at a project in Castle Yard near Holborn. Ten months later, they discovered that freeman Abell Barton had also used "very bad mortar and insufficient workmanship" at a site in suburban White Lyon Court. In July 1663, searchers inspected seven chimneys that freeman John Wallis had built in Hosier Lane. They found the chimneys "insufficient to stand" and concluded that there was no option but to tear them down and completely rebuild them in a "workmanlike fashion."[20]

As they tried to maintain standards for quality, company officers sought to increase the likelihood that consumers would employ company members. Toward that end, several companies organized labor markets for their members. In 1615, carpenter John Rayners informed his company's officers that carpenters hoping to find work had gathered at Christ Church on Sunday mornings. He noted the "unfitness" of such occasions and suggested that the company establish a meeting of unemployed carpenters on workdays at its hall similar to that of the bricklayers and plasterers in Cheapside.[21] Eight years later, a petition from 54 junior members—known as "yeomen"—of the Carpenters' Company revived Rayners's plan. The petitioners complained that master builders who belonged to the company threatened their livelihoods by hiring foreigners or joiners because, the masters claimed, there was a shortage of company members. The yeomen therefore requested that the company officers establish a meeting place "upon working days in the morning for that if any man want a workman he may presently know where to find him, or a workman may hear of a master."[22] The company's officers acted on these suggestions in 1628. They acknowledged that because company members lived throughout London, "many of the inhabitants know not in their necessity where to have one to do their work," and so they gained the City aldermen's approval to establish a daily meeting of unemployed company members along Cheapside for the convenience of those seeking to hire carpenters.[23] With the aldermen's endorsement, the carpenters' daily meeting moved to the rear of the Royal Exchange in 1674.[24]

Some consumers tried to solve the problem of how to identify skilled workers by dealing directly with a company's officers. The master of the royal works would inform the governors of the Carpenters' Company whenever he needed to hire carpenters. Although he claimed the authority to draft workers into the Crown's service, he consulted the company's officers because he believed they would know who was most qualified.[25] However, this did not always produce the desired results. In June 1615, the royal carpenter complained that those the company's officers had assigned to him were "clamorous fellows" who "came not as they should have come." A month later, he noted that those sent by the company's officers had worked effectively, except for one who was "a little peevish" and another who was "a little idle."[26]

A further solution to the problems raised by malpractice involved keeping reliable builders on retainer. Livery companies had a steady demand for workers from a variety of occupations in the maintenance of their halls and properties, and so they were in a position to add builders who demonstrated proficiency in their trades to their staffs on a continuing basis. After 1612, the governors of the Vintners' Company agreed that their staff members would carry out any repairs to the company's buildings as long as they charged no more than others would for similar work.[27] The company's staff occasionally supervised larger projects. In 1648, the officers commissioned the company's carpenter and bricklayer to design and build a new tacklehouse by the river to assist merchants in unloading ships, a project that cost more than £20.[28] Companies also allowed some relatives of company workers to inherit these positions, thereby enhancing their value. In 1627, the officers of the Grocers' Company ordered that Mary Stroude, the widow of the company's plumber, "continue the plumber's work to this Hall during her widowhood and for so long time as she shall carefully, honestly, and at reasonable rates perform the said work."[29] In 1658, they allowed Thomas Shippey, the son of the deceased company bricklayer, to succeed to his father's place because he was a "civil, hopeful, and industrious young man" who, from his childhood, was "well instructed and qualified in the rudiments of his profession by his father," who had been a skilled and experienced worker.[30]

Nevertheless, steady employment and other benefits were not guarantees of smooth relations between an institution and its staff members, especially when money was at stake. In 1627, the governors of the Salters' Company considered the bill of charges from their company's bricklayer for repairs in the company's almshouses. Although they agreed to pay his fee, they believed that he charged excessively high rates, and so they disqualified him from any future work for the company.[31] In order to reduce costs, some large employers preferred hiring builders only when they were needed. In 1613, the Carpenters' Company officers considered a complaint from a carpenter that he had been displaced from a building project at Christ's Hospital by a fellow company member. On their part, the hospital's governors informed the company's officers that their policy was "to have no appointed workmen to our house, but as occasion of work requires to take them where we please who will do it best cheap," a policy they assumed all employers would follow.[32]

The problem of identifying honest traders vexed the customers of retailers as well as builders. Even if a consumer had a recommendation for a shop, finding it could prove difficult at a time when retailers relied on their shop signs to distinguish them from competitors who often lived close by. In 1656, haberdasher Hugh Ratcliffe complained to the lord mayor and aldermen that his neighbor and fellow haberdasher George Goldham had appropriated his sign of the Beaver, which he had used for more than twenty years, when he gained the lease on Ratcliffe's shop. When Ratcliffe moved out, he took his sign with him and hung it in front of his new shop, which was next door. After Goldham established himself in his new location, he, too, put up the sign of the Beaver, thereby diverting Ratcliffe's customers into his shop. The aldermen found Goldham's ploy a violation of the City's custom and ordered him to remove his Beaver.[33] A more straightforward case of this sort occurred three years later, when barber-surgeon John Freestone set the sign of the Three Herrings atop his shop, which was on the same street as barber-surgeon John Tempest, who had already been known by that sign for many years. The City magistrates ordered Freestone to take down his sign.[34]

The officers of the Grocers' Company dealt with a variety of equally deceptive practices. One common infraction involved the sale of uninspected goods. The City's governors appointed a garbellor to ensure that all unusable parts of goods such as spices and grains were removed from consignments before they were allowed to be sold in the City, and the company's officers searched grocers' shops to ensure that they had complied with this policy.[35] If they found any uninspected merchandise, the officers would either confiscate the goods and destroy them or order the grocer in question to send them out of the country. Among those guilty of this type of mischief was liveryman William Brockbanke, whom the officers fined £40 for purchasing 40 pounds of ungarbelled cloves from a Bristol merchant in 1579. They also suspended him from the company's livery until he paid his fine and proved his conformity to the company's orders.[36]

Even if grocers had succeeded in evading the garbellor, they would still have needed to convince their customers of the quality of their goods. In 1580, the company's wardens inspected the shop of company member John Palmer and found six bags of ungarbelled rice, four of which displayed old garbellor's seals so potential buyers would think they had passed inspection. The wardens sent Palmer to jail after he resisted their inquiry.[37] In 1586, the company's officers informed the lord mayor that they had discovered counterfeit seals in the possession of freeman Edward Buckley. They believed he intended to use them to pretend old seed was new.[38] Rather than bothering with the garbellor's seal, some grocers simply fabricated their wares. In 1591, company officers punished freeman grocer Francis Sclater, who had made "counterfeit" indigo. They ordered him to sell his merchandise to a chapman "at the best price he can make," and then to turn the proceeds over to the company. Sclater eventually paid a £10 fine and took out a bond of 500 marks against such mischief in the future.[39] Nevertheless, Sclater's case did not signal the end of this form of deception. In 1611, despite the willingness of their predecessors to profit from the sale of Sclater's false wares outside London, the company's officers encouraged grocers to report anyone who traded in false indigo in order to preserve "the good of the commonwealth and credit of the government" of the company.[40]

This sort of malpractice by grocers was especially significant because it could have threatened the health of their customers. In 1616, company officers found freeman Michael Eason in possession of goods "unwholesome for [a] man's body." Upon examination, he confessed to having sold such goods to one of Prince Charles's apothecaries. The officers found that he was "very unfit, insufficient, and unskillful to deal therein," and so they concluded that "great damage and danger might come to the whole realm" if "such enormities and such evil and wicked members of the commonwealth go unpunished." They therefore committed him to prison until he sealed a bond for £100 against selling confections in the future.[41]

Moreover, grocers could deceive suppliers as well as customers. In 1622, the Star Chamber considered the case of freeman Francis Newton, who stood accused of using false weights in his shop. Nine years earlier, one Joyce Dannize had found that Newton had cheated her by nailing a piece of lead under the weight pan of a scale in his shop. As a result, whenever she sold starch to him, he paid her for twelve pounds per barrel less than she had deserved. Dannize then asked another person to negotiate with Newton "for allowance and satisfaction" for her loss. As a result, Newton "confessed the fault with tears and promised to make satisfaction" by paying her eight 22s gold pieces. Similarly, in 1610, Newton had purchased starch from one Rachel Duffield, who noticed that when he weighed her barrels in his shop, he put the hook of his weight scale "up as far as it could into the eye of the beam and thereby lengthened the one side of the beam that was there [and] gained twenty-four or twenty-eight pounds weight in every draught." She alleged in court that when she complained about this to Newton he denied that he could alter his scales. After hearing of additional examples of Newton's fraudulent practices, the Star Chamber had little sympathy for him. It found his deception, committed him to the Fleet Prison, fined him £1,000, and ordered him to make a public admission of his crimes in Grocers' Hall because the company had "suffered much disparagement and scandal" as a result of his cheating.[42]

The reputations of individual company members were also at risk in cases of this sort. In April 1628, the Grocers' officers and several confectioners who were free of other companies searched the shop of freeman John Grant. They confiscated three barrels of comfits that Grant had prepared for sale to a chapman and subsequent distribution in the country, and then tested them at Grocers' Hall. They found that most of the goods had been deceitfully mixed with flour, and when they questioned Grant about their observations, he denied any transgression. They therefore ordered him to be present at an inquest before the lord mayor and aldermen at the Guildhall. Two weeks later, Grant requested that the company forgo a trial before the lord mayor: "This cause lies so in the balance that my name, credit, and reputation and all will be weighed per it, and I, the unworthiest of your members, utterly broken and spoiled." After further consideration, the officers decided to fine Grant £10 and to dissolve the deceitful merchandise in water at a meeting of their Court of Assistants to which other confectioners would be invited.[43]

The Vintners' officers followed a similar policy when they apprehended company members adulterating wine. In a particularly outrageous case in 1610, the officers found that freeman Robert Stanley had placed "unwholesome" wines for sale at low prices to entice people ignorant of their poor quality "to the great peril of their lives." As a result, they committed Stanley to prison. In addition to punishing offenders, the officers interrogated them about the origins of their practices. Several examples from 1610 display the variety of responses to such inquiries. After James Fenton confessed to adulterating wine, the Vintners' Court of Assistants fined him £3 and asked him to identify the person who had taught him such techniques, to which Fenton offered the name of a man in Newcastle. In another case, when the officers discovered an illicit mixture of rum, raisins, and water in the cellar of Henry Sacheveral, he told them that his servant had learned how to adulterate wine from a man in the City. After the officers reprimanded Robert Johnson for a similar abuse, Johnson told them that he had learned the technique from his former master.[44] There is no indication in the court records that the company's officers pursued any of those cases successfully; perhaps the accused vintners gave names of people who were not within the company's reach—or who had never existed.

Nevertheless, there were occasions when the Vintners' officers found what they had been looking for. In 1638, James Jelly told them that before he had become an apprentice he had lived with goldsmith William Banks, the proprietor of the Dragon, a tavern in the City. While he was there, he had watched one of Banks's apprentices work with a cooper and his servant in adding honey and seeds to sherry until it "tasted sweet and drawn with sherry sack was sold for canary wine." Banks appeared at the next meeting of the company's court, and after the officers had ordered him not to sell any of the adulterated wine, he paid a fine of £3.[45] In 1647, the assistants summoned Robert Bignall, a tavern keeper in suburban Horsleydown, whom they charged with adulterating wine. Bignall sent his wife to answer for him, and she admitted that she had made the mixture of raisins and water, a trick she had learned from her neighbor Valerius Sutton. The officers told her to have her husband appear himself to pay the £3 fine and ordered Sutton—who was a member of the Goldsmiths' Company—to transfer into their company.[46]

Besides fines and inquiries about their past contacts, vintners who were caught cheating were also subject to humiliation before the company. In 1609, the Vintners' officers decided that the frequent violation of their ordinances had embarrassed the company and its government. They therefore ordered that anyone adulterating wine more than once would be set in the stocks for one hour at a general meeting of the company. In the mid-sixteenth century, the Goldsmiths' officers also punished deceitful practitioners by placing them in the stocks.[47]

The threat of being put into the stocks alone was a powerful deterrent. In January 1610, the Vintners' officers found three grocers guilty of adulterating wine for a second time and ordered them set in the stocks at their next meeting. However, when the time for their punishment arrived, the assistants decided to vote on the matter, and then the majority was "inclined to clemency in hope of their amendment." One week later, the assistants heard that their searchers had found adulterated wine in the cellar of freeman haberdasher John Smith's tavern. The officers, along with William Webb, a governor of the Haberdashers' Company, judged the wine to have been "unwholesome," and so they voted on whether to fine Smith or to give him a more "public punishment." In the end, the officers split their votes, and the company's master elected to defer his deciding vote until further consideration of the matter.[48] The presence of Webb suggests that the Vintners' officers wanted to prevent tavern keepers who were free of other companies from evading their discipline. The significance of this message was apparent in 1614, when they punished haberdasher Timothy Tanner for violating the ordinance against adding water and sugar to his wine. Tanner paid the fine that the officers levied, but he also requested that "none of his own company" be present to see him reprimanded.[49]

The Vintners' officers realized that a reputation for deceitful dealing could ruin a retailer's business. In 1629, they discussed an order by the City's lord mayor and aldermen for the inspection of banned Rhenish wines at the Guildhall. Although they had instructed their searchers to keep a record of any tavern in which they found such wines, they asked the lord mayor to take steps to preserve the reputations of vintners accused of selling them because the "drawing out of those wines by a public officer may imperil the credits and disgrace those persons in whose custody those wines are found to the overthrowing of their credits and trades."[50] Similarly, the company officers knew that they could destroy the business of vintners by denying them the right to display a bush—the traditional symbol of a vintner—outside their shops. In 1609, after hearing a report that Joan Gregory kept a bawdy house, they decided to inform the Court of Aldermen of her misdemeanors so that "she may be disfranchised and her bush pulled down."[51]

Livery company officers also understood the importance of maintaining their own reputations. In 1609, the Grocers' Company assistants learned that the accounts of their wardens for the previous year had been £368 in arrears. They questioned the individuals involved—Robert Cocks, Edmund Peshall, and Timothy Batherst—and discovered that Batherst had become financially "decayed" before he had taken office. Although Cocks and Peshall had each paid in their share of the accounts, all three wardens had sworn a bond of account jointly, and so the officers expected that Cocks and Peshall would contribute toward Batherst's shortfall. Upon further examination, they found that Batherst had been indebted to Peshall for £1,000 prior to their appointment as wardens. They concluded that Peshall must have known of Batherst's financial condition and that, instead of informing either Cocks or them, he concealed the matter.[52]

The officers of the Vintners' Company faced a similar scandal that year. William Bate, the company's renter warden, was unable to produce £219 of the company's money at the end of his term of office. Bate apparently had intermingled his personal estate with that of the company during his tenure as warden, for he explained his situation to the Court of Assistants by claiming that he had suffered several losses as a result of nonperforming loans. The officers then faced a dilemma. They could have taken legal action against Bate in the hope of recovering their funds after he had liquidated his personal assets. However, they realized that if Bate's condition were made public, it would have brought "some disgrace to the company" for having trusted Bate in the first place and would have led "to the utter overthrow and undoing of the said William Bate forever." They decided to allow Bate to repay them over an extended period "for the preservation of his credit and in hope that he may hereafter recover himself in his estate," although they expected that "if it should please God" to improve his fortunes, he would repay them sooner.[53]

Such examples cannot produce a definitive estimate of the extent to which London freemen violated their companies' ordinances. Nevertheless, they underscore the necessity that historians avoid the assumption that livery company members were inherently honest and law-abiding while interloping strangers were inherently deceitful and anarchic. Companies contained—throughout their ranks—members with diverse attitudes toward their callings. For some, livery companies were institutions that defended order and discipline and at the same time allowed them to pursue an honest living. For others, their company membership was a sort of seal of approval that could transfer their company's good reputation to themselves, giving them an advantage over strangers when soliciting business from anxious consumers. For the deceitful dealer, the expectation on the consumer's part that a company member was likely to be honest could have provided an ideal opportunity for fraud. However, once a person lost his or her reputation, it would have been difficult to regain, and the financial repercussions of scandal—for a company as well as its individual members—could be devastating. The same would have been true for the company itself if its officers had been too lax in enforcing their ordinances. Although they may at times have desired to be lenient with wayward members, their discretion was ultimately limited by their need to uphold the reputations of their company and, by extension, their honest members.[54] Cheating within a company therefore was a risky venture because companies were well positioned to humiliate a dishonest member before his or her commercial peers, and no one, not even an officer of a company, was immune to the most severe sanctions.

Decayed Freemen

As the examples of the financially "decayed" company officers (discussed above) demonstrated, economic disaster was a fact of life in early modern London.[55] Those who did not face bankruptcy personally doubtless knew of others who did. Citizens who lost their livelihoods were in a difficult position. Without a personal estate, their chances of attracting the capital required to restart a business were not favorable.[56] As a result, unemployment could send a member of a City livery company tumbling swiftly down the social hierarchy. The loss of one's career often entailed a loss of prestige. In 1630, members of the Weavers' Company said that rising numbers of apprentices and foreigners working in London were leading freemen to "forsake the trade and fall to servile labours."[57] In 1669, the journeymen of the Dyers' Company complained about the competition they faced from foreigners, claiming that some of their colleagues were being forced "after hard and very laborious apprenticeships to become porters and laborers" in order to make a living.[58] At the same time, in late medieval and early modern England, as elsewhere across Europe, a distinction was made between the deserving and the undeserving poor, between those who physically could not support themselves through work and those who could. Although there was an understanding that some able-bodied people were willing but unable to find employment, when the demands for relief strained the resources of parishes and companies for assisting the needy, preference was given to those physically unable to work.[59] In this context, salaried and casual labor became a valuable option for bankrupt company members despite its lack of prestige.[60]

The transportation of goods was one major source of such employment in London. Several trade guilds maintained tacklehouses and stationed porters at the riverside to assist merchants in unloading and transporting their goods. Also, since the reign of Henry VII, the Grocers' Company had the right to appoint the four master porters and their servants who worked at the weighhouse for foreigners' goods in Cornhill.[61] The City government took steps to ensure that citizens had an advantage in securing porterships. In 1604, the lord mayor approved a scheme to establish a Society of Tacklehouse and Ticket Porters throughout the City. He granted the society control over the movement of goods at the riverside and through the narrow streets of London. The society was not a livery company. Instead, it was an organization that offered membership only to those who already possessed the freedom of London.[62] In 1618, a mayoral proclamation against interlopers made the purpose of the society plain: it was "for the comfort of a great number of poor decayed freemen of this City (whereof there is a competent and sufficient number to perform the labors of all manner of porters without any help of foreigners at all)," and thus it was part of efforts across the nation to create work for the able-bodied unemployed.[63] In 1646, the City government estimated that there were 3,000 such porters in London.[64] Although the society's intention was to support citizens who were in financial distress, a person did not always need to go bankrupt before becoming a porter. In 1654, the lord mayor asked the Weavers' Company to admit Edward Houghton, although he had not completed his apprenticeship. The company accepted Houghton because he was a poor man who intended to gain the freedom of London only so he could work as a street porter.[65]

The selection of porters gave companies an important source of patronage. In 1583, the Grocers' Company officers desired their porters at the riverside to take greater care when serving merchants, and so they appointed supervisors ("masters") among them and required these to hire as assistants ("servants") only those the officers found to be "strong and able men."[66] Four years later, the officers informed the master porters that they were performing their duties poorly and thereupon ordered that they give priority to company members when hiring their servants. At times, the officers directed the appointment of servant porters: in 1587 they named William Stephenson a servant porter at the riverside, and seven years later they elevated him to the position of a master porter there.[67] Although the officers normally had their way in such matters, they occasionally encountered resistance. In 1634, the Grocers' officers sought to promote John Smith, "the ancientest underporter" at the waterside, to a master portership there. However, they considered the complaints of Smith's fellows that he had been dishonest and negligent in his previous duties. The officers then ordered Smith to acquire a reference from merchants of the East India Company, and after he had gained their approval, he was granted the office.[68]

There was an unsteady consensus among livery companies on making porterships the exclusive domain of their freemen. The Clothworkers' officers ordered in 1571 that all porters hired by the company would have to be freemen clothworkers; not until 1629 did the Skinners' officers stipulate that all porters working for the company must be freemen of the company.[69] In 1645, several Vintners' Company porters were charged with violating the City's ordinances because they were not members of livery companies. Four years later, the company's officers attempted to resolve the dispute by informing the lord mayor and aldermen that although "by ancient prescription" they had been able to appoint whomever they pleased to positions in the company's tacklehouses, they would willingly comply with the City's ordinances in the future. They requested that the City allow them to replace their acting porters with freemen as they retired because most of the porters were elderly and would all be replaced with freemen within a few years.[70] The Drapers' Company officers occasionally had difficulty finding members of their company to serve as porters. In 1600 they announced that they would give preference to company members when employing a porter to work at the riverside, but in 1639 they declared that freemen of their company would be hired to work as porters at the company's tacklehouse "if from time to time any of the company may be found fitting" for that service.[71]

Applicants for porterships usually were company members in financial trouble. In 1556, James Browne requested a place among the Grocers' Company porters at the riverside because he was "greatly indebted" to other company members and he lacked the means either to support his family or to repay his loans. The officers could not accede to his request because the tacklehouse had its full complement of porters, but they did promise that he would receive their support if he could find any vacant office they controlled. In 1637, grocer James Pennington—a "decayed liveryman"—sought the next available master portership in the company's control. The assistants granted Pennington's request after they had been convinced of his indebtedness.[72] The Skinners' officers appointed John Warren to be a porter in 1618 because he was a freemen of their company who had fallen into poverty.[73]

Poverty was a necessary but not sufficient qualification for employment as a porter. In 1572, when several servant porters applied to become master porter at the riverside, the Grocers' officers hired Flory

King, "an ancient man [and] one that has served in that room above fourteen years and is the skillfullest man among them all and a very honest man." They then instructed the other applicants to return to their posts and "to use themselves orderly and diligently in their vocation."[74] In 1657, the company's officers hired grocer Clement Sone as a servant porter at the riverside after considering his "ability and fitness for the service," and they rejected the application of Herbert Higgins for a portership because of his advanced age, physical weakness, and "unacquaintedness in the service." They promised instead to consider him the next time they distributed poor relief.[75] The Drapers' officers sought to hire "honest, faithful, and diligent laboring men" who were members of their company to work at their tacklehouse; the Clothworkers' officers looked to hire "able and skillful men" who were capable of the "skillful and safe handling" of goods.[76] The use of the terms "skill," "honest," "vocation," "ability," and "diligent" in the context of manual labor displayed the complexity of the relationship between the officers of livery companies and the porters. The porters were dependent upon the officers' support to a greater extent than they had been before they took up their present occupation, but—like any member of their company—they were still expected to take pride in their calling.[77]

Their continued status as freemen enabled porters to seek assistance from their companies in a variety of circumstances. In 1570, the officers of the Grocers' Company agreed to forward to the lord mayor their porters' concerns about a proposed new company of porters, and ten years later, the company fulfilled the weighhouse porters' more mundane request to have their privy cleaned.[78] In 1608, the Vintners' Company paid 20s to a porter so that he could pay a surgeon to treat his arm, and three years later, it paid 30s to another porter who had been injured while delivering wine.[79] In 1572, the officers of the Grocers' Company gave a benevolence to an old porter at the riverside who had been crippled by an accident while working. Thirty years later, they awarded a porter at the weighhouse a pension of 8d per week because he lost his right arm in a similar incident.[80] The Grocers' officers reimbursed the porters at the riverside 20s for burying two of their impoverished colleagues in 1607, and in 1657 they granted £3 to the son of master porter Thomas Phillips, who was about to receive his M.A. at Cambridge.[81] In 1666, the Clothworkers' officers presented to the City's aldermen a complaint from their tacklehouse porters against another group of riverside porters who, they alleged, interfered with their "labor to the hazard of their lives" and damaged the goods of merchants.[82]

Although many bankrupt freemen had to pursue the physically demanding work of porters, some were forced to pay fees to secure their posts. In 1644, the Skinners' officers caught an elderly master porter attempting to transfer his post to another man for £10. While they allowed the transaction to proceed at a reduced price, they warned their other porters against attempting to sell their positions.[83] After 1620, newly installed master porters associated with the Grocers' Company were required to pay the widow or child of their predecessor 4s 6d per week for six months, a sum that was increased in 1624. Similarly, in 1627, a porter at the weighhouse complained to the Grocers' officers that the weighmaster and his fellow porters had required him to pay them twenty nobles toward the maintenance of horses and carts. Since the officers discovered that the weighhouse staff had not kept either horses or carts for many years, they prohibited the collection of such fees. Nevertheless, the fact that the porters thought they could extract such a sum from a new colleague suggests that they were not all paupers.[84]

Their revived fortunes enabled some porters to enter into financial agreements with their companies. In 1609, the Grocers' officers leased a house in Emperor's Head Lane to porter Isack Gardiner for the annual rent of four marks and required him to secure a bond for the payment of an additional £25 for the lease.[85] Several porters were tenants of rooms at the weighhouse itself. In 1566, porter Thomas Skott negotiated with the Grocers' officers for the rent of a room at the weighhouse, and in 1576, porter John Tetlar sought reimbursement from the company for a staircase he built to his room there. In 1594, porter John Greene leased two rooms over the weighhouse after promising that his children would never seek charity from the parish of St. Peter Cornhill.[86]

Nevertheless, whenever porters attempted to involve themselves in commercial activities, their companies would remind them of the concessionary nature of their positions. In 1645, the officers of the Vintners' Company informed porter James Jean that if he continued to retail wines he would have to resign his portership.[87] In 1657, the Grocers' officers mediated a dispute between a group of salters and the weighhouse servants they had accused of being brokers in the hops trade. After investigating the allegations, the officers decided that instead of being brokers, two porters had received gratuities from country wholesalers for putting them in contact with City merchants and chapmen interested in purchasing hops. The guidelines they adopted prohibited porters from dealing in hops in their own right, from assisting noncitizens in the buying and selling of hops, and from maintaining a correspondence with noncitizens regarding fluctuations in the price of hops.[88]

The potentially lucrative nature of porterships gave companies considerable authority when setting out the working conditions and wages for the porters they supervised. The Vintners' Company controlled two tacklehouses that had a combined regular staff of fifteen master porters and eighteen servant porters, with additional servants hired as needed during busy periods. Although the company's officers could appoint anyone to a master portership, they usually promoted a senior servant porter. The profits of the tacklehouses—probably from the use of the tackle in unloading ships and carts—were to be divided into seventeen parts, with the company getting two parts for the rent of the tacklehouses and the remainder going to the master porters. For the delivery of wine to shops, the company set the rates of portage in 1610 at 12d per tun within the walls of the City, 16d between the walls and the bars, 2s for places between Temple Bar and Westminster, and multiples of that scale for places farther away. The officers also declared that any servant porter who left his post for more than three days without the permission of the master porters would either be demoted to the most junior porter or dismissed.[89]

The officers of the Grocers' Company maintained similar policies. They expected that the four master porters at the weighhouse would be at their post by eight in the morning, and they did not allow porters any absences without their permission. The weighmaster was to keep accounts, which he was supposed to make available to the master porters for inspection. The weighmaster was also the cashier, and he was entitled to one-fifth of the profits, with the remaining four-fifths going to the master porters. The porters were all required to be obedient to company officers as well as to the weighmaster's guidelines for their work.[90] The officers had a similar regime at the waterside, but they also required that porters rent their tackle from the company.[91] The porters were expected to divide their proceeds among themselves, a task that often generated controversy. In 1556, several porters at the waterside requested that the Grocers' Company officers call "one of their fellows" to present his accounts so that the proceeds could be divided. As a result of such controversies, the company's junior renter warden was empowered to oversee the porters' accounting procedures.[92] In 1626, Robert Jennings received additional supervision after the officers heard complaints by several porters that his illiteracy had led him to neglect his accounts.[93]

Porters squabbled over more than money. Although they had much in common, the conditions of their employment established hierarchies among them. In 1617, James Clerke, the most senior porter at one of the Vintners' Company tacklehouses, reported that Richard Church had called him a "knave" in front of some servant porters. The company's officers ordered Church to distribute 3s 4d among the servant porters in recognition of his transgression. In 1641, several of the Vintners' porters reported that they would no longer work with their colleague John Malin because he was "stubborn and fraudulent in his reckonings." Since that had not been the first complaint the officers had heard against Malin, they expelled him from his post. However, in 1645, they rehired him on condition that he improve his behavior toward his fellow porters. The company's officers dismissed Malin permanently ten years later, after he caused further disruption.[94]

Company officers monitored other forms of work-related misbehavior by porters. In 1653, the Skinners' officers admonished porter Robert Pilkington to "leave potting and idleness." After several Vintners' porters complained about one colleague's drinking in 1620, the company's officers warned him that he would be expelled from his office if he did not reform his behavior.[95] In 1572, the Grocers' officers chastised their riverside porters about the dangers drunkenness presented to merchants' wares. Other common complaints against porters addressed their mishandling goods. In 1583, the Grocers' officers disciplined their riverside porters for the unauthorized carrying of goods "to their great peril." In 1560, after grocer Ralph Pyndar complained against porters James Browne and John Browning for "negligently" throwing a butt of malmsey, the officers fined them £3 10s.[96] In 1681, William Kent, the master of the Vintners' Company, complained that some of the company's porters negligently misplaced some of his wine. The porters subsequently offered to reimburse Kent for damages.[97]

A company's disciplinary sanctions extended to the ways porters treated their employers as well as their goods. In 1562, James Browne again appeared before the Grocers' officers, on this occasion to answer a charge of acting "very unreverently" toward a company officer. They decided to imprison Browne for his "evil behavior" as an example to the other porters, but they remitted the sentence after he had apologized tearfully. Nevertheless, they ordered that in the future all porters would have to attend their court at the first quarter day every year so that the officers could evaluate their performances and decide whether to continue employing them.[98] In 1635, when liveryman Samuel Harsenett complained to the Grocers' officers that George Bright, a master porter at the riverside, had insulted him at a company dinner on Guy Fawkes Day, the officers suspended Bright from his position until he apologized to Harsenett.[99]

Such discipline reminded the porters of their dependence on the company's officers. Although complaints against porters usually resulted in contrition and forgiveness, some porters were ejected for misbehavior. In 1609, the Grocers' officers heard numerous complaints against Henry Tuttesham, who had been a porter since 1604, for being absent from his post. After considering that his fellow porters and "many others" were "much damnified and hindered" by Tuttesham's negligence, they decided to remove him from his position.[100] Even after they had been dismissed, porters could still receive the company's charity. In 1601, the officers displaced John Ratcliffe from a portership after he had failed to heed several warnings against drinking while on duty. Still, they awarded him a pension of 16d per week—which was payable to his wife—because of his poverty.[101]

Despite their dependent relationship to their employers, porters could seek redress when abused. In 1618, the officers of the Vintners' Company ordered liveryman William Abell to pay 20s to porter Hugh Clark for striking him on the nose. In 1673, when a vintner named Strawley complained to the officers that the porters had charged him excessive rates, the porters responded that Strawley's cellar was deeper and more dangerous than others. After they reminded the porters that the power to set prices rested with the company, the officers inspected Strawley's cellar and decided that the porters should be allowed to charge him the higher fees.[102]

The officers of some companies also employed porters to assist them with company business rather than to move goods around London. In 1640, the Goldsmiths' officers considered the request of Francis Robinson to be their company's porter. They decided to hire him after considering that he had been a member for more than thirty years and had lost his trade, that he had assisted them without reward for two years, and that it would bring credit to the company to have a porter.[103] The Clothworkers' officers employed one poor member as porter at their hall—which entailed attending them at their meetings and standing at their pew door when they went to church—and another as porter of the company's almshouse, presumably to assist the poor women who lived there.[104]

A unique scheme for employing decayed freemen was the Grocers' "sanderhouse," in which poor "sanderbeaters" ground sandalwood into perfume powder. In 1559, grocer Robert Hobbie leased the sanderhouse from the company for £6 13s 4d per year, and he assured the company's officers that the sander stock would be beaten "without fraud" and in such a way that "no just complaint be made upon him."[105] Hobbie's widow acquired his office, and she was in turn replaced by a series of managers who oversaw a slump in the sanderhouse's fortunes, which transformed it into a money-losing operation for the company.[106] During the ensuing decades, the sanderhouse became a steady drain on the company's finances, and its officers increasingly considered it a source of relief for financially troubled company members. In 1576, William

Young gained the lease of the sanderhouse for 40s per year, despite a much higher bid from another grocer.[107] Seven years later, the company's officers allowed Young to fulfill a debt to a widow by assigning the sanderhouse to her. Although the court considered its being governed by a woman "unseemly," she was still in control of it in 1586.[108] In 1587, the company remitted a year's rent to George Hughes, master of the sanderhouse, because of his poverty and the decline of the sandalwood trade.[109] The demand for sandalwood powder dwindled further during the early seventeenth century, and by 1658 the company sought to convert the sanderhouse into a warehouse in order to improve the company's financial condition.[110]

The charitable attitude of the company's officers toward the sanderbeaters became clear as their fortunes declined. The sanderbeaters were poor members whose wages reflected their tenuous occupation. Although the officers raised the wages of the "poor sanderbeaters . . . poor freemen of this company" because of the high cost of food in 1560, five years later they agreed to pay the sanderbeaters at a rate appropriate to their "vocation and calling" until the sanderhouse master recovered from financial problems. In March 1571, the officers distributed 5s each to the five sanderbeaters who they found lacked sufficient employment to support their families.[111]

In many respects, the company's officers treated sanderbeaters like porters. In 1572, they granted Richard Serle a pension of 12d per week as well as 13s 4d for a surgeon because of his poor health and willingness to work in the sanderhouse as long as he was able. Three years later, the officers gave sanderbeater William Angellsey a weekly pension of 14d because of his "honest painful service and charge of children." In 1578, the officers granted the sanderbeaters a raise from 3d to 4d per pound, but ordered them to employ some young men as beaters to improve the powder's quality. The officers also closely monitored the sanderbeaters' behavior. In 1583, they condemned the actions of Victor Goodyear, but they still granted a 12d weekly benevolence to his wife because she was "a good honest poor woman and labors truly" to support herself and her family.[112]

At times, the Grocers' officers felt the need to respond more severely to the behavior of individual sanderbeaters. In 1594, they accused Humphrey Bourneford of stealing a section of lead pipe stored in the sanderhouse. He confessed that he had committed the crime, and so they reinstated him to his post after he promised that he would never steal again. He kept his word, and in 1598 the officers granted him a pension of 6d per week and allowed him to remain at his post.[113] Five years later, Bourneford was promised the office of master porter at the riverside once it became vacant, but when in 1609 there was an opening, the assistants appointed someone else after having asked the other porters if they considered Bourneford fit for the job. Bourneford's frustrated ambitions soon got the better of him. In 1611, the company's officers discovered that he had mixed a foreign substance with his sander powder in order to increase his profit. After Bourneford confessed, he apologized to the court and asked for their forgiveness on account of his age and poverty, but the assistants ejected him from his post and had him imprisoned. Shortly thereafter, they denied his request for reinstatement.[114]

In addition to porters and sanderbeaters, the Grocers' officers also controlled several positions related to food distribution. In 1622, they appointed Miles Troughton, a "poor ancient decayed brother" of the company, to oversee the grain stocks the company maintained for the City's use. Upon Troughton's death in 1633, the officers hired Oliver Coxed as cornkeeper for one year and appointed widow Anne Troughton to be his assistant; they also ordered that the yearly stipend of twenty marks be divided equally between them. Nine months later, Coxed and Troughton earned a bonus of twenty nobles for their work selling the company's corn.[115] In 1633, the officers gained the power to approve the appointment of the City garbellor's assistants and to inspect their skill at judging the quality of spices and drugs.[116]

As a result of their officers' patronage, unemployed grocers who were willing and able to take up a variety of occupations could turn to the company when seeking work. In 1609, grocer Edward Owen petitioned the officers "for a sanderbeater's place, or the place of a porter at the waterside, or a garbellor," and they promised to discuss the matter with the City's garbellor.[117] Despite the claims (discussed earlier) that even a physically demanding occupation such as portering could require special skills, it was possible for company employees to transfer between posts. In 1627, sanderbeater Richard Scarlett became a master porter at the weighhouse, although four people whom the records describe as "grocers" had also sought the position.[118]

Company pensions and almshouses were also available to members who had lost their livelihoods. Here the contemporary emphasis on assisting those physically unable to work generally held true. Of the 36 petitions for relief that have survived among the Carpenters' papers for the years 1609–24, as many as 32 represented the alms-seekers as being physically unable to work on account of age or injury.[119] While petitions from freemen carpenters stressed their advanced ages and numerous injuries sustained over long careers, carpenters' widows insisted that they sought relief only because they were no longer able to support themselves by their own labor.[120] When reviewing a request for alms, livery company officers considered the state of a petitioner's family as well as his or her health. In 1629, the Grocers' officers delayed admitting Walter Curson into an almshouse because they learned he had a wife, and it would have violated company custom to grant a married man such a place. After Curson reported that he did not know where she lived and did not expect her to rejoin him, the officers admitted him to the almshouse on condition that he move out within a month of his wife's return. That decision reflected the belief that those who had families had potential sources of support besides the company, and so the officers wanted to reserve the almshouses for those who were elderly, unmarried, and poor.[121] The petition that Thomas Shanks directed to the Carpenters' Company supports this point. It claimed that he had fallen into poverty since the death of his wife, upon whom he had depended for all his necessities.[122]

Company officers were also concerned about the behavior of unmarried men and women living in their almshouses. In 1647, the Vintners' officers learned that two of their almspeople, Martin Hodgson and Isabell Pooley, had engaged in "too familiar and uncivil behavior tending to lasciviousness to the disgrace of the company's government of their almshouses." They commanded Hodgson and Pooley to avoid such activity in the future and warned them that breaking the company's regulations would result in their expulsion from the almshouse.[123] Two years later, after a company warden complained to his fellow officers that Hodgson had insulted him, the officers considered further reports of his continued "familiarity" with Pooley, which promoted the sort of "uncivil behavior" he had been warned about. They suspended Hodgson's pension and ordered him to vacate the almshouse. They also warned Pooley that if she continued to allow him into her room, they would punish her in a similar way. However, Hodgson appealed to the officers for relief sixteen months later, and after he had apologized for his past behavior and promised to obey their regulations, they readmitted him to one of the company's almshouses and paid him 10s of his suspended pension.[124]

Leniency also could inhibit the ability of company officers to control the religious behavior of almspeople. In May 1645, the Salters' officers ordered their almsmen to attend services at St. Swithen's Church every Sunday. Three months later, they heard a complaint against almsman Daniel Sutton "for his disorderly carriage and lewd life and neglect of going to church." Sutton repented his offenses, promised to change his behavior, and agreed that he would expect no further favors from his governors if he were to violate their regulations. Four months later, Sutton again appeared before the officers after they learned that his poor behavior had continued. They concluded that there was "little hope of amendment," and so they ejected him from both his pension and his almshouse. But not for long. By March 1645, Sutton had been readmitted to the company's charity after promising to reform, and according to the company's sporadic Interregnum court records, he stayed out of trouble until 1656, at which time both Sutton and an almswoman were suspended from their pensions for their "entertainment of inmates" and other offenses.[125]

Almspeople with strong ties to influential company members may have received special favor from a company's officers. In 1633, the Salters' officers admitted Bartholomew Banks into one of the company's almshouses. Five years later, they learned that Banks had often been drunk and that he had abused a company staff member. Because they considered it to be "a disparagement to the company to keep such almsmen," they threatened to expel him if he were to repeat such offenses. In 1640, the officers fulfilled their promise and ejected Banks for failing to reform. However, they reinstated him within three weeks, in part because of their respect for the memory of William Robson, a deceased company officer who had first recommended Banks for relief.[126]

Despite occasional assertions that almspeople had to be physically unable to work, they often could combine alms from the company with casual labor. In the Salters' Company, the six almsmen who lived near the company hall in the early seventeenth century were expected to assist the company's officers on feast days with "any service" such as carrying the gowns of guests.[127] They were also paid for assisting the company's officers in calling freemen to elections and in selling the company's grain in the marketplace.[128] The Grocers' officers in 1598 appointed Robert Coping, a company almsman, to be overseer of works at the company hall for the fee of 40s.[129]

Sometimes pensioners also held steadier company offices. In the Salters' Company, the appointment of a beadle could occasion a variety of shifts among almspeople. In 1645, when beadle Robert Ely died, the company's officers considered the petition of almsman William Ibbett, whom, "in respect of his knowledge in that office," they considered "to be a fit man for that place." They offered him the beadleship, along with its £3 per year salary, and then promoted almsman William Heyward to be Ibbett's assistant and receive a 20s per year stipend. The officers subsequently offered the almshouse where Ely had lived to William Grymes, "a poor member of this company," on condition that he give the company a bond securing the departure of his wife and children after his death.[130] The intermingling of the criteria for holding company offices with those for receiving poor relief was also evident when the governors of the Vintners' Company hired William Edwards as their deputy beadle in 1677 while he remained well behaved and unmarried.[131]

Some of the Salters' Company pensioners were given preference for spaces in the company's almshouses in exchange for their promise to care for their fellow residents. In 1628, the company's officers admitted John Goosey—"a poor man of this company"—and his wife into one of the company's almshouses on the condition that they care for "old Browne," a sick inmate there. As a result, John Goosey received a salary of 5s per week over and above his pension of 7s per week, and a year later, his wife received 8s from the company for burying Browne. In 1649, the company's governors granted an almshouse to Constantine Allstone and his wife after they had considered "the good condition of Allstone's wife" and her ability to assist the other almspeople.[132]

Despite their policy of excluding married people from their almshouses, the Grocers' officers followed a similar course. In 1656, they rejected Richard Darnell's application for an almshouse they controlled in Oundle, Northamptonshire, because the founder's will allowed them to admit only single men. But they admitted Darnell and his wife after they had received assurances from the churchwardens of Oundle that Darnell's wife would vacate the house if she survived him and would "in the meantime be helpful to the old men there."[133] That same year, the officers granted an almshouse place to the widow of an almsman on condition that she assist a fellow almsman who was "aged and dimsighted and troubled with lameness." However, in 1658, the company's officers reaffirmed that no married member of the company would be considered for a place in an almshouse.[134]

The flexible attitudes of company officers toward the criteria for relief and the ability to combine work with charity enabled some company members to spend much of their adult lives in their company's service. Grocer Anthony Box became a sanderbeater in 1631 and began receiving a weekly pension of 12d one year later. In 1636, the officers paid him 20s to act as a messenger between themselves and a grocer in Peterborough. Two years later, Box and sanderbeater George Bright became masters of the sanderhouse after they had sealed a bond of 200 marks to the company as security for their good performance. In 1639, Box and Bright joined the widow Troughton as the company's paid cornkeepers.[135] Box received twenty nobles on the occasion of his daughter's wedding in 1641, 20s after an illness in 1644, and after an unspecified lapse, his pension was restored in 1651. At some point in the late 1650s, sanderbeater Rowland Burfield replaced Bright as master of the sanderhouse, and Burfield and Box received income supplements of 30s or 40s from the company yearly after 1659. As the sanderhouse fell into disuse, they were referred to variously as "sanderbeaters and waiting servants" and "servants to the company."[136]

The career of Salters' Company almsman Burrell Nower took a similar course. In June 1637, the company's officers ordered him and his wife to dismiss their daughter from their almshouse because she was about to give birth and to secure two bonds assuring that they would not take in any other inmates in the future. Eight months later, Nower submitted himself and his wife to the judgment of the officers, and he promised he would "carry himself with all due respects" to the master, wardens, and others of the company and "live peaceable with the beadle and his fellow almsmen."[137] In 1656, Nower was given the job of porter at the company hall with a salary of 12d for each day that he served, which improved his material condition to such a degree that, seven years later, he gave £10 to the company's clerk to be spent on a plate engraved with his coat of arms as well as that of the company.[138]

A gift of plate was not the only way someone could express appreciation for a company's patronage. In 1611, grocer Francis Clapham became a sanderbeater, but he continued to receive occasional relief as a "poor brother" of the company, and in 1613 he began to receive a pension of 12d per week. In 1615, the company's officers granted his request for the reversion of a master porter's place at the weighhouse, and one year later, they increased his pension by 12d per week upon noting his "honest carriage" as well as the "diligence and industry" he had exhibited in the company's work. Clapham took up a master portership in 1617, and he soon joined his colleagues in a dispute with the master of the weighhouse. Although the company's records do not indicate the outcome of that controversy, in 1620 the assistants noted that Clapham had used his own money to set up in the weighhouse a desk with a Bible "for the instruction, use, and benefit of the officers of the said house." They also granted the request of Clapham and the other porters by ordering the weighhouse officers to maintain the books and table at their own expense. In 1624, Clapham in turn donated "a very fair Bible gilded" to the company, which the officers accepted with gratitude and placed on a desk in the hall's parlor.[139]

All this sheds light on the relationship between the officers of livery companies and their less fortunate members, and reveals how opportunities for casual and salaried employment in the company's service were important benefits of membership. Since they were able-bodied, sanderbeaters and porters stood to gain more income than they likely would have obtained from company poor relief alone, and they also were given limited opportunities to participate in trade. It is difficult to judge whether they considered such work to be a deviation from their callings. The conditions placed on rooms in almshouses may have encouraged the poor to pursue casual labor as long as they were physically able. This in turn may have reduced the costs for merchants who depended on porters to move their goods from the riverside to their shops. However, the frequency with which officers dealt leniently with porters and sanderbeaters indicated that they were not concerned solely with maintaining harsh discipline among their poorer members. The ability of many almspeople to combine work with relief suggests that livery company officers did not make a rigid distinction between the deserving and the undeserving poor, and the articulation of criteria for employment such as skill and honesty encouraged financially decayed company members to pursue their new occupations with pride. Besides, given the tumultuous nature of the early modern economy, the officers who watched their bankrupt colleagues compete for the right to hold such positions could not have assumed that they and those close to them would never suffer a similar plight.

Like players on a Renaissance stage, members of London's trade guilds were not always who they seemed to be. The indications of a person's association with a livery company, such as the bush outside a vintner's shop or participation in the meeting of unemployed carpenters, could have been valuable marketing devices, but they were not necessarily guarantees of quality. The officers of companies realized that a diversity of attitudes toward work contributed to varying proficiency levels among their members. It must have seemed possible to many Londoners that interloping strangers who took pride in their work could have produced goods of at least the same quality as company members who cared little about their own. In practice, the distinction between citizens and noncitizens was therefore very fine, and the petitions that defended the "honest callings" of freemen against foreigners' craftiness only confused matters further.

Diverse attitudes toward work also produced divergent views of company discipline. Those who valued discipline encouraged officers to enforce company regulations in order to keep themselves and their colleagues focused on the divine plan for their lives. But those who wished to deceive their customers may also have valued company discipline because it enhanced their companies' reputations and thereby facilitated their deceitful practices, at least until they were discovered. The enforcement of ordinances gave officers power over the lives of hundreds of people, but there were limits to their discretion. Everyone in the company was expected to conform to a certain set of behaviors, and violations—whether by shopkeepers or almshouse dwellers—reflected not only upon the individual but also upon the governors themselves. There were risks involved in leniency.

At the same time, interpretations of social relations in early modern London need to account for individuals who viewed the livery companies as sources not only of economic regulation but also of economic security during personal financial declines. Noncitizens who evaded company dues may have had one sort of economic advantage over company members, but during a period of continual economic fluctuation, for many freemen the benefits of company membership far outweighed the costs.

CHAPTER 4

Communication and Company Politics

The ability of livery companies to provide freemen with a sense of community was limited by the diversity of their members' attitudes toward work. The structure of guild governance further complicated the relationship between freemen and their companies. Following the pattern that historians have found in towns across early modern England, the direction of a company's affairs rested primarily in the hands of individuals who ranked among its oldest and wealthiest members, although the interference of powerful external actors such as the Crown—the ultimate source of corporate authority—could alter the direction of guild politics considerably.[1]

Historians have drawn a number of competing conclusions about livery company politics in early modern London. George Unwin, whose work is still a historiographic touchstone, stressed the growing power of company courts of assistants in guild affairs. This in turn gave larger capitalists increasing authority in setting the working conditions of smaller producers and retailers. For Unwin, many of London's companies were strife-filled, particularly during the seventeenth century, as older forms of craft organization gave way to industrialism, with all its inherent class antagonisms. More recent studies of company politics, focusing on the sixteenth century, have challenged Unwin's emphasis on conflict. While acknowledging that ultimate power rested with the relatively exclusive courts of assistants, Steve Rappaport argued that the liveries' ranks from which the assistants were chosen were rather broad in Tudor London. He also attributed the elite character of company government to the heavy demands that officeholding placed on officers' time and financial resources, rather than to any inherent conflict of interest between officers and members. Ian Archer found a middle ground between Unwin and Rappaport by suggesting that although important tensions arose between the governors and the rank and file of Elizabethan companies—and particularly in those companies with larger memberships—conflict tended to remain unfocused and seldom posed a significant threat to the officers' authority. Furthermore, he found that the ability of aggrieved company members to appeal to the Crown for support restrained their officers' oligarchic ambitions.[2]

Following several of those observations, this chapter analyzes the routine practices of company government from the late sixteenth to the early eighteenth century in order to gauge the ability of companies in general to cope with the diversity of their members' interests and values. This will lay the groundwork for more detailed investigations of the internal affairs of two companies—the Grocers' and the Weavers'—in subsequent chapters. Beginning with an examination of the methods of communication among company members, this chapter demonstrates that the expanding ranks of many companies during the early modern period limited the personal interaction between members and their officers. Increasingly, routine communication took written form, which enhanced the influence of mediators, such as company clerks and scriveners. Although clerks routinely acted as the conduits between company governors, company members, and others who wished to transact business with them, scriveners often worked with illiterate and semiliterate members who needed to communicate with their governors. Clerks and scriveners in London, like notaries elsewhere in early modern Europe, sometimes intermingled their own opinions and interests with those of their clients.[3]

The discussion then examines the limitations that custom and bureaucracy placed on the influence of officers in company affairs. As was true for towns, a company's members generally rose to prominence through a well-established pattern based on seniority. However, the continual turnover in personnel often brought individuals not familiar with routine matters of company government into positions of authority. Such governors relied on the advice of the company's permanent staff members, and especially of its clerk, who were responsible for managing the information that was crucial to the functioning of company government. At times, the officers' limited knowledge of company affairs influenced guild politics.

Unwin's structural analysis of guild politics led him to assume that company officers shared a single view of their authority. The hierarchical nature of company government often reduced the diversity of ideas circulating among the officers, but this chapter argues that in practice their similar economic and demographic backgrounds did not guarantee consensus. Although competing economic interests occasionally influenced the character of guild politics, some officers were receptive to ideas of lower-ranking members when determining policy. Despite the often formulaic nature of company records, meetings of officers could be quite deliberative and open to debates on all sorts of matters, including the nature of company politics itself. However, before guild officers and members could cooperate fully, they had to find ways to communicate effectively.

The Politics of Semiliteracy

Since much of the discussion that influenced company policy was never recorded, an analysis of guild politics often rests on the interpretation of texts of uncertain origin. In his study of Tudor London, Rappaport claimed that the vast majority of apprentices could write their names. However, even if most company members could do so, that would not imply an ability to craft the sometimes elaborate petitions that claimed to represent their positions. For that reason, the question of authorship impedes the interpretation of communication among the different levels of a company's hierarchy. Nevertheless, as Natalie Davis has demonstrated in the case of French pardon tales, even texts that were co-authored can be invaluable for historical investigation. By reading pardon tales as cooperative projects of defendants and scribes, Davis uncovered the "fiction in the archives," a blend of the true and the imaginary. Davis was able to identify the voices of pardon seekers because they consulted notaries not out of ignorance of how to tell a good story, but because they needed to draw on the notary's specialized knowledge of the language of courts.[4]

When in need of skilled writing, early modern Londoners often turned to scriveners. In the medieval period, professional scriveners were artisans who underwent extensive training in the ways and the handwriting of courts before embarking on careers that could involve them in the recording of legal proceedings in royal tribunals, the composition of governmental orders, and the drafting of legal documents such as bonds, deeds, wills, and insurance policies. Scriveners thus could offer knowledge for sale, and as the law of commerce expanded in the early modern period, so, too, did the commerce of law. By the early seventeenth century, "scrivening" developed into a branch of legal activity concerned primarily with investments and securities. However, since most early modern people had no formal education, and those who had been to school may have learned to read but not to write, scriveners—many of whom belonged to the Scriveners' Company—continued to practice the more common forms of legal writing such as the drafting of wills and leases. They may not have exercised a monopoly over writing legal documents, but their expertise set them apart from their contemporaries.[5]

The exercise of a craft that was difficult to monopolize was a predicament that scriveners shared with weavers. Because weaving was a labor-intensive occupation in the late sixteenth and early seventeenth centuries, the Weavers' Company encountered obstacles in its attempts to prevent nonmembers from participating in its trade. One way in which the company attempted to limit the number of weavers working in London was by controlling the entrance of apprentices to the craft. The company's regulations fixed the number of apprentices that a member could employ and required masters to use the company clerk for formally binding their apprentices, a process that gave the clerk additional income while allowing company officers to supervise apprenticeships. As a result, any weaver who bound his apprentices elsewhere would be subject to a fine equivalent to nearly twice the company clerk's binding fee.[6]

Nonetheless, those who sought to profit from illicitly crafting legal documents remained willing to assist company members in evading such regulations. An early-seventeenth-century petition from a group of weavers to the City's lord mayor and aldermen asserted that because the company's officers failed to control apprenticeship, poor-quality material was produced in London and sold throughout the country. They reported that several weavers who were freemen of other companies had, in less than seven years, bound a total of 37 apprentices to themselves with the assistance of their companies' clerks. The petitioners further charged that one of the clerks in question had proclaimed himself willing to bind 20 apprentices to a man in a single day "by reason that it was for his profit."[7]

The Weavers' officers were well aware of the problem. In 1613, they fined a weaver 20s for a variety of offenses including having a "foreign scrivener" bind an apprentice, and in 1631, they blamed the illicit work of scriveners for the excessive number of apprentices employed in their trade.[8] In 1666, the company's officers disciplined John Oakley after he confessed to binding a female apprentice at a scrivener's shop three years earlier. Not only had Oakley violated the company policy concerning apprentice binding, he also breached a regulation that prohibited company members from teaching their craft to women.[9] The officers were not immune from temptation by scriveners. In 1654, the company's assistants learned that the previous year's wardens had secretly taken their accounts to a "scrivener shop" and had them altered.[10] Such cases revealed the company's vulnerability to those willing and able to falsify documents.

Two texts from the records of the Carpenters' Company suggest that scriveners also may have influenced more licit types of communication between company officers and members. As craftsmen in the building trades, freemen carpenters stood to profit from economic growth in early modern London, but they struggled to remain dominant in their market. Such tensions were apparent in two complaints from freemen against James I's royal carpenter. The first petition introduced its authors as "us being freemen of the City of London." It listed their grievances in three numbered paragraphs and mentioned their intended audience only by references to the petitioners' need for "your graces favor" and "your graces speedy help." The second described its authors as "your Majesty's most lowly and obedient subjects, the freemen of the Company of Carpenters within your Highness's City of London," and it contained references to contemporary social relations that went unmentioned in the other petition. While the first text reported that the royal carpenter did "wholly set men and boys being foreigners at work and almost no freemen," the other petition alleged that he hired "multitudes" of "foreigners which he hath drawn out of the country from their dwellings and trades in those parts, which now lie in chambers and places in and about this City and suburbs, pestering them up (a thing very dangerous)."[11]

To read one of these petitions without being aware of the other would leave a distorted impression of the attitudes of freemen carpenters. The first appears to be the product of aggrieved freemen concerned with defending their rights without bothering to flatter their royal reader. However, the second represents deferential subjects who sought only to notify their monarch that one of his servants was doing him a disservice by trampling on the rights of his subjects, a fine distinction that would not have been lost on early modern politicians.[12] More important, rather than seeming to be the remains of two discrete petitions, the first text looks to be a rough plan for the second. Perhaps a small group of concerned carpenters met together, outlined their basic strategy, and then took what has survived as the first, poorly written petition to someone who they believed was more knowledgeable in the ways of the court. Although the second petition displays a general similarity to the first, it was inscribed by a hand more accustomed to holding a pen than a hammer. The fact that they each found their way into the archives of the Carpenters' Company, and not those of the Crown, suggests that the company's officers discovered that some members were about to appeal over their heads, and they then intervened to manage or forestall the complaint in the hope of maintaining the company's good relations with the Crown.

Toward that end, the governors of livery companies themselves sometimes sought professional advice when drafting petitions directed to the central government. In 1635, the Vintners' officers obtained legal counsel before they wrote to the Crown regarding a previous agreement in which Charles I promised to give the company control over tavern licensing in exchange for £6,000. Although the officers had paid the sum in question, they continued to have difficulties with licenses, and so they established a committee of leading members to draft a petition. After hearing the committee's report, the assistants decided to show the draft to the Recorder of London "to be penned by him lest any offensive word or matter shall be inserted."[13] And in 1684, the Weavers' Company—like other livery companies—was obliged by Charles II to defend its charter. After deliberating over their response to the Crown's action, the company's officers instructed their clerk to draft a petition based on their discussion, and "if he see cause to alter the said petition" they asked him to revise it and present it at their next meeting. At that time, the original and the clerk's revisions were "several times read over and well considered and debated" before a decision was made. Although the court's record book contains a copy of the petition that the company submitted to the Crown, there is no indication whether it included the clerk's revisions. However, when the officers sent a delegation to Windsor, the king directed the company's clerk to read their petition.[14]

A letter that carpenter Robert Wingfield sent to the Carpenters' officers regarding his unruly apprentice Luke Wassall also went through at least two drafts. Wingfield reported that Wassall behaved "very badly" and that, despite occasional warnings, he remained unrepentant. At that point in the complaint, something unusual happened: the handwriting changed dramatically. Although the signature was by the first hand, a list of Wassall's misdemeanors appeared as a postscript in a second hand, though the subject of the petition remained "I."[15] The company records contain no details of the case's outcome, but the petition itself says a great deal about communication within the company. Clearly, Wingfield was not satisfied with the first draft. If he began it himself, he employed someone else to finish it. Then again, Wingfield may have taken his story to a scrivener and asked him to compose it in the first place. He may have read the finished product, or had someone read it to him, and decided that it needed embellishment, and so he added to it himself or took it to yet another scribe. Either way, the resulting complaint was the product of at least two individuals, one of whom, Wingfield, was not confident of his abilities to write his own complaint, although he knew his case well enough not to allow it to be misrepresented.

The case of Carpenters' warden William Bonner and his apprentice Philip Davis combined elements from both of the previous examples. Sometime in 1613–14, Bonner petitioned his company's assistants about his unruly apprentice, and his charges against Davis were a catalog of vice. Davis, Bonner alleged, was a "drunkard and a great swearer, a common liar . . . a common swaggerer . . . a great tobacco taker and a common alehouse haunter . . . [and] a whoremaster by show for words spoken lying in his bed and deeds done to his fellow which [are] not fit to be spoken by man." In the company archives a letter from Davis was attached to Bonner's statement that offered his side of the story. Davis claimed that Bonner had been making "evil reports" of his behavior to the company with the intent of seizing some property his father had given him on condition of his continued good behavior in London. Davis then complained that he was "wronged and cannot of my self have redress" without the officers' help "because he is a man of good fashion outwardly to the world's eye, and I am but at this time a poor apprentice not able to manifest my cause." Davis went on to say that he was "almost desperate, nay I will rather violently destroy myself than thus to live, yet I desire not to be posted over any more from one to an other, but rather honestly to serve out my time with him what ever I did endure, only let me have a good report to the world to the comfort of my friends."[16] There is no evidence of the officers' decision in this case, but if the written record is a true indication of the controversy's nature, it boiled down to Bonner's word—and reputation—against those of his apprentice.

This matter was complicated further by Davis's subsequent claim that he did not write the aforementioned complaint against his master. In a letter composed in a hand different from that of the attack on Bonner, Davis alleged that he had shared some of his complaints against his master with someone who offered to write to the company on his behalf. However, the resulting petition "was made so contrary" to Davis's intent that he decided to suppress it. Bonner soon discovered the document and, after dismissing Davis from his service, took it to the company's governors himself as evidence of his apprentice's unruliness. Davis, who found himself without money and friends, was then forced to seek charity from the company's officers, largely because he had been unsuccessful in finding someone to help him write a petition.[17]

The political weakness of an allegedly abused apprentice is also apparent in the story of William Nichols. Sometime in 1615, Nichols reported to the City chamberlain that he had served his master, William Freeman, for five years, but according to his petition, "in all that time he hath not been put to work in that manner whereby he might become a sufficient workman towards the maintenance of himself and his family," and his master often threatened to send him to Bridewell for his disobedience.[18] His complaint was a serious one, but it was taken to the wrong court: the chamberlain therefore asked the Carpenters' officers to deal with it first, and to refer it back only if they could not resolve it.[19] Nichols's complaint reveals the difficulties facing apprentices who felt that they had legitimate grievances against their masters, and raises the question of how apprentices learned to complain.[20] Perhaps an aggrieved apprentice would consult his peers or seek the advice of a skilled writer, as Philip Davis apparently did. Even if Davis fabricated or embellished upon the role of the scribe in his story, the fact that he thought the court would believe his tale suggested that contemporaries were aware that such things could happen. These cases display the complex power relations between master and apprentice, but they also demonstrate that complaining was an art and that the presentation of a complaint to the proper audience was at least as important as its composition.

Petitioners sought advice from scriveners because they lacked skill in presentation, not because they did not know what they wanted. They maintained some control over the representation of their views even though the words used may not have been their own. Such a strategy was familiar to artisans like carpenters who would normally proceed on a building project with only a general idea of their client's wishes. Not surprisingly, the Carpenters' papers contain examples of complaints not only from carpenters but also against them. In a case reminiscent of the way apprentice Philip Davis criticized his scribe, one Nicholas Davies complained to the court that he had agreed with carpenter Owen Hoor to build his house in a watertight manner, but Hoor "did not do it sufficient . . . [so] that your petitioner can not lie dry in his bed." Davies then asked the court to help him to gain satisfaction.[21] A complainant, like a householder, communicated a basic plan to a craftsman, but he did not lose sight of his objective, and he expected value for money.

While handwritten complaints could display a petitioner's individuality, requests for alms were the most common type of communication between members of the Carpenters' Company and their officers, and their uniformity suggests that scriveners were involved in their construction.[22] In addition to emphasizing the petitioners' physical debilities, the petitions had several other structural similarities. Their introductions all situated the petitioners in a dependent position relative to their readers. Twenty-seven of the 36 petitions discussed in the previous chapter began with the phrase "to the worshipful master, wardens, and assistants of the Carpenters Company of London, the humble petition of . . . " Of the 9 that did not conform to that pattern, all but 2 either neglected to mention the assistants or described themselves as "poor" rather than as "humble." The others included a request for a small loan by John Patey, a carpenter trying to recover from a long illness, and the petition of a widow who had been living in Ireland, circumstances that may account for their idiosyncratic styles. The closing of each petition reaffirmed the relationship between the humble petitioner and the worshipful governor. All the petitions except two stated the petitioner's intention of praying to God on behalf of the officers, although the fact that one of these ended with "etc." underscores the formulaic quality of these texts.[23] Since only one individual had two petitions included in the sample—and they were written by different hands—the apparent plagiarism that filled the charitable subgenre of the local literature of complaint must be explained.

In an era when old age was synonymous with poverty, the ability to gain poor relief was essential to survival.[24] A request for alms from a livery company was therefore not a rare phenomenon in London, and a successful petition would help not only the applicant but also his or her parish, the other major source of poor relief at the time. Perhaps, then, parochial officials, who would have been well aware of the criteria typically applied to such petitions, assisted their parishioners with their appeals. However, of the petitions included in the above sample, only three mention a parish. The widow Cooke notified the assistants that since her husband's death she had been an "honest woman and a long householder in Saint Katherine Colemans Parish, never being relieved with one penny by their parishioners." Marjorie Eaton included several references from the officers of an unnamed parish with her request for charity, and Katherine Hughes reported that she was the recipient of 4d per week from the parish of St. Dunstan's in the East, and she included a petition from the minister, churchwardens, and several of the parish vestry along with her request for company charity.[25]

In addition to their parochial officers, elderly Londoners probably had contact with someone who drafted or executed the will of a person to whom they had been close. If not a minister, then perhaps a scrivener could write an alms petition. The involvement of scriveners, accustomed to dealing with wills and other standardized legal documents, could account for the formulaic quality of these texts, and it would also explain the legalistic expressions scattered throughout the alms petitions. For example, the concluding sections of the petitions from Alice

Miller and Elizabeth Benson both began with the phrase "the premises considered"; that of William Pyndon asked for a pension "as others in like case have."[26] Indeed, the petitions all resemble implied contracts in which the petitioner promises to pray for the company officers in exchange for their charity.

Writing, or finding someone else to write, a brief yet compelling argument may have been the best way for a poor person to gain the attention of company officers. In 1610, the Haberdashers' governors announced that in the future they would receive petitions from those seeking charity once a year only, at their St. Katherine's Day meeting, just prior to the feast at which the names of the newly elected master and wardens were announced to the livery.[27] In that same year, the Grocers' officers ordered that "for the more speedy dispatch of the weighty affairs and business" of their Court of Assistants, anyone seeking charity from them would first have to approach the company wardens.[28] The determination that charity was no longer considered a "weighty" affair may have signaled a deterioration of face-to-face contact between members of different social orders, but it may also have reflected the expanding volume of business for the officers. Rather than have alms-seekers appear before the entire court—the members of which were businessmen, not professional bureaucrats—the wardens would meet them individually. Thus, by bringing a concise, clearly written petition with them to their meeting, alms-seekers could have seen themselves as cooperating with officials who had growing demands on their time, thereby improving their chances of gaining relief.

A written petition also offered flexibility to those who felt uncomfortable presenting their requests in person. In her petition to the Carpenters' officers of 1611, Jane Redding, who described herself as a "poor widow," noted that "I thought good to write my mind to you because I cannot deliver my mind by word of mouth."[29] Elite members of companies were not immune to such concerns. When Lawrence Greene wrote to the Grocers' assistants in 1621 seeking to avoid serving as company warden, he claimed that he had wanted to appear before them personally, "but being privy to mine own imperfection of speech, I have so far presumed of your patience as to entreat that this paper may excuse my absence, and deliver that which my bad utterance and bashful disposition does disable me to perform."[30] In 1648, after reading a petition for charity from former liveryman Francis Easterly, the Vintners' officers awarded him £10.[31] Easterly's petition earned him some financial relief, but it also saved him the potential embarrassment of appearing in his poor state and beseeching his former colleagues.

The preceding examples all suggest the ways in which written communication among company members increased the sense of distance between them and their officers. As communication became more formalized, it became less personal. The trend away from face-to-face contact also limited the officers' direct awareness of their members' concerns because it heightened their dependence on mediators such as scriveners and clerks for information vital to their decision making.

The Personnel of Administration

The administrative authority of livery companies rested in the hands of their wardens and assistants, who met together in courts of assistants. The number of assistants and wardens varied from company to company. Typically, there were between twelve and twenty assistants and two to four wardens. Some companies had "renter" wardens, usually among the more junior assistants, who were responsible for collecting and disbursing revenue from their company's properties. Such companies would also have "upper" or "master" wardens, who were among the most senior assistants and were primarily responsible for their company's affairs and finances. Assistants held their positions for life or until they were prevented by illness or other factors from serving, and wardens generally rotated back to the assistants' ranks after a year in office.[32] The frequency of full court meetings varied among companies, but between meetings committees of assistants appointed by the full court carried out a variety of tasks.[33] Also, the wardens at times held weekly courts on their own to deal with developments relating to the company; the Grocers' wardens held such meetings to resolve any "debates or controversies" and for "the avoiding of suits in law" involving company members. If the wardens could not handle such matters themselves, they would refer them to the next full court meeting.[34]

Members of a court of assistants were generally drawn from the ranks of a company's liverymen. In most cases, a company's court of assistants had the power to elevate junior members into their company's livery, but in practice such promotions followed a well-known pattern based on seniority and wealth. Although there was room for courts of assistants to exercise discretion in such appointments, the Grocers' officers posted a table of the company's assistants and liverymen in the parlor of the company hall, "for the better satisfaction of those of the livery concerning their due place and turns upon occasions."[35] Occasionally, placement sparked controversy. In 1617, the Grocers' assistants heard liveryman Andrew Troughton complain that he was ranked after three colleagues who joined the company "long after him and were his neighbors and parishioners," which produced "some disparagement to his credit and reputation among his neighbors." After the company clerk had confirmed Troughton's seniority, the assistants revised his placement and affirmed that new members of the livery should be ranked according to the expiration of their apprenticeships and years in the company. In 1629, Francis West the elder requested that he be ranked ahead of Francis West the younger, "according to his antiquity." After they examined the company's account books to determine the timing of their admission, the assistants complied with the elder West's request, "finding that it was no otherwise than a mistake in the first placing of him."[36]

This emphasis on custom constrained the officers' discretion in promotions. In 1613, the Grocers' assistants considered why Anthony Soda had not been chosen as a warden in 1608. They noted that while "no fault was to be imputed to the said Mr Soda," because of that "omission" from the wardenship Soda had been "without cause overmuch both disgraced and displaced." Soda then gave the company a "free gift" of £40, and the assistants pledged that he would be restored to his rightful place and chosen to be the upper warden at the next election.[37] In 1661, the City aldermen rebuked the Apothecaries' officers for taking two members into their assistants who were not among their most senior liverymen.[38] Seniority remained the common basis for promotion to the most influential livery company offices into the eighteenth century. In 1705, the City's lord mayor and aldermen considered the case of two Saddlers' liverymen who complained that the officers of their company had promoted members into the company's assistants who were their "juniors." After consulting with the legal advisors of all parties, the City governors ordered the company's officers to take the liverymen as assistants because of their seniority.[39]

The common assumption that seniority led to status within companies enabled officers to use their members' concern for place when disciplining them. In July 1622, the Grocers' assistants determined that liveryman Raphael Busby should have joined their ranks "by course and antiquity," but his "contentious spirit and uncivil and unreformable carriage and behavior" disqualified him and made him "unworthy to bear any place of authority" in the company. One month later, when Busby asked the company's officers to select him as an assistant "according to his antiquity" because he would be "much discredited in his reputation to be debarred from the same," they denied his request because he refused to amend his behavior.[40]

Although some members had an overriding concern about place, others were willing to overlook small deviations in rank. In 1609, the Vintners' assistants were unsure of the seniority of three members in line for a wardenship. The controversy involved vintners Gent, Bonham, and Gale, and though Gent had been the first to be admitted to the livery, he had lost his seniority "by reason of his disobedience and negligent attendance." Bonham and Gale allowed him to take precedence because they preferred "the good quiet and benefit of the company before any private respects."[41] In 1622, the Grocers' assistants learned that Benjamin Bacon claimed precedence over his follow liveryman John Langham, "alleging that Mr Langham had always given him place" since they had both become liverymen. After Langham had confirmed Bacon's claim, the assistants adjusted their ranking accordingly.[42]

Although seniority within a company was a major criterion for elevated status, service in other offices in the City could accelerate a member's rise in a company's hierarchy. In 1597, liveryman Vincent Norrington was promoted to the ranks of the Grocers' assistants because he had become the treasurer of Bridewell Hospital. However, before elevating Norrington, the assistants first gained the assent of Nicholas Stile, the next liveryman in line for promotion.[43] The avoidance of a City office could also lead to promotion within a company. Freemen who paid a fine instead of serving as sheriff of London and Middlesex were allowed to avoid Grocers' Company offices for a fine as well, and they would then be ranked in the company's hierarchy next to those who had already served as wardens.[44] The process of basing a company promotion on external factors such as service in City offices could spark controversy. In 1612, the Goldsmiths' Court of Assistants had to call an official of the City to resolve a dispute between Sir William Herrick and Alderman George Smithes over the order of seating at their dinner. After hearing that the Privy Council had declared that an alderman should have "precedence before the knights commoners" anywhere in the City, Sir William refused to remain for dinner.[45]

The motives for avoiding company offices varied among the senior members of livery companies. Some may have considered such service to be more onerous than paying the fine for avoidance, but others claimed to be unqualified for posts of authority.[46] As mentioned above, when Lawrence Greene wrote to the assistants of the Grocers' Company after they had chosen him as warden in 1621, he sought to avoid the office because of his "defects of utterance and audacity, which are both requisite in him that shall be the mouth of so public and grave an assembly." The Grocers' assistants received a more typical excuse in 1605 from their colleague Anthony Box, who requested that he be passed over for an office because he lived in the country.[47] In 1623, grocer John Woodward paid £100 to the company in order to avoid serving in company administrative offices because he had lost his hearing, and renter warden Andrew Field paid 100 marks and William Lake paid £50 to avoid wardenships "in respect of their years, weakness of body, and far distance of habitations."[48] Of course, such excuses may have been a polite veneer over the petitioners' desire to avoid fines as well as offices, or their lack of respect for the other officers. A member of the Blacksmiths' Company agreed to pay a fine in order to avoid serving as a company warden in 1699 after he called the other wardens and assistants "blockheads, fops, etc." and accused them of receiving bribes.[49]

The high turnover among guild officers, and particularly the annual rotation of wardens, placed considerable responsibility on their staff members. The discussion of low-ranking company offices in the last chapter emphasized their importance as sources of casual employment for company members. However, some officers were instrumental in the normal functioning of company business. Beadles, for example, acted as messengers, providing a crucial link between the officers and their members. The Drapers' officers came to realize this to their great cost in 1609 when they discovered that vital information—including the names and ranks of freemen, as well as how much money each owed the company—was kept only in "the breast and knowledge" of their recently deceased beadle.[50] In 1614, the Vintners' officers appointed an assistant beadle because the company's membership had so increased that it could no longer be served by only one beadle. The senior beadle of that company was also charged with standing outside the door during assistants' meetings to convey messages from those who had business to bring before them and to ensure that no one would attempt "to hear the secrets of the court."[51] Nominally in the service of a company's officers, a beadle might be suborned by other interests. In 1703, the assistants of the Blacksmiths' Company were amazed to learn that their beadle had been employed by a group of liverymen to purloin a copy of the company's bylaws, presumably to assist them in their ongoing dispute with the officers.[52]

While a company's beadle stood watch outside court meetings, its clerk was inside, taking notes. Normally, the clerk was the only person who had not risen through the company's ranks who had access to its records. In 1595, the Skinners' assistants declared that no one except the company's wardens could peruse the company's records, but this order was amended twenty years later when the assistants granted their clerk a key to the room where the records were kept so that he might "always have access" to the company's books. The responsibilities—and authority—of the Skinners' clerk continued to grow during the century until, by 1684, he was granted "the whole custody" of the company hall.[53] Company officers knew that they entrusted their clerks with information that in the wrong hands might damage the company's interests. In 1577, the Skinners' assistants instructed their clerk to conduct an investigation into allegations that staff members had embezzled the quarterly fees paid by journeymen and nonfreemen. In 1609, the Vintners' assistants ordered their clerk to conceal the fact that the company's renter warden had lost a considerable amount of its money, and in 1637 their clerk recorded the assistants' plans to have "some discreet men" attempt to purchase wine from coopers in order to entrap them in illicit retailing.[54]

Company officers reminded their clerks how important their positions were. The oath of the Vintners' clerk required him to remain loyal to the monarch and to the officers of the company and, when recording the proceedings of company courts, to keep "all things secret."[55] In 1577, the Grocers' assistants ordered their clerk not to give copies of their orders to anyone without their permission. After they had appointed John Bunbury, an attorney of the Court of Common Pleas, to their clerkship, the Grocers' assistants admitted him to the freedom of their company and required that he take out a £500 bond "for his safe keeping and just and true account of all such monies, writings, evidences, and other things" with which they would entrust him.[56]

The potential influence of company clerks attracted the attention of politicians. Clerks were instrumental in company lobbying efforts, and they knew of attempts by companies to maintain ties with Privy Councilors and to lobby Parliament on the company's behalf.[57] In 1646, the assistants of the Grocers' Company instructed their clerk to consult their counterparts from other companies so they could coordinate their efforts in seeking repayment of their £100,000 parliamentary loan. Keeping such tactics concealed from the central government was not an easy task because important politicians were eager to place their own clients in clerkships. In 1578, the Grocers' assistants promised to appoint George Southaik as their clerk after they found him to be "an honest man and of good experience" who also enjoyed the support of the Earl of Leicester. In 1633, the Crown asserted its right to inspect the records of livery companies in its investigation of offices and fees, but it also found that maintaining ties to company clerks was useful.[58] In that same year, the Vintners' assistants received a letter from King Charles, requiring them to grant their company's clerkship to one Herbert Fynch when the post next became vacant. They appointed a committee to reply that "their predecessors have not at any time disposed of that place in reversion and they humbly desire to continue that custom." But they assured Charles that when a vacancy occurred, Fynch would be their preferred candidate.[59] Companies may have expected preferential treatment from well-placed politicians whose advice they took when appointing company staff members. In 1640, the Plumbers' officers accepted the nominee of Sir Robert Heath, one of King Charles's Sergeants-at-Law, to be their clerk, and they then hoped that Heath would assist them in settling a suit in the Star Chamber and obtaining a new charter.[60]

In keeping with the skill and trustworthiness the post required, company governors tried to promote clerks whom they had already known. In 1647, the Vintners' assistants awarded their company's clerkship to Will Doughty, who had been the assistant to their clerk John Child for eight years.[61] When Doughty resigned eight years later, the assistants appointed Philip Hinton, who had served both Doughty and Child.[62] In 1639, the clerk of the Salters' Company died, and the assistants granted the position to Edward Stretchly, a freeman of the company and the assistant to their former clerk. They reported that "though diverse other able men made suit for the same place," he was selected because of his considerable experience in the company's service.[63] In 1644, the Grocers' clerk informed his employers that his assistant had died. They allowed him to nominate his personal aide, Francis Harris, to be his new assistant and to receive the reversion of the company's clerkship.[64] Six years later, the clerk reported to the assistants that he was 79 years old and too frail to continue in his office, and he reminded them of their agreement to give the post to Harris. The assistants agreed unanimously, and after they called Harris into the court, the new clerk's appointment was confirmed by handshakes from all the wardens and assistants present, signifying their trust in him.[65] The governors of companies encouraged their clerks to train their successors, and they took care to prevent them from vacating their posts prematurely. In 1683, James Cole, the clerk of the Weavers' Company for eighteen years, nominated his assistant, Charles Burroughs, for the reversion of his post. The company's assistants granted Cole's request, but reminded him that they expected him not to turn over his duties to Burroughs until he was physically unable to continue.[66]

Company staff members were reimbursed in a variety of ways. Besides their fees for routine matters such as binding and freeing apprentices, the Grocers' clerk and beadle received stipends on the company's first quarter day every year. Typically, the clerk and beadle would be called before the assistants and then dismissed from the court while their performance was evaluated. They would then be recalled, formally readmitted to their posts, and awarded their stipend.[67] In addition, the Grocers' clerk could expect the assistants to contribute toward the costs of maintaining his personal staff, and he controlled access to the garden and tower by the company hall, a perquisite that might gain him favor from members.⁶⁸ Furthermore, clerks could expect assistance with their personal rent. In 1700, the clerk of the Joiners' Company told his employers that it was unusual for a company clerk in London to pay for his own housing, whereupon they allowed him to live in one of the company's houses rent free.⁶⁹

Companies also extended benefits to their clerks' family members. In 1621, the Grocers' assistants awarded their clerk's son an exhibition worth twenty nobles per year at Balliol College, Oxford, and in 1623 they granted him the reversion of his father's place because he had been "trained and bred" to hold the office and would assist his father during his old age and sickness. In 1631, the assistants granted the younger clerk twenty nobles per year for "his better encouragement" in the company's service. Thirty years later, the company's assistants compensated the son of another of their clerks for helping his father organize a company ritual.⁷⁰ When the Blacksmiths' clerk resigned in 1655, the company's governors chose his son to replace him, and in 1702 they appointed their clerk's father to be their beadle after considering the requests of several people—including three liverymen—for the post.⁷¹ Clerks may have used their influence to help their friends as well as their families. In 1650, the clerk of the Vintners' Company reported that a friend of his offered to lend £70 to the company at 7 percent interest, and the officers accepted those terms.⁷²

However, there were limits to a clerk's influence. In 1611, Grocers' clerk John Grove informed his employers that Andrew and Paul Bayning had together donated £200 to the company with which to purchase land whose rent would support a fellowship at Cambridge for two poor scholars. Toward the "more speedy performance and execution" of that bequest, Grove suggested that the assistants purchase a parcel of land that he knew of in Northamptonshire, which he offered to lease from the company personally. The assistants thanked Grove for his offer, but after seeking "a better bargain for the company," they apparently purchased land elsewhere. Five years later, the Grocers' assistants noted that they had received several petitions from suitors for the reversion of their company's clerkship. The assistants believed that Grove, who was infirm at the time, was encouraging those requests because he hoped to direct his office to someone "for mere affection or private profit to himself." Because they feared this would deprive them of their right to appoint a clerk when the position became available, the assistants resolved not to grant any reversions to the clerkship. Grove's successor, John Bunbury, may have acknowledged his employers' well-established skepticism in the way he asked them to grant him a lease on a company property in 1630. To buttress his case, Bunbury asserted that for the previous fourteen years he had worked exclusively on the company's behalf "ever aiming and seeking the profit and welfare of this worshipful society." The assistants were amenable to his offer at first, but subsequently felt that Bunbury had the better end of the bargain and sought to renegotiate it.[73]

Although a clerk may not have gained a personal advantage in all aspects of company business, his position could continue to produce benefits long after the end of his active employment—and even after the end of his life. In 1639, the Vintners' assistants decided that because their clerk had lost his hearing, he needed to hire an assistant. Nevertheless, they promised him that he could continue to receive the other benefits of his office during his lifetime because he had served the company faithfully.[74] Thirty years earlier, the assistants had allowed the widow of their recently deceased clerk to remain with her children in the clerk's house for one year and then to receive £40 for herself and £40 to be divided among her children when they reached adulthood because of her poverty and her husband's diligent service.[75] In 1614, the assistants allowed a clerk's widow to live in a room above the clerk's kitchen rent free, and they gave her a benevolence of £6 and a pension of 20s per quarter.[76]

Clerks could express their appreciation of the value of their offices through gifts to their companies. After the Weavers' clerk died in 1693, the assistants considered 22 applications for the post. They narrowed the field to three attorneys, and after an election, they awarded the clerkship to Case Shewell. One month later, Shewell, acknowledging "the great respects this court showed him in their free election of him," presented £100 to the assistants for the relief of the company's poor or for "other such uses" as the assistants should think fit, which they "very kindly" received.[77] Some clerks expressed their loyalty posthumously; in 1618, the estate of Grocers' clerk John Grove donated £100 to the company.[78]

The prominence of clerks in company affairs made them the object of members' praise and criticism. In 1643, assistant Rubin Bourne wrote to the Grocers' Company to avoid a wardenship because of his poor health, but he also went out of his way to praise the service of the company clerk, John Bunbury. Bourne claimed that "I am not Homer to commend Achilles nor Augustine to praise Ciprian, nor Melancthon to extol Bucer . . . [but] he is worthy that you should do something for him . . . because though his pains have not been less yet his benefits by our court have been less this year than ever they have been."[79] However, such feelings were not universal. As we saw in the previous chapter, in the early seventeenth century the Weavers' clerk accepted payments from strangers to whom he bound apprentices in violation of the company's rules.[80] And in December 1621, the Grocers' wardens heard the allegations of grocer Raphael Busby regarding an agreement that they had allegedly negotiated between Busby and Roger Gwynn, one of the assistants. Busby charged that the clerk had falsified the agreement and forged his signature. The wardens found Busby's accusations groundless, and after considering the harm done to their clerk by the charge, they fined Busby 40s and ordered him to apologize publicly for his slander.[81] The Joiners' assistants also defended their clerk against charges brought by a group of liverymen in 1700.[82]

However, clerks were not always guiltless. In 1584, the Grocers' assistants reprimanded their clerk, George Southaik, for allowing dicing and cardplaying in his house and in the company's tower. They also ordered him to permit such games to be played only at tables in the company garden and "in no secret place, and that there shall no man bowl within this garden unless they be of this company or some of the honest and ancient neighbors which dwell here near about."[83] In 1616, the Grocers' assistants apprehended John Beyd and his family living in the company's tower without their consent but by permission of the clerk, for which the clerk was "much blamed in open court." In 1630, the Salters' assistants dismissed their clerk, Richard Rothram, because he had "misdemeaned himself." Although the court's records offered no details of Rothram's alleged infractions at that point, nine months later the assistants required him to repay £16 he had taken from two company members "and detained," presumably without the assistants' permission.[84]

The role of clerks and beadles in the administration of company affairs challenges the notion that the governors of companies were increasingly powerful, self-interested oligarchs. Legally, courts of assistants were responsible for the conduct of company business. In practice, the high turnover rates of company officers meant that the permanent staff bore a considerable amount of the companies' administrative burden. Individual clerks and beadles often worked for companies for decades, thereby lending cohesion and continuity to company affairs. Staff members were well compensated for their efforts, and they sometimes used their unique command of company business to advance their own interests and those of their friends and relatives. Ultimately, the influence of a company's staff on administrative affairs is difficult to assess, but it is evident that the clerks' and beadles' indirect control of the channels of communication curbed the ability of company governors to determine events.

Decision Making

The authority of company governors flowed from their control over company policy and patronage as well as from their ability to discipline and punish members. Like local governors throughout early modern England, the officers of livery companies could exercise discretion, and their control of patronage gave them influence on the lives of their members. Nevertheless, coupled with their reliance upon their clerks and beadles for information, disagreements among officers limited their ability to exploit their inferiors.

Company court records rarely detail the procedures that lay behind the governors' decisions, but the examples of voting that have survived suggest that there was no fixed method of achieving consensus. The Salters' assistants employed a variety of means for distributing their company's religious patronage. In 1638, they granted a lectureship under the company's control according to the choice of the wardens, assistants, and "diverse of the livery and yeomanry of this company (being the representative body of the commonalty thereof)." Five years later, the assistants considered the opinions of company members who had attended sermons by five candidates for the lectureship, and then placed the names of all the ministers "in competition, and it fell by lot upon Mr Wilkinson." In 1650, Wilkinson resigned, and five ministers sought to replace him. The assistants decided that they all should be put in nomination, and each member made "his strike upon a paper presented to him with the names of the several ministers showing his approbation," after which the two candidates who received the most "hands" were placed in a runoff.[85] When selecting their wardens, the assistants of the Blacksmiths' Company also voted by placing strike marks on a line next to the name of the candidate they supported.[86]

Any confusion over such procedural matters could complicate company politics by exacerbating confusion as well as disagreement among governors. In December 1622, the Grocers' cook died, and the assistants considered several candidates to fill the vacancy. Lord Mayor Peter Proby, a member of the company, nominated his personal cook, William Norringrost. However, Sir Humphrey Handford, a former lord mayor and a grocer, recommended his own cook, Francis Acton, who enjoyed King James's endorsement. Sir George Calvert, the king's principal secretary, informed the assistants that Acton had been Queen Anne's cook, and he notified them that the king expected a report on Acton's nomination that would "be such as will give his Majesty contentment." Nevertheless, the assistants put Acton and Norringrost into an election "by the balloting box." At first, Acton received nineteen votes to Norringrost's fourteen, but a new election was called because some assistants claimed to be unacquainted with the method of voting and therefore "were mistaken in putting their balls into the box." The subsequent round of balloting was inconclusive—although Norringrost received nineteen votes to Acton's eighteen, the assistants discovered that only 35 persons were in the room at the time. Apparently, both the lord mayor and the senior warden of the company had assumed that their offices entitled them to vote twice. After further discussion, the assistants agreed that "there can be in a Court but one casting voice or ball and that in case of a difference when the persons in choice are even." The master warden then yielded the right to cast the deciding vote to the mayor, but the assistants decided to follow the advice of Alderman Sir Thomas Middleton that a third election should be held "by scrutiny, that is, the suitors names to be written and every assistant to give his score" to the candidate he supported.[87]

This procedural change failed to resolve the issue. Although Acton received eighteen votes to Norringrost's seventeen, the assistants allowed the mayor to cast his deciding vote for Norringrost, after which the assistants declared the matter "unresolved" and deferred a decision until another court. This apparent violation of the recent agreement was overturned three weeks later. After Sir George Calvert demanded an explanation from the assistants for the delay, they asked their company clerk to read the record of the various votes, after which it was "agreed by the whole court without contradiction of any one person" that Acton had been "duly by scrutiny elected and chosen cook."[88] Although the interest of King James no doubt complicated the matter, the inability of the Grocers' senior members to agree on the best candidate contributed to the confusion regarding the procedure.

The appointments process was further slowed by the common practice of promising someone that he or she could fill a post once it became vacant, which allowed one set of company officers to limit the patronage available to future officers. In 1624, the Grocers' assistants ruled that they would no longer grant reversions to university fellowships. During the next six years, however, four such grants were made, and the assistants' decision in 1630 to deny a grocer's request for reversion on the grounds that it violated the company's policy was only a halfhearted attempt at reform. The following March, the assistants granted such a reversion with only a warning that it would not preclude "all others their rights of reversions thereof formerly granted." During the next year, the assistants granted three additional reversions and ordered the wardens to ensure that those who held reversions for university exhibitions would receive them according to the order in which they were granted.[89] In this way, the granting of reversions became a self-perpetuating process, with each cohort of governors expecting that future assistants would comply with their wishes just as they had carried out the wishes of their predecessors.

The administration of patronage sometimes gave clerks influence in company decisions because they were better informed than their employers about procedural matters. The Grocers' assistants asked their clerk to search the company's records in 1612 to determine the procedure for granting university fellowships—forestalling any awards until they had received his report—and they also instructed him to search the records regarding their patronage of the mastership of the weighhouse.[90] In the next year, the assistants asked Lord Mayor Thomas Middleton, a grocer, to recommend the schoolmaster of Oundle for preferment to a benefice. Middleton promised to do his utmost and asked the company's clerk to remind him of his pledge. In 1616, the Grocers' officers asked their clerk to catalog the company's property and funds devoted to the support of younger company members and to notify them of any outstanding reversions to university exhibitions. In 1649, the assistants instructed their clerk to determine whether an applicant for a loan from the company's funds had received one previously, which would have disqualified him for additional support.[91] The Joiners' officers in 1704 ordered their clerk to search the company's records for information on the procedures for appointing the company's beadle.[92] Such examples suggest that company officers depended on their clerks to manage information essential for distributing company patronage.

In addition to consulting their clerks, company governors sometimes also solicited the views of members generally before making policy decisions. As in the cases of the distribution of their religious patronage (discussed above), the Salters' assistants agreed to purchase a property to convert to a new company hall in 1641 after they had consulted the company's livery and yeomanry.[93] The Vintners' assistants, many of whom were wholesalers, sought the opinion of retailing vintners before speaking on their behalf. In 1634, a committee of Vintners' assistants appointed to ask the Crown to suppress tavern licensing called for more money to be devoted to their effort, and their request was approved at a general meeting of company members.[94] In 1635, the assistants called a meeting of retailing vintners to discuss King Charles's proposal to add a 1*d* tax on every quart of wine they sold. The assembly rebuffed the proposal, and "the younger sort" then nominated fourteen individuals to represent them with "such ancients" as the assistants appointed to consider how to respond to the king. At a subsequent meeting, "the generality" of the company and other wine retailers agreed that the proposed tax would ruin them, and so the assistants considered petitioning the Crown on the matter.[95] Such willingness of company officers to consult their members on important policy matters was a further check on any oligarchic ambitions they may have harbored.

On other occasions, company members sought the support of their governors for their own initiatives. In 1620, a group of retailing grocers presented a list of grievances to the officers of the Grocers' Company. They requested the advice of the assistants and sought their help in submitting a bill to Parliament to overturn monopolists. The assistants agreed that a bill of that nature should be drafted in the company's name, and they instructed the petitioners to seek legal advice for formulating the legislation, pledging to contribute company funds to the cost of the action.[96] The company thus could be a conduit for members' ideas rather than an institution firmly controlled by its governors.

Although some members may have been eager to participate in policy making, poor attendance at general meetings often impeded communication within companies. If governors had been motivated by the desire to shape company affairs in a self-serving manner, they would likely have been encouraged by members' apathy. However, governors employed a variety of means to improve attendance. In 1614, the Vintners' assistants elevated twelve men to their ranks because so many of their colleagues had died that they wasted time at meetings waiting for a quorum.[97] In the Salters' Company, assistants who were absent from meetings were liable for a 12*d* contribution to the company's poor box, and those who were tardy were fined 6*d*.[98] The officers of the Grocers' Company fined members—the "generality" as well as the livery—who were absent from quarterly meetings. The senior warden could also use those meetings as an opportunity to exhort his colleagues to attend more regularly. At the conclusion of an address to the company in 1626, Warden Humphrey Smith informed his "younger brethren" that while he formerly had not bothered to attend company meetings, "God has his ends in human things as in divine," for when he finally did join a quarterly assembly and heard a "grave, wise, and religious exhortation," it prodded his conscience about his having neglected his duty to attend meetings.[99] In the Blacksmiths' Company, by the end of the seventeenth century the governors had drifted out of touch with the company's affairs to such an extent that their clerk had to propose that they meet at least once a month in addition to the regular court meeting.[100]

Some companies offered incentives for attendance. In 1633, the Salters' assistants agreed that for the "increase and continuance of love" among the wardens, assistants, and livery of the company, liverymen as well as assistants would be invited to dinner on quarter days, the occasion for the company's regular, general meetings.[101] The assistants of the Vintners' Company agreed in 1622 that the "love and affection" among members was hindered by infrequent general meetings. They therefore resolved that all the assistants and their wives, along with the widows of assistants, would dine together on two quarter-days every year. However, not all such meetings had amicable results. In 1633, the assistants observed the "rude and unbrotherly behavior" that Raphael King directed at a fellow assistant. According to one witness, King offered his colleague "most base and uncivil language, threw tart upon his bond, and offered him many uncivil touches with his knife and trencher which few men would have born with patience." The assistants ordered their beadle not to call King to any further meetings until he conformed to their orders.[102]

Dinners also offered governors an opportunity to display their distance from their more humble colleagues. The Vintners' assistants repeatedly instructed their company's almspeople not to approach them at dinner after their meetings, warning them that violators would lose the benefit of the company's charity. It is unlikely that the policy reflected the governors' contempt for the poor: in 1623, the company's assistants fined George Cholmeley 6s 8d for saying "he was rich and cared not what happened to poor men."[103] Rather, the exclusion of almspeople probably was designed to maintain the hierarchy of influence within the company, and poor company members would not have been alone in suspecting that their governors discussed company business during their private meals. In 1705, a group of five liverymen of the Weavers' Company, all of whom had recently been involved in efforts to reform the company's charter, appeared with their wives at the inauguration dinner for the new wardens and bailiffs. Although the routine invitation of the company's livery to the inauguration dinner had been "discontinued time out of mind" and replaced by a dinner for the liverymen and their wives on the company's election day, the five men refused to leave.[104] The exclusive nature of such meetings and dinners therefore had the potential to spark controversy among members concerned about the direction of company affairs.

Company members who felt that their governors had ignored their interests sometimes held meetings of their own. In September 1630, a group of 30 members of the Weavers' Company met at the Black Boy tavern in Cornhill to discuss their grievances against their governors. According to a subsequent petition, the authorship of which is uncertain (because of factors discussed earlier), they met "in the fear of God" and with respect for their oaths as freemen of London. After discussing ways to find a legal means to make their governors enforce company regulations against interlopers, they took a voluntary collection toward the costs of a lawsuit.[105] When their governors learned of this meeting, they complained to the lord mayor that the freemen met "for some evil purpose" designed to interfere with company procedures.[106]

Of course, company governors themselves were also capable of trying to block members' efforts to influence company affairs. In 1628, the lord mayor and aldermen considered a complaint by Robert Marchant, a liveryman of the Tylers and Bricklayers' Company, who accused his company's governors of promoting several men into the ranks who had been company members for fewer years than himself. The City magistrates concluded that the company governors had been guilty of a "plot" intended "irregularly and preposterously" to exclude Marchant from the assistants in order to prevent him from ever becoming a company warden—since wardens were always elevated out of the ranks of the assistants—and from enjoying the perquisites of that office, such as the right to take on an additional apprentice. They ordered the company assistants to add Marchant to their ranks.[107] In the end, Marchant refused, suggesting that he brought the matter before the lord mayor and aldermen only to remind his company's officers that there were limits to their discretionary powers.[108]

The desire of members to remain involved in company affairs, the customary nature of participation in company rituals, and the complexity of the decision-making process within companies were all checks on the power of company governors. Their dependence upon clerks for information and their practice of calling meetings of their general membership on important occasions demonstrated that the self-selective nature of their offices did not necessarily lead to the promotion of their interests at the expense of those of their members. Furthermore, as the example of the addled selection of the Grocers' cook revealed, the governors of companies were not always united in their own views. While the potential for oligarchic rule was present in livery companies, the practices of guild governance meant that it was a potential that often remained unfulfilled.

Livery companies were governed by a few of their wealthier, more experienced members. Although they were positioned to name their successors, governors were constrained by the well-known patterns of precedence within their companies and the difficulties of recruiting colleagues willing to serve in positions of authority. Rather than seeking an exclusive command of power within their companies, courts of assistants sometimes called general meetings to discuss common issues such as petitions to the Crown or the construction of a new company hall. On such occasions, company governors may have been disappointed by members' lack of interest instead of feeling threatened by any diffusion of their authority.

Their limited command of their company's past policies and procedures posed a further challenge to the power of guild officers. It is impossible to determine the extent to which clerks manipulated company patronage. However, as assistants' routine business increased, they clearly came to rely on the experience and advice of staff members who were primarily responsible for managing company information. Staff members were also important points of contact between company members and their governors, at times providing alternative access to company policy making. Since company members embraced diverse attitudes toward their governors and governments, the diversity of channels of communication available to them fostered company ties.

Nonetheless, the complexity of communications and politics within livery companies limited their potential to offer members a sense of community. The ability of companies to overcome such challenges is the focus of the next two chapters. Although this chapter drew on examples from a wide array of companies over two centuries, each of the next chapters offers a study of a single company so that the response of their members to change over time may be followed in greater depth.

CHAPTER 5

Religion, Economics, and Tolerance in the Grocers' Company

The sixteenth of July 1574 was a typical first quarter-day for the Grocers' Company of London. During their morning meeting, the company's assistants reappointed their clerk and beadle for another year, arranged for the auditing of the wardens' accounts, and sold several leases on company property. After lunch, Warden Richard Thornhill delivered, in the words of the court's minutes, an "excellent exhortation" to a general assembly of the company. He began by reminding his audience that the company's founders had been moved "by the word of God" to devise "very godly and wise ordinances" designed to keep them in "brotherly love and verity." Thornhill then warned the company that the neglect of that inheritance would produce such "contention and disagreement" as would lead to the "dissolution and overthrow" of all governments from companies to commonwealths. He concluded his address by declaring his desire to maintain the company's "good government and continuance in worship." Following Thornhill's remarks, the clerk read the company's ordinances to the assembly, and the meeting ended.[1]

Thornhill's speech reflects the attitude of company officials toward the problem of disunity within the company. He argued that the company was part of the foundation of the social order, and that any controversies among members would undermine the entire structure. In order to evaluate his sentiment's resonance among his fellow company members, this chapter analyzes the company's internal politics from the Reformation through the Civil War and the Revolution. Although many trade guilds experienced disagreements over the direction of company affairs, tensions within the Grocers' Company were largely the product of antagonisms between those who considered it an essential part of their lives and those who felt that they could better pursue their interests elsewhere. As a case study, this chapter assesses the company's ability to remain a source of meaningful association for its members throughout a tumultuous century and a half. In particular, it analyzes the ways in which officers such as Thornhill sought to encourage members to tolerate their colleagues' different religious opinions and economic interests.

Tolerance could not be taken for granted in early modern London. According to Susan Brigden, London's livery companies were catalysts for religious change during the Reformation. Reflecting their origins as medieval fraternities, early Tudor livery companies included in their religious life chantries, obits, and funeral processions, all of which maintained spiritual links among members both living and dead. Nevertheless, cells of evangelical—that is, proselytizing Protestant—members whose personal beliefs surfaced during the Reformation developed behind the facade of guild unity. The spiritual cohesion of the companies therefore declined, and although religious goals continued to be "piously invoked," Brigden found that the economic functions of livery companies "may often have been incompatible with their spiritual purpose." In his recent study of secularization in early modern England, C. John Sommerville argued that "the religious character" of guilds "ended" once the government seized corporate property that had been devoted to the support of religious observances. Crucially, the Chantries Act (1547) ensured that there would no longer be any "spiritual benefits" given to those who made gifts to their companies.[2]

The Grocers' Company deviated from this pattern. The records of the company's Court of Assistants are not extant for the period before 1556, but the wardens' account books and other records allow the company's religious life to be surveyed after 1511. As expected, the theological components of the company's ceremonial practices evolved throughout the sixteenth century, but they did not change as dramatically as Brigden and Sommerville predicted. Chantries, obits, and funeral processions were important features of the company's pre-Reformation spiritual life, but they were only a few of the commemorative forms that affirmed the shared heritage and values of company members. Many of these forms survived, and continued to evolve, far into the seventeenth century. The persistence of such practices enhanced the potential for unity among grocers by encouraging them to identify themselves with their company and its traditions. The Reformation caused company officers to alter the forms of their ceremonies, but they succeeded in maintaining many of their meanings.[3]

There were many reasons why the officers of the Grocers' Company, like urban elites elsewhere in Europe, would have desired to maintain the appearance of unity, even had unity been only a distant goal.[4] According to London's customary trading policies, members of companies did not have to pursue the trade that gave their company its name. By the early seventeenth century, such flexibility enabled the Grocers' Company to claim jurisdiction over the trade in goods from sugar to rhubarb and from perfume to gunpowder.[5] As a result, diverse economic interests among freemen were a constant challenge to the company's officers. Most important, mixed loyalties among the grocers surfaced in the later sixteenth and early seventeenth centuries, when a determined group of apothecaries defied the company's authority over the drugs trade. Despite the company's best efforts, King James created an Apothecaries' Company in 1615, and it soon absorbed one-fifth of the Grocers' Company membership. Against the backdrop of such commercial disputes, references to the company's benefactors and calls to godly unity were more than invocations of piety; they reminded members that the integrity of their company rested on their ability to abide the religious and economic differences they had with their colleagues. To a degree that the recent historiography has not anticipated, such calls found a receptive audience.

The Politics of Clerical Patronage

The roots of the Grocers' Company stretch back to 9 May 1345, when a group of pepperers formed a fraternity dedicated to the honor of God, the Virgin Mary, Saint Antonin, and all the saints. Their corporate status was elevated in 1428, when Henry VI issued a charter to "the freemen of the mystery of grocery" in London. The king placed the company under the direction of three wardens and empowered the freemen grocers to choose the wardens' successors. The company soon created a court of assistants to work with the wardens in the management of the grocers' affairs.[6] As a corporation, the company could acquire property in its own name, which allowed it to administer the estates of deceased members. During the ensuing decades, members often entrusted the company with the management of their chantries, obits, and other spiritual bequests. By the early sixteenth century, the company's religious portfolio included two chantry priests, six obits, and the advowsons of two London parishes, St. Stephen Walbrook and All Hallows Honey Lane.[7]

In her examination of the Reformation in London, Brigden suggested that the company's parochial appointments may have displayed its members' attitude toward religious change. In 1525, the grocers named Robert Forman rector of All Hallows, an office he held until his death in 1528.[8] Forman was a committed evangelical whose sermons attracted the attention of reformers across London. He also stood at the center of an illicit book trade that circulated the works of Luther, Wycliffe, Hus, and Zwingli throughout London. Forman's involvement in this operation led to his arrest and imprisonment in 1528, but the intercession of Anne Boleyn ensured that his life ran its natural course.[9]

Although Forman was a leading reformer, his appointment casts only a dim light on the spiritual disposition of company members on the eve of the Reformation. In the absence of Court of Assistants' records, there is no evidence of how his appointment was approved. The surviving records indicate only that the wardens presented Forman to the bishop of London on the company's behalf.[10] The selection of Forman for All Hallows could have suggested either that conservative assistants were outvoted by their reform-minded colleagues, or that only the evangelicals among the assistants were aware of Forman's views. For example, John Petit, an influential reformer with close ties to Forman, had been a company warden in 1519, and he may have served as Forman's patron among the assistants.[11] The wills of two wardens have survived, but even if they are accurate representations of their makers' religious views in 1525, they do little to clarify the politics behind Forman's selection. William Campion, the senior warden, set out his will in 1530. In a typically Catholic fashion, it reported that he bequeathed his soul to God, Saint Mary, and all the saints in heaven. It also stated that he left 10s to the Society of Jesus in St. Paul's and £4 to the Grocers' wardens for a dinner among the livery after his death. Campion's will included a gift for his son-in-law, Edward Murrell, another of the wardens who presented Forman to the bishop.[12] By the time Murrell composed his will twelve years after Forman's appointment, his views on purgatory—or the views of the person who actually penned his will—had diverged from Campion's. Like Campion, he left a sum to the company to fund a "recreation" among those grocers who attended his funeral, but he bequeathed his soul to Jesus "in whom and by the merits of whose blessed passion" he placed his "whole trust of clear remission and forgiveness" of his sins.[13]

Even if Murrell had been an active religious reformer in 1525, he also was a member of a court of assistants that continued to maintain chantries, conduct obit masses for deceased members, and accept new spiritual bequests. The will of John Billesden was completed in 1522, and it left the weighhouse for foreigners' goods and other properties in the City to the company with the stipulation that it maintain two chantry priests in a suburban London church. Billesden had served as a warden of the company in 1517 and 1518, and the witnesses to his will included two wardens of 1522 as well as future upper wardens William Campion and Nicholas Lambert.[14] In 1523, John Drayton's will bequeathed properties to the company in order that it keep a chantry priest at a church in London. The will named Campion and Lambert as executors of Drayton's estate, and it implored the company's wardens to carry out his will as they would have wanted their own wills fulfilled.[15] At the close of the decade, William Butler left the company some land with which to fund a chantry priest in a Bedfordshire parish church. Butler served as upper warden nine times during the period 1511–33, and his long career in the Grocers' government suggests that he felt a strong attachment to the company. It also must have given him a firm sense of the opinions circulating among the assistants. Although he had been warden before, during, and after the evangelical Robert Forman's tenure at All Hallows, Butler's will demonstrated that he believed that the company would carry out his traditional spiritual wishes. According to the subsequent wardens' accounts, Butler's trust was well placed.[16]

After Forman's death, the company's ecclesiastical nominations displayed no clear pattern. Dr. John Coke followed Forman at All Hallows in 1528, and his seven-year career there was marked with scandals, most notably in 1532, when he became embroiled in a City-wide tithes dispute and preached against the royal divorce. His subsequent arrest and imprisonment in the Tower did little to dissuade him from his conservative views, which he often shared with his parishioners during confession.[17] After Coke's resignation, the company appointed Thomas Garrett, Forman's curate and assistant in the evangelical book trade, to the rectorship. During his tenure at All Hallows, Garrett continued to pronounce his evangelical views until they cost him his post and his life in 1540.[18]

The years following the Act of Six Articles (1539) brought confusion to most English people, with the church on the defensive and traditional forms of worship in decline. Across London, the number of wills that included bequests for chantries and obits plummeted, and spiritual endowments were increasingly allowed to lapse; at All Hallows, an income provided for a chantry priest was left unutilized after 1540.[19] Despite such trends, the Grocers' Company continued to fulfill its spiritual obligations to deceased members until King Edward seized their chantry assets. During 1547, the company spent more than £37 on fourteen obits, and it distributed more than £63 to seven chantry priests; such totals compare favorably with those of the other years for which records are available.[20]

Nonetheless, the company may have acquired by mid-century a reputation for being hospitable to evangelicals. In his late-sixteenth-century history of the Reformation, John Foxe suggested that the Protestant martyr John Lambert had considered joining the Grocers in 1533, but he provided no evidence for how Lambert developed his interest in the company.[21] Although several influential evangelicals were members of the company, the surviving records do not indicate that they played leading roles in the company's affairs. In 1540, four grocers were indicted under the Six Articles, but only one of them, John Blage, was among the junior liverymen of the company in 1536, the year closest to 1540 for which a company roster has survived.[22] Perhaps the strongest evidence for the company's acceptance of evangelicals came in 1547, when it nominated Thomas Becon for the St. Stephen's rectorship, a post he held until he was deprived of it because he married in 1554. Becon had been an outspoken reformer who fled London during Henry's final years, and his appointment only weeks after Edward's accession indicated that some in a position to influence the assistants' decision were well connected among evangelicals.[23]

The survival of Court of Assistants' records from the middle of Queen Mary's reign adds greater detail to the company's religious policies. Despite the progress of reform under King Edward, Mary's accession allowed those who were not convinced by the new faith to express their views once more. In May 1556, a man identified as "Parson Jennings" offered to bequeath his house to the company if it would use the property's annual rents to maintain an obit for him, and the assistants formed a committee, which included Protestant Richard Grafton, to consider the offer. Although no record of the committee's report survives, Jennings returned to the court six months later and offered the grocers £40 with which to carry out his will. The assistants decided that what he offered would not have been "profitable" to the company, and so they thanked him "for his good will" and told him they would not accept it.[24]

Nonetheless, the Grocers' officers remained receptive to other bequests with spiritual implications. In 1556, Sir William Laxton left his estate in the hands of the assistants in exchange for their agreement to use its proceeds to establish a free school and an almshouse in his native town of Oundle, Northamptonshire. Laxton's will required the almsmen to be beadsmen, and although it did not specify what Laxton wanted the beadsmen to do, the term traditionally referred to people who were set the task of praying for the souls of the dead.[25] A former lord mayor who had served seven terms as company warden between the years 1534 and 1553, Laxton should have been well placed to gauge religious opinion among his colleagues.

During Queen Elizabeth's reign, the company took steps to encourage a preaching ministry, one of the centerpieces of the Puritan reform program, by sponsoring two divinity students at Cambridge. The company required their scholars to preach in London at least once during the tenure of their fellowship, at which time they were to acknowledge the support they had received from the company.[26] Of course, this policy may have been no more than a test of a scholar's ability. In August 1589, the company's officers required Bernard Robinson to preach before them so that they could "judge his worthiness of their exhibition conferred upon him." Robinson traveled to London to deliver a sermon on the company's election day in 1590. After leading the lord mayor, several aldermen, and the livery of the company from Grocers' Hall to St. Stephen Walbrook, he delivered a "good sermon," which pleased the assistants so much that they gave him £3 6s 8d for his travel expenses.[27]

The case of Edmund Campion indicated that the sermon was a test of orthodoxy as well as of talent. In July 1568, the company informed Campion that his sermon was long overdue, warning him that he would lose his fellowship if he did not "utter his mind in favoring the religion now authorized." By October, Campion informed the company that because "he dare not, he cannot, neither was it expedient he should preach as yet," he would resign his fellowship.[28] Although the embarrassment of offering their unwitting support to Campion, who later became one of Elizabethan England's leading Jesuits, accounted for the loosening of the company's preaching requirements for scholars, their reliance after 1566 upon the recommendations of divines such as John Whitgift indicated their desire to remain in the Protestant mainstream.[29]

The assistants' support of divinity students required them to rely on references from outside experts, but their clerical patronage led them to weigh opinions from overlapping groups of parishioners and company members. In 1563, the assistants considered the request of a minister named Sheriff for the rectorship of St. Stephen Walbrook. Sheriff's principal reference was from Miles Coverdale, who had been a leading translator of the Bible into English during the 1530s, an activity that probably brought him into contact with Assistant Richard Grafton. However, Sheriff's appointment was delayed because Edward Jackman, one of the company's assistants and a parishioner of St. Stephen's, was not present for the discussion. Jackman did attend the next assistants' meeting, at which time Sheriff was passed over for the benefice in favor of Richard

Leyfield.³⁰ The court record mentioned no reason for Sheriff's failure, but it was unlikely that Coverdale's influence impeded his candidacy, because in subsequent years the assistants included Coverdale among four "famous and learned men" the company nominated to judge the qualifications of candidates for the rectorship of All Hallows.³¹

A nomination that involved the broader membership of the parish took place in December 1562, when Thomas Becon—who had returned to his former benefice at some point after Queen Elizabeth's accession—asked the company for permission to turn his position over to his curate, Philip Pettit. Becon described Pettit as "well learned and of good behavior" and "one that well pleases the parish and they are well contented with him." Three months later, the assistants received a petition from some parishioners of St. Stephen's that asked them to appoint Pettit upon Becon's retirement. The assistants complied with that request in May "because of the good report of the worshipful parishioners . . . and for the towardness that he bears for the setting forth of God's holy words." Pettit's cause may also have been advanced by the willingness of two assistants—one of whom was a City alderman—to guarantee that he would fulfill the company's expectations.³²

At the turn of the century, the St. Stephen's parishioners again cooperated with the company in replacing their rector. In July 1601, the parishioners requested that the company present Roger Fenton to the bishop upon the resignation of Henry Tripp. The assistants—who had heard a sermon by Fenton two weeks earlier—encouraged the parishioners to proceed "in the said cause as they have begun according to the ecclesiastical laws," after which their request would again be considered "with all love and favor, according to the worthiness of the said Fenton." Although "the said cause" remains unclear, the parish records indicate that one Lawrence Greene had been authorized to join with the church wardens in paying the parish's costs for "the removing of Mr Parson Tripp." Greene may have served as a liaison between the company and the parish in this regard, for he had recently joined the company's livery. In any event, the negotiations between the parishioners and Tripp produced an amicable separation. In August, after Tripp resigned, the Grocers' assistants named Fenton to the benefice expressly because he was recommended by the parishioners.³³

The assistants' clerical appointments did not always meet with such broad approval. In 1625, they granted Aaron Wilson the benefice of St. Stephen's.³⁴ Nine years later, King Charles elevated Wilson to a vicarage in Plymouth and requested that the company not name a successor to the St. Stephen's rectory until they had consulted with him. The assistants expressed their willingness to comply with the king's request, but they also considered a petition from several parishioners that nominated three candidates to succeed Wilson.[35] Two months later, Charles again wrote to the assistants and asked them to nominate Thomas Howell, a royal chaplain, to the vacant rectorship, but the assistants also had the petition of Thomas Saxby, who was their clerk's son-in-law and one of the parishioners' nominees. The assistants then interviewed Howell, who informed them that although he intended to continue occupying the rectorship of a parish in Surrey—a more valuable post than St. Stephen's—he would reside in London during the winter and provide for a "learned preacher" to fill his place there the rest of the year. The assistants then offered Howell time to reconsider his position, but he pressed them to an immediate vote, which Saxby won with a "plurality of hands."[36] Two weeks later, the assistants received a letter from King Charles indicating that he was "much displeased" by Saxby's election. When they informed Saxby of the king's position, he asserted that he had no doubt of his legal right to occupy St. Stephen's, "but now seeing his majesty is displeased with the said choice, he therefore did freely and willingly surrender" his election, after which the assistants gave him a gift of £20 and presented Howell to the bishop.[37]

Howell's relations with the company and with his parishioners were strained throughout his tenure. In February 1636, the assistants chose not to reimburse him the £80 he spent on repairs to his rectory, and two years later, Howell refused to preach before the company at their annual liturgy.[38] In March 1641, a petition from "the most part" of the parishioners notified the Grocers' Court of Assistants that they anticipated that their parish's rectory would be vacant in the near future. They requested that the assistants make sure to name "an able learned and conformable divine" who would be nominated by "the greater part of the voices of the parish." After the assistants debated the parishioners' proposition, they remained concerned that it would involve their "giving away their power and freedom of election in confining themselves to one man." Nevertheless, the assistants pledged to give particular consideration to the parishioners' candidate when the post became vacant.[39]

When the assistants met to discuss the vacancy two months later, the St. Stephen's parishioners presented them with a list of five candidates for their rectory. The assistants agreed to consider the nominees, if they could do so legally and without undermining the company's right to present a candidate to the bishop. They then added five nominees of their own to the list, and they held an election that narrowed the field to two finalists: Michael Thomas, a nominee of the assistants; and William Strong, a nominee of the parishioners. After further debate, the court decided to resolve the contest with a ballot, in which Thomas received fifteen votes to Strong's thirteen. After the assistants installed Thomas as their appointee, they read a letter on his behalf from a member of Parliament that denied allegations from an unnamed source that Thomas was "a time server and a bower to our late devised altars" and certified that he was "utterly averse from all those late innovations" in the church.[40]

The election of Thomas did not end the controversy. In October, three members of the company—Samuel Warner, William Underwood, and Richard Rogers—requested that the assistants show them the documents that would confirm the company's power to nominate someone to the bishop for the St. Stephen's rectorship. Upon questioning, the three members declined to reveal their intentions, and so the assistants turned aside their request, suggesting that they might sue the company at law if they questioned its rights to the advowson. The assistants also moved to suspend Warner, a liveryman of the company, for "his malicious practices and scandalous and abusive words against this court." Three weeks later, the assistants received a petition from "the greater part" of the parishioners of St. Stephen's that praised their rector, about whom "anything we know or ever could hear by diligent enquiry is [that he is] a man without taint in his doctrine, life, and conversation." The petitioners concluded by suggesting that "though there be some few in the parish that aim at the bringing in of some other in his place if possibly they could," they continued to support Thomas.[41]

The assistants subsequently confirmed their support for Thomas and then considered their decision to suspend Warner. They alleged that Warner had complained to one of the bishop's officials that Thomas "was an unworthy minister and no real honest man would give testimony in his behalf." In response to this charge, Warner claimed that because he had a poor memory he could not recall the precise words he had spoken, "but his opinion is still that the said Mr Thomas was a very unworthy minister." Although the assistants found Warner's behavior to have been "rash," they decided to forbear punishing him until some "worshipful persons" had spoken with him. Five weeks later, the assistants asked him to accept their judgment so that they could reinstate him, but Warner, "standing upon his justification and centaurily maintaining his own opinion," refused to conform. The assistants therefore continued his suspension from the company.[42]

The dispute surrounding Thomas lingered into the next year. After Thomas assumed his post, some of his parishioners refused to pay their tithes until the company's control of the advowson was confirmed. Thomas ended the stalemate by accepting a more valuable benefice elsewhere, and the assistants named Thomas Warren—whose sponsors remained unidentified—to replace him in March 1642. Controversy over the St. Stephen's rectorship arose again at the end of 1642, when the estate of grocer Edmund Turville provided £10 per year to support a monthly sermon for the parish. The Grocers' assistants appointed the rector Thomas Warren to the lectureship, only to learn that several parishioners had kept him out of the church and employed "illiterate mercenary fellows to supply the cure to the contempt of Mr Warren." The assistants therefore appointed a committee to lobby Parliament on Warren's behalf, hoping they would receive support from those who previously had sought the company's assistance for Parliament's cause. This effort achieved some success, for Warren retained his post until January 1644, when he resigned "by an agreement betwixt him and the parish." The assistants subsequently considered a petition from several parishioners on behalf of Humphrey Chambers, who, they claimed, was "a man generally affected and desired by the parish." While they maintained their right to control the advowson, the assistants held an election between Chambers and another candidate, whose supporters were not identified, which Chambers won.[43]

Samuel Warner's position in the company also became an issue in 1644, following his election as a City alderman. After the court allowed him to give "satisfaction for that which caused his suspension, not in open court, but privately" to a committee of aldermen and company wardens, the assistants elevated Warner to their ranks.[44] Of course, much had changed since Warner had been suspended from the company. By 1644, the crisis of the Civil War had altered the composition of the company's assistants considerably, likely bringing into power individuals more sympathetic to Warner's religious views.

Despite Warner's return, the company's assistants continued to assert their control of the St. Stephen's advowson. After Humphrey Chambers resigned the rectorship in 1647, the churchwardens and the parishioners of St. Stephen's supported Samuel Tomlinson for the post, but the assistants chose a minister named Watson by "general consent." The assistants' decision came immediately after they had heard Watson deliver a sermon to a company assembly. However, support for Watson may not have been unanimous, for at the next assistants' meeting they complied with a warden's request to allow "Mr Tomlins"—presumably the "Tomlinson" endorsed by the parishioners—to preach before the company on the morning before the selection of the company's wardens. Nevertheless, the court decided that even though "Tomlins" would preach the sermon that day, the usual stipend would be paid to the rector of St. Stephen's "as heretofore it has been accustomed."[45]

All of this demonstrates the pitfalls of assuming that the officers or other members of a livery company shared a view of religious change. Throughout the period being considered, the Grocers' assistants were concerned both to uphold orthodoxy and to maintain working relationships with parishioners and monarchs. Although the limited evidence surviving from the early sixteenth century precludes assessing whether the same had been true during the early phases of the Reformation, historians should not assume that the company was "evangelical" simply because it appointed prominent Protestants or because a few of its members supported innovation. Rather, it seems likely that the company's patronage decisions throughout the period were the results of discussions and agreements among assistants of diverse theological opinions and varied degrees of religious intensity. Some assistants may have been more concerned than others with the company's religious policies, and as long as the company was in the mainstream, an indifferent majority could have allowed a committed minority to direct the course of the company's religious patronage.

Religion and Company Unity

Religious patronage was not the only theological issue that brought to light the diversity among company members. The disputes that swirled around religious ceremonies during the early modern period transformed the company's social customs. Practices intended to enhance feelings of shared values could, in the unsettled atmosphere of the English Reformation, excite further controversies.[46] Although the company's late medieval rituals often fostered a sense of commonality among members by encouraging prayers for the souls of the company's benefactors, the abolition of the doctrine of purgatory during the Reformation loosened the connection between the company and its traditions, which in turn tested the loyalty of its members.

The semipublic state of the religious, social, and political events surrounding the selection of the company's wardens presented the assistants with a set of particularly thorny issues. The typical practice early in Queen Elizabeth's reign required the company's aldermen, wardens, assistants, and livery to assemble at Grocers' Hall in their livery gowns and then to proceed to St. Stephen Walbrook to hear a "service sung by solemn note." Afterwards, they returned to their hall, "where they drank according to the old custom" and nominated the wardens for the following year. At nine in the morning on the next day, they would again meet at their hall in their gowns and return to St. Stephen's to hear a sermon by the rector and to receive communion. They would then return to their hall for dinner and the selection of the wardens.[47]

Because the assistants often marked their wardens' election with a feast for the company and invited dignitaries, it was crucial that they resolve their differences during the previous two days.[48] However, things sometimes went awry. In 1557, Upper Warden Thomas Bowyer was asked to select his replacement from two nominees the assistants had appointed. Rather than accept the honor and authority of this position, Bowyer complained about his share of the costs of the upcoming feast, and so he resigned his office altogether. As a result, the court fined Bowyer £6 13s 4d for having "moved and stirred sundry inconveniences amongst the whole company."[49] In this context, the company's officers may have hoped that their ceremonies would display their unity, but they must have also realized that unity was not a thing they could take for granted.

Funerals could also demonstrate diversity and change as well as unity and stability among the grocers during the Reformation.[50] The company's ancient ordinances required all liverymen to attend the burials of their deceased colleagues, but the practice may have diverged from the policy. A survey of the wardens' accounts for the third, sixth, and ninth years of each decade from 1510 to 1600 produced no evidence that a liveryman was ever fined for being absent from a funeral, although the accounts usually did include the fines of those who were absent from other company meetings such as quarter days. The wills of Grocers' wardens also suggest that the company's attendance at funerals was optional rather than mandatory. In 1537, Edward Murrell left money for a dinner for those liverymen who accompanied his body to the cemetery, an indication that he may not have expected all of them to attend. Ten years later, the will of Andrew Woodcock made no reference to the company, although it gave his executors the ambiguous instructions to bury him "without pomp" but with "four or five priests and clerks" to receive his "body at the church door with psalms." A clearer expression of the testator's wishes came in 1558, when Thomas Bowyer instructed his executor "not to trouble" the members of the Grocers' Company to attend his burial.[51]

Despite Bowyer's attitude, the company still knew how to participate in funerals. In 1556, the diarist Henry Machyn reported that the funeral procession of grocer Sir William Laxton included the lord mayor and aldermen, all of whom found refreshment at Grocers' Hall after the burial. On the next day, three masses were said for Laxton, and they were followed by, in Machyn's estimation, as "great [a] dinner as I have seen at any burying." In 1560, the diarist noted that the "masters of the company of the Grocers" and several "priests and clerks singing" accompanied the body of a grocer named Hansley. Despite such traditional ceremony, Bishop John Jewel, an outspoken critic of the doctrine of purgatory, preached over Hansley's corpse. The assistants' decision in 1616 to allow liverymen to request the attendance of the company's officers at the burials of their wives was further evidence of their interest in funerals; the only requirement for this "commendable work of charity" was a gift to the company of at least £6 13s 4d.[52]

The controversy that developed over the use of the company's hearse cloth suggests that the assistants considered funerals opportunities to focus members' spiritual interests on the company. Traditionally, the assistants allowed the hearse cloth to be used only for the burial of former wardens, but in 1564 they allowed the widow of liveryman William Bridger to "have the best cloth," although they noted that her request was unusual. The exclusivity of "the best cloth" may have been an attraction for some grocers, but others were upset by its theological implications. In October 1573, the Court of Assistants considered a report that some people were offended by some aspects of the hearse cloth, and so they authorized the wardens to "take away such things as are unlawful and to set good things in their place." In May 1575, the court instructed the wardens either to sell the cloth and acquire a new one of velvet or redesign it so it would include "the company's arms and other good things as they shall think good." In October, they sent the hearse cloth to an embroiderer to be altered, and although the records do not offer details on the changes, they suggest that the wardens adopted a design that included the company's arms.[53]

Their reinvention of the feast of Saint Antonin also revealed the assistants' concern for the company's spiritual life. The ordinances of the medieval fraternity which lay at the company's roots required every member to attend mass on the saint's feast day in May.[54] In the early sixteenth century, the wardens' accounts contain sporadic references to dinners and processions on that day, but they also suggest that the form and content could vary from year to year. In 1519, the company spent £3 3s 8d, donated by a deceased member, on the dinner, and although it was not common for an individual to fund the dinner, the range of expenditure usually did fall between £3 and £4.[55] While the Church of England under Henry VIII and Edward VI had discouraged the celebration of feast days, Queen Elizabeth took a less restrictive policy toward them.[56] The Grocers' Company held a fairly steady course through the confusion. The assistants continued their traditional observation with worship and dinner throughout the Reformation, and each year they appointed two liverymen to provide the meal. In 1563, the Court of Assistants agreed that the feast day would "be kept on the Tuesday in rogation week being the 18th day of May," at which time the liverymen were to meet at Grocers' Hall at eight in the morning and proceed in their gowns to St. Stephen Walbrook to attend mass, after which they would return to their hall to dine together "according to the old custom." Not everyone was eager to embrace this custom. William Ormeshaw, one of the stewards for the dinner that year, refused to pay his share of the expenses, claiming that "he would rather spend £20 and lie in prison than to be one of the stewards for it was but a slavery." The company's assistants subsequently fined him 40s for his "unfitting words."[57]

If Ormeshaw's complaint had been theological in nature, he may have received comfort in 1576. At that time, following the lapse of a City government moratorium on company dinners, the company's assistants decided that the custom of having the liverymen worship and dine together in May should be continued not for the saint's feast but "in commemoration of the beginning of the company" on 9 May 1345. Since the company's origins lay in a fraternity dedicated to Saint Antonin, among others, its first meeting was possibly intended as an observation of its patron's feast day a few days later. In any case, the assistants' subsequent practice of referring to the reformed custom as "the feast of St Antonin alias the commemoration dinner by an anniversary solemnity in commemoration of the beginning of this worshipful company" reflected their continued association of their patron saint with their company's founders.[58]

Commemoration was an individual as well as a collective act. After the Reformation, the company could no longer maintain chantries and obits, but it could still offer members a means for perpetuating their memories. Sir William Laxton's will not only endowed a free school and an almshouse, but it required the company to see that the school be "perpetually . . . called the free grammar school of Sir William Laxton knight Alderman of the City of London" and that the schoolmasters, ushers, and beadsmen be similarly named.[59] The company complied. In 1593, the schoolmaster was ordered to display Laxton's arms on the school, and although beadsmen were archaic, in 1638 the company reminded the almshouse residents "of the foundation of the memorable benefactor Sir William Laxton" and ordered them to perform "their duties towards god and praying for their benefactors."[60] As late as 1650, the company's inspectors recalled for the schoolmaster and the students the "pious and worthy act of the founder" in fostering their education, and noted the company's continuing obligation "for perpetuating the memory of such a benefactor by their liberality, care, and oversight of the due performance" of his will.[61]

The company's ability to commemorate deceased members extended beyond those whose gifts were as large—or whose wishes were as explicit—as Laxton's. In 1570, Edward Jackman left the company £40 to be spent on a plate that would have his arms engraved "upon it whereby it might be known to be [his] gift." Four years later, Henry Cloker arranged to bequeath a house to the company in return for its agreement to spend the proceeds on gilded ale pots with his name engraved upon them. In 1614, grocer Philip Rogers left a bequest to fund a dinner for those liverymen who attended his burial. However, since he was buried in Surrey, none of the livery attended him, and so the company applied his donation to the purchase of plate "to remain forever . . . in remembrance of the testator's love" for the company.[62]

After 1568, those who bequeathed land, money, or other substantial gifts to the company would have their names read at a company meeting at least once a year. Although the form of the ceremony was similar to that of a collective obit, a member would not have to be dead to be counted a company benefactor. In October 1617, Sir Stephen Soame was present when the wardens registered him "among the worthy benefactors of the house" because he had contributed £500 toward a new ceiling for the company hall. While adding to the company's ornaments, some benefactors became ornaments themselves. In 1613, the assistants arranged for "pictures of famous and worthy magistrates and benefactors of this company" to be painted and displayed in Grocers' Hall "for continuance of memory of them to future posterity."[63] The company's commemorative efforts were similar to those of other London trade guilds.[64]

Guild leadership was not a prerequisite for memorable gifts. Those who sought to avoid serving in company offices could give a piece of plate and be added to the register of benefactors. In 1656, Peter Hulme, who had escaped both the City aldermanry and the wardenship of the company, bequeathed a 60-ounce silver salt cellar to the company, which the assistants "lovingly accepted" and added to the inventory of company plate.[65] Two years later, the assistants declared that anyone who had avoided the aldermanship would not have his arms displayed in the company hall unless he made "such a signal demonstration of his good will to the company" by which they could consider him to have been a benefactor.[66]

Such Interregnum bequests came against a background of financial disaster for the company. In May 1643, facing mounting debts, the assistants approved the sale of up to £1,000 worth of company plate, but they agreed that "when the troubles of this kingdom shall be composed" and the company's financial position stabilized, "the several parcels of plate shall be repaired and made good to remain a memorial in this Hall according to the gifts and intents of the donors." Four months later, the assistants ordered a further liquidation of company plate, but they recorded "the donors' names and weights thereof," so they could replace them once "the peace of this kingdom" was restored.[67]

And so, while the Reformation transformed the religious practices of the Grocers' Company, it did not divide members into opposing camps of conformists and heretics. The company continued to offer a sense of community to individuals with a variety of attitudes toward theology and religious practice. Those troubled by aspects of the company's ceremonies—such as the hearse cloth, funeral processions, or Saint Antonin's feast day—could either seek reform or avoid participation, but they would still be considered members. The relationship between the living and the dead grocers changed noticeably with the attack on the doctrine of purgatory, but the company found ways to maintain the memories of its deceased benefactors long after the abolition of chantries and obits.

Economic Change and Company Loyalty

One explanation for the company's apparent religious cohesion may be that most of its members chose not to express their religious views through an institution primarily concerned with trade. If post-Reformation companies were focused on economic matters, then perhaps members were willing to abide each other's theological differences as long as they remained beneficial commercial contacts. However, in the case of the Grocers' Company, such an argument would have to account for the internal economic conflict that gripped the guild during the later sixteenth and early seventeenth centuries, conflict that highlighted the significance of tolerance for the company's survival.

The "mystery of grocery" over which the company had authority covered a wide range of goods. The company's ordinances indicated that the wardens inspected powders, confections, plasters, cinnamon, and "all sorts of things that belong to the . . . craft."[68] As with many issues of rights, the proof was in the practice. A key moment in the company's evolution came in 1540, when King Henry empowered the officers of the College of Physicians to enter the home of any apothecary and to correct any false practices that they found. However, if such correction required the confiscation or destruction of merchandise, then the physicians would need the prior approval of the Grocers' wardens.[69] The company's involvement in the apothecary trade stemmed from its members' dealing in such items as treacle, spices, and distilled water, integral parts of the early modern pharmacy. According to contemporary medical theory, when people became ill, they were to seek a diagnosis from a physician, who would prescribe a purge to redress the balance of their humors. Depending on the prescription, the patient then consulted either a barber-surgeon or an apothecary. The physicians struggled to prevent barber-surgeons and apothecaries from prescribing cures as well as treating patients, and so they were anxious to extend their control over those groups whenever possible. They achieved a second victory in 1553, when Queen Mary authorized them to correct apothecaries without the assistance of the Grocers' wardens if the physicians found them to be uncooperative.[70]

In response to the erosion of their jurisdiction, the Grocers' officers tried to convince the physicians that they were willing partners in the regulation of the apothecary trade. In March 1566, the wardens expressed their knowledge that any failure on their part to punish grocers who sold poor-quality pepper, cinnamon, and "other drugs such as rhubarb" would damage the company's reputation. Throughout the later sixteenth century, the wardens took grocers who were "expert apothecaries" when inspecting those suspected of selling "evil wares and unwholesome spices," established an annual dinner for those who assisted them in their searches for illicit confections, and occasionally consulted physicians as well.[71] The wardens tried to inspect all apothecaries at least three times per year, and they fined grocers who violated their regulations and ordered any seized goods to be sent abroad or destroyed.[72] The presence of apothecaries among the Grocers' officers and the continued membership of royal apothecaries in the company established an uneasy compromise between the company and the physicians.[73]

Nevertheless, the Grocers' Company had to defend its remaining authority over the apothecaries throughout Queen Elizabeth's reign. In March 1563, the assistants instructed the wardens to seek counsel about a bill that the physicians had introduced into the House of Commons that would have required the apothecaries to join their college. At this point, the conflict involved the Grocers' officers defending some of their members against an outside agent, but by the end of the queen's reign, the terms had shifted dramatically. In March 1588, the assistants agreed to support any "reasonable" attempt by the apothecaries to strengthen themselves against the physicians. However, by the following February, a group of apothecaries—probably anticipating the physicians' next move—suggested that a separate company for the apothecaries would be the best solution to the continuing controversy. The court replied that the idea "was not well liked," and so they "commanded" the apothecaries "upon their oath taken in this house not to proceed further in their suit" unless it was approved by the court. In the meantime, the assistants established a committee to consider the apothecaries' proposals for the reformation of abuses within their trade. This committee included wardens, assistants, and some of the more outspoken apothecaries such as Robert Morer and Anthony Soda.[74] The committee was still active in 1592, when the assistants again considered the apothecaries' interests.[75]

In 1605, the assistants hoped to resolve the controversy by obtaining a new charter that spelled out their jurisdiction over the apothecary trade. Their actions bore fruit in 1607, and the preamble of the new charter claimed that King James had acted in response to a request from "the Mystery of the Grocers and Apothecaries of the City of London" for improved regulation over their trades. The resulting charter created "one body corporate and politic in reality, deed, and name, by the name of the Wardens and Commonalty of the Mystery of Grocers of the City of London."[76] In other words, the charter asserted that the king united the Grocers' Company and a noncorporate group known as "the Apothecaries" by their mutual consent.

The new charter resolved little. The dispute erupted again in 1610, after several apothecaries submitted a bill to Parliament that would have given those apothecaries who were free of the Grocers' Company the power to regulate their trade. When the assistants learned of this move, they summoned a group of the company's leading apothecaries—including Assistants Robert Morer and Anthony Soda—and asked them if they were involved in the plan "to sever and divide themselves" from the company and "alter the government thereof which hath continued many years of their forefathers in unity, love, and concord." The apothecaries denied participation in the scheme, but they went on to request the reform of "some abuses committed by some persons exercising their art and mystery." The assistants replied that they were as prepared as ever to conduct such reform, after which the apothecaries departed. Then, as if to prove their point, the assistants punished two grocers for selling defective treacle. One of the accused, Nicholas Warren, responded to the assistants' charge by remarking that "he knew twenty more in and about this city who used the same as he, and that they were not called in question for the same as he." The court asked him for their names, but Warren refused, "saying he would not be accounted so base as an informer or promoter." At that, the court had him bound over to the City's lord mayor for imprisonment.[77]

After the apothecaries' bill of 1610 failed to win parliamentary approval, the Grocers' assistants continued to inspect apothecaries with little controversy. The lull ended in April 1614, when the assistants considered a petition from some apothecaries who claimed that because they had no authority in the Grocers' Company, their complaints had gone unheeded, and that abuses in their trade would continue as long as the grocers and the apothecaries remained "one body politic." The assistants consulted the three apothecaries in their ranks—Anthony Soda, Robert Morer, and Roger Gwynn—and they in turn claimed surprise at the allegations, particularly in light of the charter of 1607. The assistants therefore reassured themselves that the petitioners had been "few in number," were "not of the most skillful and proficient men" of their trade, and sought to hold "principal places in the company before their due desert or calling."[78]

Two months later, the assistants received a clearer indication that they faced a revolt when apothecaries William Quick and Daniel Darnelly refused to join the Grocers' livery. Their defense was that they supported a separate apothecaries' company and could not change their position without disgracing themselves. The assistants then reminded them of the oaths they took on admission to the Grocers' Company, imploring them to consider the danger that "their endeavors and attempts might bring not only to themselves and this company in particular, but also to the whole city by altering a settled government." Unbowed, the two apothecaries refused to cooperate. The assistants received some belated consolation in July, when apothecary Thomas Whitely agreed to join the Grocers' livery.[79]

During the next decade, the assistants' efforts to prevent division in their company bore little fruit. Perhaps because of his concern for the condition of his royal apothecaries, King James looked favorably upon the apothecaries' petition of 1614, and over the next few years he issued a series of proclamations which gave control over the retailing of drugs to a new Apothecaries' Company. The Grocers' Company sought to impede its rival at every step, and it continued to inspect treacle and other apothecary wares, but it was fighting a losing battle. The Grocers' best hope lay in Parliament's opposition to the Crown's intrusion in economic affairs, but in many respects antimonopolist sentiment was not on their side. They incurred a major setback in July 1616, when a grocer sold defective drugs to one of Prince Charles's apothecaries. From that point onward, the grocers were on the defensive against those they termed "the separate apothecaries." In 1619, the Crown created a committee of four members of the Grocers' Company, four "apothecaries unsevered," and four "apothecaries of the separation" to draw up lists of goods that would fall under their respective jurisdictions. Later that year, the Grocers' officers granted 100 marks to "diverse apothecaries true and faithful members and brothers" of the company to defend themselves against suits brought by the Apothecaries' Company.[80]

The Grocers' Company's prospects brightened briefly in 1624. The House of Commons Committee on Grievances narrowed the range of goods under the Apothecaries' Company's jurisdiction, but the Grocers' assistants soon acknowledged defeat by seeking a reduction in their contributions to City loans because of their reduced membership. Although it is difficult to assess the validity of their claim that more than one-fourth of their membership left during the dispute, it seems plausible that as many as one-fifth of the grocers joined the new company.[81]

The exhortations that Warden Humphrey Smith delivered to quarterly meetings of the company in 1619 and 1626 summed up the nature of its predicament. In the first, he began by arguing that the privileges and benefits that his audience had received from the company's founders ought to have been "motives and chains to move and tie the whole body in all love and obedience to observe the good and laudable orders and ordinances" of the company. He then rebuked them for their past poor attendance, claiming that there had been some quarterly meetings at which, besides the assistants, there were fewer liverymen than "Noah had persons entered the Ark with him." By 1626, the departure of the apothecaries confirmed Smith's fears. Most of his remarks on this occasion echoed his previous speech, but he stressed that members should tell the officers about any disputes that broke out among them, claiming that the wardens would try "to reconcile them even in the beginning lest they prove as the nature of all evils are, worse and worse in time." He then drew their attention to the dispute between themselves and the apothecaries, and suggested that "it was at first but the private quarrel of some few two or three, and yet, by siding and partaking, a rent and division was made in the company and so the company drawn into the quarrel to defend their own rights and privileges to their great trouble." Smith then wished the apothecaries well, and expressed his hope that despite all that had occurred they would "return again unto us, and that we and they might lovingly, like brethren, join together for a true reformation of all our abuses as once it was well intended without separation." He was sure this "would be pleasing unto God and for the quiet and peace of the whole society."[82]

This controversy posed a particularly difficult challenge for those apothecaries who did not want to join the new company. In 1629, Thomas Christie complained to the Grocers' assistants that by joining the new company, he had been deprived of the benefits and privileges he had received from his former guild. When Christie had joined the

Grocers' livery, the wardens had promised him that they would refund his £20 entrance fee if the apothecaries subsequently separated themselves from the grocers. Christie therefore asked the officers to refund his fee because he had remained a part of their company long after the creation of the Apothecaries' Company in the hope that he would be "engrafted again into his original, and much desired, Company of Grocers." The officers complied with his request upon condition that Christie rejoin their livery if the two companies were reunited.[83] Christie's dilemma highlighted the difficulty of assuming that the conflict in the Grocers' Company divided "grocers" and "apothecaries" into two groups that had clear, irreconcilable economic interests. Instead, it appears that Warden Humphrey Smith was correct in observing that the conflict hinged on attitudes and personalities and that the separatist apothecaries pursued objectives that were not necessarily in the best interests of all apothecaries.

Rivalries among members who were involved in overseas trading further exacerbated economic tensions within the Grocers' Company. As Robert Brenner has argued, during the sixteenth century the Merchant Adventurers dominated London's overseas trade, which centered on cloth exports to continental Europe. Relying on Crown concessions, a group of traders—including some Merchant Adventurers—came to prominence through their involvement in the luxury-centered Levant, Spanish, and East India companies during the late sixteenth and seventeenth centuries. According to Brenner, during the early decades of the seventeenth century, an entirely new constellation of traders emerged to challenge the leadership of the Levant–East India merchants. These newcomers undermined the older companies by smuggling goods from areas that fell within their monopoly and by taking advantage of the growing tensions between the Crown and Parliament to develop new companies trading with the Americas.[84] Some members of the Grocers' Company participated in each of these overseas trading companies as both investors and directors in the early seventeenth century.[85]

The evolving relationships within and between these groups of traders created numerous occasions for members of the Grocers' Company to associate in ways that may have undermined the interests of their fellow guild members. Controversies arose when the chartered trading companies used their political connections to ensure that they did not have to compete with smaller dealers. In 1620, when several retailing grocers refused to redeem their orders for currants from the Levant Company, they were challenging the power of many merchants who were, like themselves, members of the Grocers' Company.[86] However, in the 1630s the relations between company members involved in trading syndicates that would later emerge as open rivals did not disrupt the company's affairs. In 1631, the assistants allowed John Sadler and Richard Quiney to pay £50 each to avoid joining the company's livery and serving in company office. Sadler and Quiney told the Grocers' assistants that they were partners in a business that required them to be away from London frequently. Indeed, it was about this time that Sadler and Quiney began building a major tobacco-trading business in America, an activity that would later bring them into conflict with the East India Company and therefore with leading members of the Grocers' Company.[87] Similarly, John Warner, an active merchant in the American trade who would be a leading London supporter of Parliament in the 1640s, maintained collegial ties with the Grocers' Company throughout the period. He gained the company's freedom in the early 1610s, received several small loans from the company thereafter, and joined its livery in 1627. As was customary, when Warner became a sheriff in London in 1639, the assistants added him to their ranks and allowed him to borrow the company plate.[88]

Internal company politics remained generally placid during the 1630s, though there were some disputes among commercial rivals. The most significant controversy of this sort involved Samuel Warner, the brother of John, who would himself become a leading figure in London politics during the Civil War. Samuel Warner joined the Grocers' Company in 1614 and took several small loans from the company over the next decade in order to develop his family business.[89] Warner also employed illicit means to expand his trade. In January 1627, he was apprehended after accepting the delivery of several smuggled casks of cloves, nutmeg, and pepper removed from a ship recently returned from a voyage for the East India Company.[90] During the next three years, Warner refused to cooperate with the East India Company's efforts to resolve the matter in a "friendly manner" until the Court of the Exchequer found him guilty of violating the company's trading monopoly and fined him £200. After this, he apologized to the company's officers and sought relief from his fine.[91] The dispute dragged on until 1631, when he was forced to seek the pardon of the East India Company in order to reduce his fine. This controversy doubtless came to the attention of leading members of the Grocers' Company, who likely had little patience for smugglers seeking to undermine their investments. It must have been no surprise when, a few months after his surrender to the East India Company, the Grocers' assistants denied his request to avoid their livery and all other offices.[92] So when Warner and the Grocers' officers became embroiled over the St. Stephen's rectorship a decade later, it was the culmination of a long period of misunderstanding between the parties.[93]

Grocers' Company members followed a variety of courses when the Civil War gripped London. Some, like Thomas Soames, a Grocers' assistant since 1631 and a major investor in the Levant Company, stayed on. As sheriff of London in 1638, he refused to arrest those who failed to pay the Crown's unpopular Ship Money assessment, thereby winning considerable prestige throughout the City. Though a critic of the Crown, by 1643 he supported those in Parliament who favored peace. Soames remained active in City and company affairs—he loaned the Grocers' Company £4,000 in 1647—but some of his prewar colleagues disappeared for considerable periods. Thomas Northey joined the Grocers' livery in 1620 and its assistants in 1633, and he became a wealthy Merchant Adventurer. When the assistants appointed him to be one of the six auditors of their wardens' accounts in early June 1642, they apparently had overlooked his absence for the preceding six months.[94] In addition to John and Samuel Warner, the ranks of the Grocers' assistants contained several leading supporters of Parliament's cause in London. While Randall Manwaring, who had been a Grocers' assistant since August 1640, served as a colonel in the City militia, American trader Richard Waring, who had joined the company's livery in 1627 and had become an assistant in August 1643, served on a parliamentary commission in the 1640s.[95]

As described earlier, the company's Interregnum governors spent their time attending to many of the same kinds of business that preoccupied their predecessors. After the Restoration, several of the company's assistants resigned unceremoniously in response to the Crown's purge of Interregnum local governors. More important, perhaps, assistant Thomas Northey attended a court meeting on 22 August 1662 after an absence of two decades.[96] As was the case with the Reformation, the Civil War had the potential to fracture the company, but individual positions on national events seem to have had little lasting influence on the company as a whole.

The exhortations of wardens such as Richard Thornhill in 1574 and Humphrey Smith half a century later suggested to their audience that tolerance, based on godliness and common economic interest, was the foundation of the Grocers' Company. Their speeches may have sounded like attempts to make grocers feel guilty for their lack of concern for the company, but it must have been evident by the early seventeenth century that if the company was to survive the various commercial disputes dividing its members, it would need to maintain their sense of shared heritage. This was the only thing, it sometimes seemed, that members had in common. Toward that end, the assistants mediated religious controversy by reforming the company's policies gradually in response to both internal and external factors. The assistants' commitment to maintaining the appearance of orthodoxy enabled them to serve the needs of members who held various and often conflicting theological opinions. They expressed a similar attitude in economic matters. Although the loss of the apothecaries was a great defeat for the Grocers' Company, for more than a generation they had succeeded in meeting the needs and desires of apothecaries who expressed a willingness to form a separate company.

The message conveyed in the exhortations was that a failure to keep the past in sight would lead to chaos in the future. If the foregoing discussion were reconstructed into a narrative, the assistants' emphasis on the commemoration of the company and its benefactors would often coincide with their attempts to dissuade apothecaries from leaving the company. However, rather than reducing religion to a reflection of social relations, this chapter has argued that the Grocers' officers drew on the legacy of the company's founders and benefactors in their efforts to hold their community together.

In this light, the frankness of the wardens' exhortations is their most remarkable aspect. Rather than trying to assert their authority over the economic lives of their dissatisfied members, the wardens admitted their difficulties and requested the members' cooperation in overcoming them. After all, this discussion has been possible only because a series of records known as the Orders of the Court of Assistants contains conversations and debates as well as pronouncements and commands. The assistants realized that although every citizen of London had to be a member of a livery company, the success of their community depended on members' willingness to esteem the company's benefactors as well as its benefits. Freemen grocers were not required to become benefactors of the company themselves, but they were expected to uphold certain shared values.

The importance of the ethos of tolerance for the company's internal political relations suggests the ways in which the company contributed to the cohesiveness of metropolitan London during a century and a half of religious, economic, and political change. Primarily, it offered members a community in which to assess their relationship to such changes in a nonconfrontational way. Of course, the company's internal politics cannot be analyzed in isolation, and its survival depended at least in part on the availability of other communities—such as the Apothecaries' Company, the East India Company, and the parishes of All Hallows and St. Stephen's—to which disgruntled members could also turn for meaningful association. Nevertheless, the company continued to present to its members a community in which they could find common ground with colleagues of diverse religious opinions and economic interests; it remained for each of them to decide whether to accept what the company offered. At times, most notably during the Civil War and Interregnum, some members felt compelled to avoid the company. However, the essential functions of the company continued, and when the crisis ended, members such as Thomas Northey returned, reaffirming by his presence that while individual members could come and go, the company might live forever.

CHAPTER 6

Economic Competition and Politics in the Weavers' Company

The preceding chapters have analyzed the ways in which livery companies offered a sense of community to metropolitan Londoners during two particularly tumultuous centuries. In the case of the Grocers' Company, officers encouraged members to tolerate colleagues' differences, a process essential to the guild's survival in the face of religious innovation and commercial rivalries. The officers largely succeeded in providing a forum in which members could resolve their differences, even if their efforts did not prevent some from leaving the company. However, it cannot be assumed that the experience of the Grocers' Company was typical of other trade guilds in early modern London. This chapter examines the internal politics of the Weavers' Company, a guild that has been considered an example of the indifferent governance and addled relations that marked seventeenth-century companies.[1]

Weaving was a labor-intensive and largely suburban trade in early modern London. As such, it exposed company members to the challenges often noted in complaints about metropolitan expansion. Controversies over technological innovation and the admission of immigrants—primarily "strangers" from other countries—fueled debates among company members throughout the early modern period. In particular, the influx of religious refugees from continental Europe often led freemen to accuse their officers of doing too little to limit access to the trade. From the outbreak of religious war in France during the early 1560s to the revocation of the Edict of Nantes a century and a quarter later, alien settlers contributed greatly to the metropolitan economy, but their presence was not always welcomed by their English hosts.[2]

Throughout the sixteenth century, strangers often associated themselves with London trade guilds. These aliens would pay dues to the companies and pledge to obey their regulations, but they were prohibited from establishing shops on their own until they had obtained the status of denizen. The Weavers' Company was a leader in this process, admitting between eight and ten aliens in a typical year during the early decades of the seventeenth century into a guild that was, by the 1650s, registering some 320 apprentices every year.[3] The question of whether the admission of aliens was a threat or a benefit to company members energized guild politics well into the eighteenth century.

Although there are large gaps in the company's records for the early modern period, the documents still provide a solid basis for an analysis of its internal politics during an era of great change. Without denying the significant divisions between the company's yeomanry and its governors, this chapter emphasizes the importance of reform, which often emerged from controversy and confrontation, for the company's survival. Furthermore, because the historiography often portrays the strangers as a problem that the company's members had to overcome, the officers' inability to exclude noncitizens from the trade has been seen as a failure on their part. This chapter argues instead that the company's assimilation of immigrants, whether intentional or not, enabled it to continue offering its members a sense of community that could adjust to metropolitan expansion.

The Politics of Innovation

As part of her efforts to spur economic development, Queen Elizabeth encouraged weavers from continental Europe to relocate to England.[4] While the queen hoped that the aliens would provide a boost to the flagging English textile industry, English weavers were not entirely enthusiastic about her idea. Economic rivalries between strangers and natives largely explain why, in 1595, Huguenot weavers became a main target of a series of riots that rocked London. Historians have often attributed these disturbances to xenophobia intensified by economic dislocation.[5] Although it is impossible to gauge the motives of all the rioters, the faith of some native weavers encouraged them to take a generous view of the strangers—as long as they conformed to local law and custom. In a letter of June of that year, several freemen weavers requested that the elders of the French Church in London exhort the French weavers to obey the Weavers' Company's orders. According to the freemen, the French weavers were "Christianly entertained amongst us, even as the members of [the] mystical body of Jesus Christ, and citizens whereof that heavenly and celestial body." The authors complained that the aliens took advantage of their hospitality and violated a variety of company ordinances, thereby threatening the natives' livelihoods. "To be brief," the freemen continued, the strangers did not live "like Christian brethren, nor like friends, nor like good neighbors." The freemen then reminded the church elders that when English Protestants had fled to "the well-governed city of Geneva" during Queen Mary's reign, its magistrates had prohibited them and other aliens from entering the market until ten o'clock in the morning. They reported similar moves in cities in Germany, France, and Flanders, "which we speak to their commendations, for as good men had never purchased privileges, as to suffer every one to infringe it."[6] Aliens may have borne the brunt of the riots of 1595, but only the oddest sort of xenophobes would have praised foreign governments while criticizing the policies of their own.

Whatever their causes, the controversies of the mid-1590s may have spurred a reformation in the Weavers' Company policies. In 1594, the assistants granted twenty of the company's yeomen the right to meet at the company hall in order to join in enforcing the company's ordinances, and as early as 1595, they ordered strangers to occupy no more than four looms either in their own homes or elsewhere and prevented them from employing any weaver who had not been admitted to the company.[7] Nevertheless, the company's officers may not have implemented such policies to the satisfaction of all their members. The company's records are sparse for the fifteen years that followed the 1595 riots, but they suggest that the controversy continued into the next century. A draft of a petition to the City's lord mayor from the company's yeomen in 1610 complained that although they had exercised their duty to search out violations of the company's ordinances, their officers refused to act on their reports of aliens who established themselves as weavers without having first served a seven-year apprenticeship. They therefore urged the lord mayor to summon the company's officers and convince them to change their attitudes.[8] In 1614, a petition to the company's officers from a group of freemen asserted that because the yeomen had not been conducting their searches in recent years, "there are now many offenses committed in the company," and it requested that the yeomen's searches be revived in order to restore "great unity and concord in the company." In response, the officers appointed twenty yeomen to conduct a search.[9]

Nevertheless, a complaint from company members to the elders of the French congregation revealed that some weavers considered the strangers to be largely responsible for the decline of the trade. The freemen noted that King James encouraged the settlement of the aliens by allowing them to work in London, but they alleged that the aliens took advantage of their tolerance by violating London's customary trading policies. In particular, they claimed that while the strangers were allowed four looms each "whereby all men may have a competent living," some of them occupied as many as ten, thereby causing unemployment among English weavers. Throughout their argument, the petitioners tried to appeal to a sense of shared morality between themselves and the elders. The English weavers claimed that they held neither "malice or hate for any nation," but because of those immigrants who "live without government, which we know no Christian congregation will allow," their souls were troubled by "these extravagant strangers that come among us in multitudes of no faith, of no Church." They therefore suggested that the elders hold the aliens to the same standards as their hosts, for "God commanded Moses [in] Leviticus 24 'Thou shall judge a stranger by the same law thy self art judged.'"[10]

The company's yeomen also raised objections to the aliens' use of new types of looms. Foremost among a long list of allegations against the strangers was a claim that "by an engine or loom" they brought from the Continent and set up in the metropolis, the aliens had eliminated the work of an estimated 486 weavers. According to the complainants, the products of such looms were poorly made and therefore injured consumers and undermined trade. They also claimed that the engine loom had been invented in Holland, where the government had quickly prohibited it because it replaced the single loom, on which many children and old men relied for employment.[11]

The freemen further accused the strangers of employing women illegally. As early as 1578, the Weavers' Company ordinances demanded that "no manner of person or persons exercising [weaving] shall keep, teach, instruct, or bring up in the use, exercise, or knowledge of [weaving] any maid, damsel, or other woman whatsoever" under penalty of a fine of 6s 8d for each offense. In their complaint, the native weavers claimed that the immigrants employed women to sell their goods from door to door rather than in common marketplaces, which was a violation of London's customs. This allegedly gave the aliens an additional advantage over less productive company members who were, as a result, forced to abandon their trades and seek work as laborers, "leaving their wives and children in most lamentable misery."[12] In other words, one indication of the differences between native and stranger weavers was that the newcomers were willing to employ their women in a way that undermined the ability of the freemen to support their own. This clash of economic interests was therefore cast as a clash between two systems of gender relations within the domestic economy.

It is difficult to establish the veracity of such charges. Detailed records of the company's Court of Assistants survive for the years 1610–19, and they indicate that the assistants took steps to regulate strangers. In 1612, the assistants adopted a measure that limited them to the occupation of no more than four single looms at any one time. They enforced this ordinance periodically during the remainder of the decade. In 1613, they ordered stranger John Lewars "to give over his mill or engine whereof he makes tape"; in 1616 they fined stranger John Trowle 20s for "excessive looms"; and in 1618 they fined a "newly arrived stranger" 5s for using five looms.[13]

In addition to inspecting their looms, the assistants monitored other economic activities of strangers through the decade. Before they would admit an alien as a journeyman, they would check that he was "of good fame and name," skilled in his trade, and a member of a foreign congregation.[14] In January 1611, the assistants ordered an alien to pay his entrance fine as a journeyman or return to his native land. Five months later, they warned a journeyman stranger to "repair into his country" or be sued by the company. Between December 1612 and December 1613, the court ordered four aliens—including John Lewars, whom they had told to stop using a tape engine—to join the company, and the following February, they fined John de Marie 20s for employing three unbound strangers as journeymen. The assistants pursued similar policies until the end of the decade. During 1614 and 1615, they took action against only one alien, but in 1616 they fined a weaver 13s 4d for employing three strangers as journeymen, charged a stranger 20s for employing three others, and arrested two strangers for practicing the trade before they had been admitted to the company. During the next year, the officers ordered a weaver to present the apprenticeship records of two aliens he had employed as journeymen, they punished three other weavers for hiring strangers, and ordered three journeymen and three other aliens to stop weaving in London. In 1618, the assistants disciplined eight strangers, and in 1619 they barred Peter Ewstaius of Antwerp and Andreas Bartholomew of Liège from weaving in the metropolis.[15]

While they enforced the company's ordinances, the assistants cooperated with City and Crown efforts to minimize the threat immigrants posed to freemen's economic rights. In 1615, the assistants informed the lord mayor that alien weavers employed their own countrymen, to the detriment of the English. However, when company officers would go to search the strangers' workshops, they would "send their servants abroad into the fields and hide them by other means out of our sight." The Weavers' officers acknowledged that the aliens were fellow Protestants who deserved refuge in England during the wars of religion in France, but they questioned having to encourage immigrants nearly two decades after the Edict of Nantes had established a limited tolerance for Huguenots in their native land. They then requested that the lord mayor ask King James to stem immigration in order to remove another nation's surplus laborers from England.[16]

The king acted on such complaints in the later years of his reign. In 1622, he established a commission to ensure that strangers would not threaten freemen.[17] Among those who cooperated with the royal investigation were the Goldsmiths' officers, who produced a list of 188 noncitizens working in greater London. Although they tried to enforce their ordinances, they claimed that because the strangers hid throughout the metropolis, their searches were constantly impeded, and the livelihoods of freemen goldsmiths were threatened.[18] A group of freemen weavers made a similar report to the elders of the French and Dutch churches. They complained that when the company's officers went to search the houses of alien weavers "they shut their doors against them" and then used their churches' political connections to gain royal protection from prosecution.[19]

During King Charles's reign, the Weavers' officers became the focus of complaints from the company's members. The sixteen yeomen who were empowered by the company's ordinances to conduct searches of the craft often reported that the officers undermined their efforts to regulate alien weavers. In 1626, the yeomen alleged that they had warned their officers that one Roger Plush had recently arrived in England and planned to practice their trade. Despite their promise that they would admit only strangers who had been "of some good continuance in their congregation," the assistants admitted Plush while the yeomen were absent from their proceedings. The yeomen also alleged that the officers harassed their members by searching them and then demanding higher payments than the ordinances allowed.[20]

The yeomen subsequently accused the officers of profiting from putting their personal interests ahead of the company's. In a series of statements that probably date from the early years of King Charles's reign, the yeomen complained that members would bind apprentices to themselves, turn them over to serve with strangers, and then inform the chamberlain of the City that the apprentices had served with them when the term of their apprenticeships had expired. The yeomen claimed that freemen—including some company officers—were motivated to engage in such illegal practices "for some private end to themselves" and that, as a result, the metropolis was becoming overpopulated and prices were rising beyond the means of honest weavers.[21] On 13 September 1630, a group of 30 company yeomen met at a pub to discuss ways in which to present their grievances to the City government. Three yeomen subsequently appeared before the lord mayor and reported that because the company's officers took bribes from strangers "to allow them to use the trade of weaving there are many now [where] if the orders were put into execution there would not be any." They asked the lord mayor to use his influence with the company's officers to eliminate abuses in the trade.[22]

In their own defense, the bailiffs, wardens, and assistants of the company argued that their policy of admitting strangers into the company was designed to enhance their control over their trade. They claimed that efforts in recent years to limit the numbers of aliens working in London had failed to stem their flow. They therefore asserted that the best way to regulate the economic activities of the strangers was to bring them into the guild, thereby increasing the officers' ability to enforce company ordinances. They denied the yeomen's allegations that they profited personally from their admissions policies, and they insisted, "upon their credit and upon their consciences," that they sought "to reduce the strangers into obedience and conformity of life and to have them live under government in such manner as the free men and members of their own company."[23] The officers may have been making a conciliatory gesture in 1633 when they confirmed the power of the company's yeomanry to conduct searches. However, of the thirty yeomen who had agitated against the officers in 1630, only two were among the sixteen yeomen the officers appointed to conduct searches.[24]

The yeomen were not the only Weavers' freemen disappointed with their officers. In 1633, a group of liverymen protested against the election of anyone who had previously been a bailiff or warden—the most senior company offices—to either of those posts. Rather than being jealous of the officers' positions, the liverymen claimed that their action represented their "woeful experience" of the officers' negligence in punishing offenders against the company's ordinances and of their accepting bribes for turning apprentices over to aliens. The protesters concluded their argument by suggesting that the officers had neglected their responsibility to use the company's revenues for the benefit of its poorer members, and they expressed their desire that the assistants elect bailiffs and wardens who "will be better husbands for the company" and reform the trade.[25]

Two years later, a series of petitions, from groups such as "the generality of the native born" weavers of London, suggested that little had changed. The petitioners rehearsed the litany of complaints against aliens, whom they considered to be "a commonwealth without government." As usual, the main causes of the petitioners' concerns were the employment of strangers who had not served apprenticeships to the trade, the propagation of multishuttle looms, and the general evasion of the company's ordinances.[26] In a letter to the king's attorney general, some weavers attributed the decline of their trade to the assistants' choice of aliens to be company bailiffs, some of whom were inexperienced in the trade. The yeomen also continued to attack the company's fee structure, claiming that while three or four apprentices used to spend 6s 8d for a breakfast for their governors when they were made free of the company, in recent years the officers had charged each new freeman 5s 4d and a silver spoon that weighed at least one and a half ounces. When the City's lord mayor and aldermen examined the controversy, they ruled that the company's officers should charge each new company member only 3s 8d.[27] For their part, the assistants represented some of their members' concerns in a petition to the aldermen that accused strangers of pursuing the trade in and around London, whereby "the bread is taken out of the mouths" of English weavers.[28]

The matter was resolved for a time when King Charles reaffirmed the company's rights in 1638. He empowered the officers to "moderately rate" themselves and the members in order to defray the costs of searches and other company business. He also pardoned them "for all errors or offenses in any matter touching the government of the said company," and he allowed them to collect from each new freeman a silver spoon, which was to be used for poor relief and other charitable purposes. The king further ordered that strangers should not be granted the status of master weaver unless they had served an apprenticeship of seven years, and he published a new set of duties on silk imports that assessed aliens at a higher rate than natives.[29]

In the midst of the continuous allegations and counterallegations, the critics of the company's government achieved at least one significant victory. An undated petition from the "commonalty of the company of weavers" accused Thomas Pell, the company's beadle, of binding twelve apprentices to himself within the space of two and a half years and then turning them all over to foreigners to serve their apprenticeships.[30] Although there is no evidence that these charges had any immediate effect, Pell was disfranchised from the City in January 1637 after a weaver testified that he had been the beadle's apprentice and that Pell had falsely informed the City's chamberlain he had served his apprenticeship.[31] This embarrassing development may have inspired the Weavers' officers to appear more responsive to members' demands: they secured confirmation from the lord mayor and aldermen that all weavers in the City were under their supervision.[32]

These disputes intensified during the ensuing decade. The records of the Court of Assistants do not survive for the period 1642–48, but when they recommence, they indicate that the company remained embroiled in controversy. The assistants continued to carry out the company's normal governing functions, such as freeing apprentices, prosecuting interlopers, and ordering alien weavers to join the company.[33] However, in October 1648, the officers believed that some "ill affected" freemen plotted "to overthrow the ancient approved government of this company, the known laws of this kingdom, and their respective oaths when they were made free of the City of London." They took up a collection among the assistants and liverymen to be used in defense of their authority. During the following February, the assistants canceled the annual dinner for the assistants and livery because "great divisions at present" threatened to destroy the company.[34]

A pamphlet written by "the commonalty of the Corporation of Weavers of London" (1648) sheds light on the nature of these divisions in the company. It claimed that the company's royal charters vested authority in the commonalty and that the company's officers—whom they called "our Egyptian task-masters"—could not demonstrate any justification for assuming the governing authority. It listed various "oppressions and abuses" committed by the officers, including the admission of alien masters, and asked "all conscientious godly men" in the House of Commons to establish the "freedom of elections being both legal and rational" in the company. In response to such demands, the government revised the company's ordinances in 1649, placing the election of its officers in the hands of 140 "representatives" who were selected by all ranks within the company. The new officers made modest headway against members' long-standing complaints. They stopped demanding silver spoons from freed apprentices, set limits on the number of apprentices that each weaver could keep, and reformed aspects of the company's finances.[35] However, they continued to admit "foreign brothers," and they assessed them the same entrance fee as apprentices.[36]

The records of the Court of Assistants survive for the period 1650–54, and they reveal the officers' continued efforts to enforce company ordinances. In June 1651, the assistants reprimanded three weavers, whose nationalities were not listed, for employing women at their looms, and in April 1653 they summoned Hugh Daniell, a Frenchman who lived in Petticoat Lane, because he had been accused of illegally using the trade. They subsequently sued him for ignoring their summons and for putting "an Englishman out of work." Two months later, the court discussed the company's policies toward strangers and decided to differentiate between two groups. The assistants looked favorably upon those who had left their native countries "for conscience sake and others who have here inhabited many years and married English wives and in the late war have manifested much affection to the Commonwealth by adventuring themselves in the public service." They were more critical of those who had recently immigrated and who were "not members of the church" and yet employed themselves in weaving "to the great damage and dishonor of the Commonwealth and prejudice of this corporation." The assistants decided that strangers who belonged to the first group could be admitted to company membership, pledged to take legal action against the second group, and agreed to ask the elders of the French and Dutch churches to assist them in discouraging additional immigration.[37]

Sixty years after the riots of 1595, the admission of strangers remained a controversial issue in the Weavers' Company. The limited surviving records preclude any firm analysis of the competing claims of various groups of officers and yeomen, but sporadic reform efforts and the disfranchisement of the company's beadle indicated that some complaints had merit. Although strangers remained central to the controversies, the company's yeomanry directed their criticism not only at immigrants but also at company members who took advantage of the aliens' plight by hiring them as journeymen before they had been properly bound to the company. It is difficult to evaluate the response of the company's officers to the yeomen's complaints. Although some officers may have profited personally from the exploitation of strangers, the ability of others to reduce immigration was limited by the sympathy many weavers felt toward Protestant refugees as well as by the Crown's desire to infuse the aliens' skills into the English textile industry.

The Restoration of Controversy

The Stuart Restoration overturned the company's Interregnum government, with its expanded basis for participation in company politics, but the new assistants continued to take steps to redress their members' grievances. In particular, the yeomen still played a leading role in the enforcement of the company's ordinances. In January 1661, the officers appointed sixteen yeomen to inspect "any place or places whatsoever within the jurisdiction of the said company when and as often as they shall think fit." In addition, the searchers could sue anyone for violating the company's ordinances—provided that the bailiffs had first approved the grounds for such proceedings—and they were empowered to collect membership fees from journeymen. The yeomen took their mandate seriously. In March, the assistants allowed three yeomen to sue four weavers who had never been admitted to the company, and in the following June, a weaver who was accused by the yeomen was summoned to appear before a future court meeting. Even though the yeomen were not always credited with initiating such regulatory activity, the assistants took action against interloping strangers throughout the Restoration period. In June 1662, the court fined three weavers for employing aliens, and in July they investigated the background of eleven strangers. In January 1663, the assistants complied with the request of representatives of the Dutch and French churches not to take action against a member of the French congregation who had been "persecuted for his religion in Paris," but they insisted that the case could not be used as a precedent that the company had repealed its requirement that only strangers who had been in England for ten years would be admitted to the trade.[38]

The company's officers also monitored engine looms. In November 1666, the assistants initiated a lawsuit against a Southwark weaver who operated four of the looms. In January, when the assistants received a complaint about another engine loom, they encouraged the yeomen to investigate the matter and to report back to them. Eleven months later, the assistants again inquired into the prevalence of engine looms. After hearing complaints from shopkeepers who disliked the materials produced by such looms as well as from other members of the company, the assistants formed a committee that included liverymen and yeomen to ask the Crown to suppress the use of the engines. In October 1670, the assistants considered a petition from the yeomen that complained of "the great evils" that resulted from the use of broad or tape looms as well as the importation of fabric, and the assistants agreed to petition Parliament on their behalf.[39]

At the same time, the assistants continued to monitor aliens. Because the Crown maintained its support of strangers, the assistants cooperated with officials of the alien churches. In June 1667, two weavers certified their membership in the French church and paid 11s 10d to become journeymen in the company.[40] In March 1668, the assistants asked several foreign members to assist in collecting contributions from members of the French church for rebuilding the company hall.[41] Eight months later, the assistants decided that no alien should be admitted as a member of the company unless he had been resident in England for three years, could prove that he had been trained as a weaver according to the customs of his country, and was a member of the French or the Dutch church. However, they did suggest that in some cases they would show compassion for those who had been in England only for one year.[42] In December, some elders of the alien churches asked the assistants to be lenient toward the requests of their fellow Protestants "by reason of a persecution in France." The assistants replied that they had always been hesitant to disturb members of the alien churches, but they now believed that the foreign weavers were encouraging more strangers to immigrate "under pretence of persecution." Nevertheless, they reaffirmed their willingness to welcome the aliens "if that calamity shall really happen." The assistants exercised discretion in the coming months, admitting some strangers but rejecting others.[43]

The officers published new ordinances regarding the admission of aliens in May 1670. They subsequently encouraged the company's yeomen to be aggressive in finding aliens who violated the rules. In August, the assistants paid 5s to a man for warning aliens to conform to the company's ordinances; in February 1673, they fined a weaver in the Minories 5s for employing six foreigners; and in 1674, they decided that no alien could become a master unless he paid the company £5. Rather than considering these actions representative of a campaign against the aliens, the elders of the French and Dutch churches thanked the assistants for their "civility" in dealing with the strangers.[44]

The company's officers also continued to take action against female weavers. In 1664, Jonas Slickland admitted to the assistants that he had been employing four women, for periods of up to fifteen months, after they discovered his illicit activity. Three years later, Robert Harper confessed that he had employed a woman for two or three years.[45] However, during the late seventeenth and early eighteenth centuries, the assistants apparently changed their policy and began to bind female apprentices at the company hall. Although some of these women may have been assigned to work with the wives of members, possibly in the wives' own trades, or in auxiliary tasks such as winding and spinning yarn, during the period 1664–1706 more than 125 women were bound as apprentices in the Weavers' Company. A few of these women completed their apprenticeships, became free of the company, and then took on apprentices themselves, a practice officially allowed only to widows.[46]

Along with aliens and women, engine looms remained the chief source of competition for freemen. Some weavers exhibited their hostility toward engine looms in a series of riots in 1675. The disturbances began on 9 August, when groups of between 30 and 200 people destroyed looms throughout the metropolis, and they continued through 13 August, when royal guards finally restored order. Subsequently, at least seven individuals were sentenced for rioting at the Middlesex Quarter Sessions, and eleven more were sentenced at a session of Oyer and Terminer in London.[47] Although the rioters focused on engine looms, the session records are vague about their occupations. Of the nineteen people examined at the Middlesex sessions, three were identified as "silk weavers," but eight were called "laborers," four were "yeomen," two were the wives of "yeomen," one was the wife of a "laborer," and one was not given an occupational identity. It is possible that some of those called before the sessions were involved only peripherally in the actions against the engines, for the court records suggest that very large groups gathered around the scenes of violence.[48] In addition to several machine-breakers, the ranks of the Weavers' Company contained several victims of the riots, including one company assistant.[49]

According to Richard Dunn, the rioters were motivated in part by the failure of the Weavers' officers to suppress the engine looms.[50] As discussed above, the assistants had on several occasions considered complaints from the yeomen regarding these machines, and had supported their efforts to petition Parliament for their suppression. Of course, there is no way to determine whether all the yeomanry found those efforts sufficient. But before historians conclude that the company's officers were not up to the challenge, their response to the events should also be considered, for their silence may have spoken volumes. On 9 August, the assistants were informed that "several persons, many of them weavers by trade" were gathered in Spitalfields. They declared themselves "altogether ignorant" of the rioters' intentions and concluded that the meeting was "unruly, disordered, and tumultuous." They decided to "disown and protest against" it, and they asked the lord mayor to suppress the meeting.[51] Although this response suggests that the officers opposed the riots, the company's records did not indicate that any of those the courts punished were ever disciplined by the company, suggesting that the assistants may have been ambivalent about the destruction of machines whose spread they had opposed publicly for years. Indeed, despite the fact that at least one of their colleagues had been a victim of the machine-breakers, the assistants offered financial support to several company members imprisoned for their involvement in the riots.[52]

The assistants then took action to support the further suppression of tape looms. On 25 October, they considered a petition from several yeomen in Southwark who complained that they "exceedingly suffer by the use of the engine looms" and asked the assistants to lobby Parliament to prohibit the use of the looms in making silk ribbons. After the yeomen withdrew from the court, the assistants empowered the bailiffs and wardens to comply with the yeomen's request. Two weeks later, the assistants considered statements from "diverse masters of the trade" and from "apprentices and journeymen" that also asked them to petition Parliament to suppress tape looms. The assistants granted this request, and on 13 December they authorized a petition to the Crown calling for the prohibition of tape looms in working silk and cotton ribbons. The assistants demonstrated their willingness to sponsor such measures by paying 50s to a solicitor for his help in drafting the petition.[53]

They also continued to limit the employment of foreigners and aliens. On 15 November, one Lewes Lecompt was found employing six foreign weavers who had not been admitted to the company. The assistants ordered him to dismiss the foreigners, after which he agreed to pay a fine of 40s.[54] The following April, the assistants decided that no alien would be admitted to the company as a master unless a full Court of Assistants agreed, and then only "upon some weighty grounds and reasons." The court upheld this motion the following January after noting that several aliens defied their authority by taking on apprentices before being admitted as masters. The assistants reminded themselves that the Crown had only authorized the admission of aliens as journeymen, and they agreed that the company would take legal action against any who were found usurping the status of master. There is a gap in the company's records between 1678 and 1683, but thereafter they show the assistants serving a writ on one Peter LeMoyne for binding four apprentices although he was only a journeyman. LeMoyne subsequently paid a fine of £5 10s, dismissed one of his apprentices, and bound the other three according to the company's ordinances. In the summer of 1684, the assistants fined Henry DeBoard 40s for binding an apprentice although he had only been admitted as a foreign journeyman, and they warned a French Quaker who had served one year of an apprenticeship while in Germany to stop weaving or be indicted.[55]

Given the sporadic nature of such incidents in the company's records, it is difficult to evaluate the effectiveness of the officers' efforts to limit strangers' employment. Nonetheless, the officers appeared willing to cooperate with their members in enforcing the company's ordinances. In March 1685, the assistants considered a complaint from several freemen against foreigners who employed more French than English weavers. The officers turned the list over to the company's beadle, and the next day they disciplined eight aliens, including one who claimed ignorance of the company's ordinances because he could not understand the English language.[56] However, strangers with special skills were offered exemptions to the company's ordinances. In January 1683, the bailiffs and wardens considered admitting two Frenchmen who claimed to be able to weave lutestring, alamode, and other silk materials according to French techniques. The officers expressed their willingness to encourage new production methods and gave the men six weeks to demonstrate their skill, after which they would consider admitting them.[57] Eight months later, one of the men produced a sample of alamode silk that the officers predicted would enhance English industry. They granted him the status of a foreign master free of charge, stipulating only that for at least one year he employ Englishmen in the production of such material.[58]

The revocation of the Edict of Nantes in 1685 sent a new wave of religious refugees to England.[59] Two pamphlets recorded its significance for the company. In 1689, a broadside from "the Corporation of Weavers at London and Canterbury" urged Parliament to defeat proposed legislation that would have prohibited the nobility and gentry from wearing silks and stuffs during seven months of the year. They claimed that such a policy would cause widespread unemployment among the hundreds of thousands of people involved in various aspects of the weaving of silk and hair. In addition to those who had served a seven-year apprenticeship to the trade and who had no other occupation by which they could support their families, the petitioners also suggested that the legislation would harm the French Protestants who had sought refuge in England. An anonymous tract from "diverse liege-master weavers" similarly complained that the Weavers' Company officers had disregarded several ancient statutes when they allowed aliens—many of whom had not served apprenticeships of seven years—to establish themselves as master weavers and to take aliens as apprentices and journeymen. When the authors brought such complaints to the assistants, they were told that "King Charles did by his counsel order us to admit aliens, so they would not desist till they had order to the contrary." The complainants then referred to a statute of 1689 that declared "the execution of laws by regal authority, without consent of Parliament" illegal, and they concluded by arguing that the removal of aliens from their trade would not discourage the immigrants because a statute passed during the reign of Charles II had allowed aliens to enter several manual trades, including the weaving of hemp and flax.[60]

The company's records are not extant for the final years of the century, but when they recommence in the early eighteenth century, they show the assistants on the defensive once more. On 6 November 1704, "diverse of the livery" told the officers that although they had been "fully satisfied with the faithful, impartial, and regular proceedings" of the court, "diverse others of the livery" had collected money from company members in order to take legal action against the assistants for having "usurped their privileges and acted against the interests of the trade by admitting foreigners." The assistants condemned the complainers' "clandestine and base" attempts to "seduce and withdraw the affections of others from this court," and they appointed a committee to prepare to meet this challenge.[61]

One month later, the court received a series of complaints from "diverse liverymen" that continued the controversy. The liverymen accused the assistants of violating the company's charter and ordinances by admitting aliens and others who had not served formal apprenticeships, preventing the livery from participating in the election of wardens, failing to prosecute interlopers, and refusing to call a general meeting of the company to inspect the company's charter.[62] The gaps in the company records preclude a detailed analysis of these charges, but there is some evidence that they may not have been well founded. In 1700, the court disfranchised two foreigners who had presented false evidence of their qualifications to be master weavers. There were no other records of enforcement, but in April 1701 the court ordered the commencement of seasonal searches and the convening of weekly courts. Similarly, each of the company's three previous elections had taken place at a general meeting of the bailiffs, wardens, assistants, and livery. The livery were present for the election of the bailiffs, but only the bailiffs, wardens, and those assistants who had been bailiffs participated in the wardens' election. These procedures were in keeping with the company's ordinances.[63]

In March 1705, the assistants learned that they had all been served with Court of Chancery subpoenas for a case that several members of the livery brought against them.[64] Ten weeks later, the plaintiffs suggested that three of their number meet with three of the assistants to seek a settlement of their differences. The assistants complied, but these negotiations did not settle the issue. On 29 June, the assistants called a general meeting of the livery and master weavers, but many journeymen attended as well, allegedly at the instigation of three plaintiffs in the Chancery suit. Although the overcrowding of the hall prevented any quiet discussion of the controversy, the clerk read a statement from the assistants. It defended them against the charge that they had neglected the election procedures outlined in the company's agreement with Charles I in 1638 by claiming that their "forefathers" had thought these procedures would jeopardize both "the trade and company," and so ever since the company's officers had "acted by other charters and ordinances." This statement was hotly debated, after which the assembly agreed that committees from the two opposing sides should meet and consider the issue.[65]

The formation of these committees exposed the divisions among liverymen. At a meeting of the assistants and livery on 9 July, liverymen argued among themselves over the appointment of members to the committee to represent their interests in negotiations with the assistants. The "complainers"—probably those who had begun the Chancery suit—claimed that they should control the livery's committee, but other liverymen would not agree to this plan because "they have as much right to give their vote for anything concerning the good of the company and trade as the complainers." After a "long confused debate," the meeting was dismissed without a result. In October, the company's officers reported to the City's lord mayor and aldermen that three liverymen had refused to serve as stewards for an upcoming company dinner, and had then claimed that the company's ordinances empowered them to pay only 40s to avoid that service rather than the £14 that had become the "accustomed" fine in recent years. The City magistrates found that the liverymen should pay £14 each to avoid serving as stewards, and ordered them to comply with the rulings of their company's officers or face imprisonment.[66]

Little progress was made in resolving the ongoing conflict between the Weavers' officers and liverymen until the following February, when first the assistants and then several liverymen attempted to write a new company charter. A committee of assistants considered the liverymen's proposal three months later, and after a discussion of the assistants' objections, both the liverymen and the assistants agreed to present a draft charter to a general meeting of the livery.[67] The new charter was approved at the meeting by "a great majority," but it was noted that "some" seemed to be dissatisfied. However, the dissatisfied liverymen declined the assistants' subsequent offer of a poll of members' views on the issue. During the next winter, the assistants presented the new charter to be sealed, but they learned that the Duke of Newcastle, Lord Privy Seal, was respecting a caveat against it from a "Mr Diggs on behalf of diverse of the livery and other weavers in Middlesex." Newcastle ordered the assistants to call a meeting at which each liveryman would confirm his approval or disapproval. At that time, the charter was approved "by a majority of near thirty to one," but Newcastle ordered the assistants to inform him of the specialties practiced by those who voted. At a meeting on 9 June 1707, the charter was approved by a margin of 65 to 17, but the record did not specify the trades of the voters.[68] The subsequent appeals of the company's officers to the City's lord mayor and aldermen to require a member of the Clothworkers' Company who wove for a living to transfer into their company suggests that the resolution of the crisis over the new charter improved relations between the various ranks within the company.[69]

The meetings and debates of the early eighteenth century recalled the controversies that had surrounded the company's government for more than a century. Against this background, the riots of 1675—like the riots of 1595—seem to be part of a multifaceted conversation involving native and alien weavers of both sexes, the company's officers, and the national government. As such, they resolved little, but they encouraged the officers to govern the company in a way that maintained support from a sizable portion of its membership. As the voting on the new charter demonstrated, as late as 1707 the company's officers could muster the allegiance of an overwhelming proportion of liverymen.

The variety of perceptions of economic competition invigorated the internal politics of the Weavers' Company throughout the period under consideration. Alien artisans may have been welcomed when they were religious refugees, but not all English weavers could agree on the amount of economic freedom that the strangers should have. Part of the difference may have been related to economic position. Some weavers could have profited from developments that decreased production costs, such as growing numbers of artisan weavers and the introduction of engine looms, while others could have suffered economically as a result of such innovations.

Without denying that economic competition influenced the company's internal politics, this chapter has emphasized the assistants' responsiveness to calls for reform. Throughout the period considered, the company's officers took steps to regulate both strangers and engine looms. The dissatisfaction of journeymen with such efforts was apparent, but yeomen's continued role in company affairs through the late seventeenth century suggests clear limitations to any efforts by a mercantile oligarchy to oppress native English weavers. If anything, the series of large, boisterous meetings in the early eighteenth century gave the appearance of a company whose politics were livelier than they had been a century earlier.

More important, whatever the character of its internal politics, the company survived the steady growth of the metropolis. Its sheer size combined with the willingness of some of its members to seek redress of their grievances outside the confines of the company itself—through petitions to the Crown and Parliament, the publication of pamphlets, and riots—meant that the Weavers' Company affairs could not have escaped the notice of Londoners generally. For that reason, after more than a century of public controversy, the desire of members to pack themselves into Weavers' Hall in search of reform suggests that many believed that the company's officers were not completely unresponsive to the desires of their members. Furthermore, despite the continued controversy surrounding aliens in the metropolis, the Weavers' Company policies provided them with a way of maintaining and participating in the traditional economic institutions of metropolitan London. Although innovation challenged native weavers, it also encouraged them to view the Weavers' Company as a means for coping with change. In these ways, the company continued to offer a sense of community to its members.

CONCLUSION

Metropolitan Communities

In recent years, historians and literary critics have suggested that the relationship between the early modern City of London and its suburbs and liberties was largely antagonistic. They have regarded the rapid growth of the suburbs during the sixteenth and seventeenth centuries as both the cause and the consequence of the inability of London's livery companies to enforce their regulations in areas beyond the lord mayor's jurisdiction. According to this view, the suburbs attracted immigrants who undermined traditional sources of community such as trade guilds and heralded the coming of modern society, at once more individualistic, enterprising, and exploitative. When discussing such changes, scholars have tended to assume that there were primarily two identities available to early modern Londoners: the "honest freeman" and the "illicit stranger."

This book has questioned several of the assumptions underpinning such arguments. Although some early modern Londoners decried what they took to be the licentiousness of suburban society, others found ways to incorporate the suburbs and liberties into the ideological and governmental systems through which ministers and magistrates cooperated to govern the City. More important, rather than feeling threatened by the economic developments in the suburbs, freemen of the City often considered them sources of opportunity. Since they lived and worked in the suburbs and liberties of London, many freemen relied upon their livery company connections to participate in markets throughout the metropolis. Thus, the companies provided their members with ways to benefit from metropolitan expansion throughout the sixteenth and seventeenth centuries.

But this was only one advantage that livery companies offered their members. The officers of trade guilds—such as the Bakers' Company—may have exercised their discretion by allowing their members to charge London prices in the suburbs while striving to limit the opportunities of strangers there. Furthermore, the companies offered their members a variety of valuable perquisites such as pensions and charitable assistance for themselves and their widows, as well as opportunities to secure casual and salaried work as porters, sanderbeaters, or minor company officials if their fortunes decayed.

The variety of company members' experiences contributed to the diversity of their attitudes toward work. Historians have assumed that freemen had incentives to maintain the standing of their companies, but it is now clear that some members took advantage of their companies' reputations in order to cheat their customers. From a distance of four centuries, it is impossible to assess the motivations of the cheaters; some may have been in desperate financial straits, and others may have been avaricious. In either case, their varied responses to the opportunities provided by metropolitan expansion created divisions among citizens as well as between some citizens and some strangers.

The examples of the Grocers' and the Weavers' companies each demonstrate the shortcomings of research that emphasizes the antagonism between freemen and strangers. The main sources of tension in the Grocers' Company were the rivalries among the company's members, such as the controversy surrounding the creation of the new Apothecaries' Company, which produced fissures that expressed themselves in conflict. The Weavers' officers, on the other hand, faced not only similar rivalries among members but also the challenge of coping with large numbers of alien weavers in metropolitan London. Despite the constant complaints of members against their officers, the company survived the challenges it faced because religious sympathy and deep-rooted loyalty to the company facilitated compromises among the various factions.

The diversity of members' interests influenced the political life of the livery companies. Rather than being dominated by merchant oligarchs who were unconcerned with yeomen's interests, company politics remained accessible to members with a variety of interests and opinions throughout the early modern period. Perhaps the most important political division within companies was between those who cared deeply about their company and those who did not. Not everyone who had the wealth and the connections to join the ranks of their company's governors chose to do so, and, as the example of the Weavers' Company demonstrated, the officers of companies could not overlook the interests of their broader membership. In noneconomic matters, such as the allocation of religious patronage, officers of the Grocers' Company had to balance the interests of members with divergent views while remaining receptive to the suggestions of non–company members such as parishioners and the Crown. While doing so, they also found it useful to remind members that their guild offered them a connection to the memories and legacies of their deceased predecessors. In that way, the company provided members the opportunity to participate in a community that was potentially timeless.

The flexibility of livery company policies helped early modern Londoners cope with changing times. Companies encouraged, rather than enforced, consensus among their members, often allowing those punished for violating their company's ordinances to apologize for their transgressions and remain within the ranks of the company. Companies offered members a useful association with individuals who shared many aims, but the ability of companies to accommodate a diversity of individual interests was the key to their survival during two centuries of far-reaching religious, economic, and social change. Further, the fact that company membership and civic freedom were conjoined meant that the guilds' economic interests and the City's political and judicial interests could never go their separate ways. If they did nothing else, companies offered early modern Londoners the knowledge that the expansion of London from a primarily walled town to a metropolis was not necessarily a threat to their livelihoods or their values.

Ultimately, the cohesiveness of the metropolis depended on the attitudes of individuals. Institutions such as livery companies may have helped Londoners imagine how an entity as expansive as greater London could function smoothly, but in order for the guilds to have been meaningful associations—communities—they had to maintain the loyalty of their members. Each member participated in shaping his or her identity in relation to the company. Those who cared little about their guild's ideals but remained affiliated with it for personal advancement considered it a loose association modern social theorists would label a "society." Those who identified closely with their guild's traditions and values found it a "community." For these reasons, the trade guilds of early modern London had the potential to be metropolitan communities.

Reference Matter

Notes

The following abbreviations are used in the notes:

APC	*Acts of the Privy Council*
BL	British Library
CHA	Clothworkers' Hall Archive
CLRO	Corporation of London Record Office
CSPD	*Calendar of State Papers, Domestic*
DHA	Drapers' Hall Archive
EICCB	East India Company Court Book
GHA	Goldsmiths' Hall Archive
GL	Guildhall Library
LMS	Lansdowne Manuscript
MHA	Mercers' Hall Archive
OIL	Oriental and India Office Library
PCC	Prerogative Court of Canterbury
PRO	Public Record Office
SHA	Salters' Hall Archive
SkHA	Skinners' Hall Archive

Introduction

1. Von Gierke; Tönnies; Bell and Newby, pp. 21–53; A. Macfarlane et al., pp. 1–27; Lyon; Anderson.

2. Finlay; Finlay and Shearer, p. 45; but see also Harding, "Population of London," pp. 111–28. For the utility of viewing "early modern" London as covering the period 1550–1700, see Harding, "Early Modern London," p. 34.

3. For reasons that will be discussed further in Chapter 1 below, in this study the term *City* refers to the City of London, the territory under the di-

rect legal supervision of the lord mayor and other civic officials of London. *Liberties* were the several small areas, both within and without the borders (or *bars*) of the City, that were exempt from the lord mayor's jurisdiction, such as Blackfriars, the Minories, and Paris Garden. *Suburbs* were areas in Middlesex and Surrey that were contiguous to, yet beyond, the City's limits. The term *suburbs* will often be used generically to refer to all areas in the metropolis outside the lord mayor's jurisdiction.

4. BL, LMS 160, fols. 95r–96r; GL MS 4655/1, fols. 25v–26r. These issues and texts will be discussed in greater depth in Chapters 1 and 2 below.

5. Rappaport, pp. 46, 62, 187, 231; Pearl, *London*, p. 43, and "Change and Stability," pp. 12–13. Rappaport and Pearl are the main proponents of the notion that London's rapid growth was inherently stable. On the use of the terms *strangers, aliens,* and *foreigners,* see I. Archer, *Pursuit*, p. 131. Since the relationship of strangers and foreigners to livery companies was, for the most part, similar, in this study the terms will sometimes be used interchangeably.

6. For example, Jonathan Dollimore based much of his criticism on a catalog of "far-reaching material and ideological changes in Elizabethan and Jacobean England—in particular the breakup of hierarchical social structures with a corresponding increase in social mobility"; see Dollimore, p. 175. For a discussion of the reliance of Dollimore and other critics on outmoded interpretations of early modern English economic and social history, see Cressy, "Foucault," pp. 121–33.

7. Agnew, pp. 50–55; Mullaney, esp. pp. 36 n. 14, 45. On economic and social relations in Renaissance English texts generally, see Wells, pp. 37–60; Leinwand, pp. 3–80; Hutson, *Thomas Nashe*, and "Displacement"; Haynes; and Howard.

8. On spatial differentiation and potential for social conflict in metropolitan areas more generally, see Perlman; and Merriman.

9. Kaplan and Koepp, eds.; Scott; Mackenney; Farr; Zimmerman and Weissman, eds.; Nussdorfer, *Civic Politics*; Safley and Rosenband, eds.; and Sortor.

10. See the discussion of guilds and their historiography in I. Archer, *Pursuit*, pp. 100–148.

11. On the construction of community in parishes, see Alldridge.

12. Prominent among the works that have influenced the analysis of the "self" here are: A. Macfarlane, *Origins*; Greenblatt; Davis, "Boundaries"; and Roper, esp. ch. 1.

13. For a recent discussion of this historiography, see Berger, pp. 1–12.

14. On office-holding generally, see Wunderli, "Evasion"; for women's economic roles nationally, see Laurence, pp. 108–43. Company office-holding will be discussed in Chapter 4 below; gender relations in guilds will be considered particularly in Chapter 6.

Chapter 1

1. Power, "Social Topography"; Harding, "New Types of Urbanism." For suburban growth during the medieval period generally, see Keene.
2. Pearl, *London*, p. 43; Beier, "Engines of Manufacture," p. 153.
3. Wells, p. 39; Agnew, p. 50; Mullaney, pp. 21–22, 45; Howard, p. 12; Manley, *Literature*, pp. 1–20, esp. p. 16, where he spoke confidently of the "unregulated suburbs, with their population of casual laborers and unassimilated artisans, immigrants and paupers."
4. Collinson, *Birthpangs*, p. 32; Brigden, *London*, p. 639.
5. Pearl, *London*, pp. 45–68; on the status of women, see Rappaport, pp. 36–42.
6. PRO C2 James I/A6/21.
7. Levy.
8. Pearl, *London*, p. 28.
9. Boulton, *Neighbourhood*, pp. 9–12.
10. Pearl, *London*, pp. 23–31.
11. BL LMS 74, fol. 68r, 26 July 1593; Pearl, *London*, p. 25.
12. Wunderli, *London*, pp. 7–23; J. King, p. 45.
13. Johnson, pp. 37, 57, 331; Houlbrooke, p. 5; I. Archer, *Pursuit*, pp. 250, 252.
14. I. Archer, *Pursuit*, ch. 6; Griffiths; J. Archer, p. 85; Shoemaker, *Prosecution*.
15. Lindley.
16. I. Archer, *Pursuit*, pp. 149–51.
17. GL MSS 12818/1–2, fols. 37–40, for nursing at Uxbridge, Westminster, and High Holborn; fols. 271r, 275r, 280r, for apprenticeships at Bermondsey, Clerkenwell, and Barking; admissions: 4 May 1622, St. James Clerkenwell; 23 April 1623, from St. Margaret's Westminster; 11–21 April 1625, from St. Andrew's Holborn; 16 December 1625, from Lambeth; 1 April 1626, St. Leonard's Shoreditch.
18. GL MS 15361. W. K. Jordan's study of charity offers many examples of individual acts of charity undertaken by London citizens but directed to areas outside of the City.
19. See Slack.
20. Brett-James, pp. 249–67.
21. Barroll; Healy.
22. Northbrooke, p. 103.
23. For a recent discussion of attacks on theater generally, see Levine, esp. pp. 10–25.
24. White, pp. 46, 93–94.
25. Gossen, pp. 32–33, 47.
26. Whetstone, sig. Aiv.
27. Dekker, *Wonderful Year*, sig. Di; Milton.
28. Clapham, *Epistle*, sig. C4. Clapham's views sparked a controversy and landed him in prison for a time; see Collinson, *Birthpangs*, p. 22; Clapham, *H. Clapham*, and *Doctor Andros*.
29. Squire, pp. 10, 21.

30. The authorship of this work is uncertain, but it has been attributed either to William Prynne—whose *Histrio-Mastix* was the greatest attack against the early modern theater—or to his comrade Henry Burton; see *Short-Title Catalogue*, vol. 1.
31. Burton, p. 28. Although the title suggested that Burton was interested in plays, the only example concerned with the theater involved a carpenter who slipped off a stage and broke his neck while working at an Oxford playhouse on a Sunday (p. 12).
32. Nashe, sigs. O2, T3, V1, X3. For the contemporary practice of comparing English towns to Jerusalem, see Collinson, *Birthpangs*, esp. pp. 28–32.
33. Quoted in Thompson, p. 293. See also Seaver, *Wallington's World*, pp. 45–66, for Wallington's providentialist views.
34. *Londons Lamentation*, sigs. A2–A3.
35. Gadbury, sig. A4; on Gadbury's astrology, see Curry, pp. 72–81; E.N., *London's sins*, and *London's plague-sore discovered*, p. 7.
36. Sandcroft, pp. 3, 6; Elborough, sigs. B2, C2.
37. Quoted in Collier, 1: 209n.
38. Quoted in Gildersleeve, p. 15.
39. Mullaney, pp. 1–25. Crown support for theater was similar to its support for traditional festivities in the face of criticism from moral reformers; see Hutton, pp. 123–25.
40. Halliwell-Phillips, pp. 354–55.
41. Gildersleeve, p. 164; BL LMS 20/11.
42. *Analytical index*, pp. 352–53.
43. *APC*, 1592–93, p. 21.
44. Stow, 2: 72. For recent discussions of Stow's view of London, see Power, "John Stow"; I. Archer, "Nostalgia"; and Manley, "Sites."
45. Larkin and Hughes, eds., 2: 466–68.
46. *Analytical index*, p. 43.
47. Barnes, pp. 1332–45. Ian Archer found that Southwark vestries took action to restrain building; see *Pursuit*, p. 185.
48. *APC*, 1591, pp. 157–58.
49. *APC*, 1591–92, p. 145.
50. *APC*, 1597–98, pp. 427–28.
51. Smuts, pp. 133–35; for the development of London's western suburbs during the seventeenth century, see Stone, "Residential Development."
52. BL LMS 169, fol. 130r.
53. BL LMS 160, fol. 95r.
54. Ibid.
55. BL LMS 169, fol. 132r; for Crown attempts to control building, see Barnes.
56. BL LMSS 160, fol. 95r, and 169, fol. 130r.
57. BL LMSS 160, fols. 95r–96r, and 169, fols. 131r–32r.
58. BL LMS 160, fols. 95r–96r. The language of the petitions suggests that their authors were concerned primarily with male immigration to London.

59. BL LMS 169, fols. 131r–32r.
60. BL LMS 169, fols. 130r, 132r.
61. Pearl, *London*, pp. 30–37; *CSPD*, 1635–36, pp. 359–60. For a somewhat different interpretation of the king's suburban initiative, see K. Sharpe, esp. pp. 245–49, 403–12.
62. PRO SP 16/363/88.
63. *Analytical index*, pp. 227–28; and Brett-James, pp. 226–28. Brett-James has a critical view of the City's motives, although he admits that "there is no record of refusal" by the City. The reaction of citizens to the New Corporation will be discussed further in the next chapter.
64. PRO PC 2/50/71.
65. Brett-James, p. 244.
66. Ibid., pp. 268–95.
67. *Declaration and Motive*. The broadside's authors claimed to have the support of "reverend divines and other worthy persons" for their plan. For the background of the militia committee's efforts, see Pearl, *London*, p. 268; and Brenner, p. 452.
68. CLRO Jor. 40, fols. 108r, 109v.
69. Quoted in Pearl, "Puritans."
70. GL MS 11655, pp. 14–15. More generally, see Reddaway, *Rebuilding*; and Kellett, pp. 382–83. On the common use of such language in early modern complaints against immigrants, see Manley, *Literature*, p. 97.
71. The quotation is from CLRO Rep. 78, fol. 126v, but see also CLRO Reps. 80, fols. 120v–21r, and 82, fol. 113r.
72. S. Macfarlane, pp. 252–53; Dunton, *Night-Walker*.
73. Shoemaker, "Reforming the City," p. 100.
74. J. Woodward, pp. iii, 72–78; CLRO Reps. 104, p. 252, and 112, p. 91.

Chapter 2

1. The proposals of 1610, a series of petitions to the Crown addressing the problems associated with rapid suburban growth, are discussed in Chapter 1.
2. Kellett, pp. 381–85. Kellett asserted that the reform proposals of 1610 "indicate a precise and accurate awareness of the problems facing the City by the early 17th century" (p. 382).
3. Ashton, pp. 163–65 (quotation on p. 164).
4. Pearl, "Change and Stability," pp. 12–13. Pearl claimed that before concluding that "three-quarters of the adult male householders in the City were freemen," she allowed for "some freemen having settled in the suburbs," although she did not explain how she arrived at that estimate. Like Pearl, L. D. Schwarz—who shares the view, found in most of the historiography, that guilds were ineffective economically—suggested that political concerns, and particularly the desire of individuals to participate in City politics, continued to be primary motivations for joining livery companies in the eighteenth and early nineteenth centuries; Schwarz, *London*, pp. 210–16.

5. Rappaport, pp. 46, 62, 187, 213. Rappaport's argument supports that of Unwin, *Gilds*, pp. 244–51. Like Rappaport, Gervase Rosser subscribed to the view that London's suburbs "lay outside the realm of effective control" of City authorities, and so commerce in late medieval Westminster was "unconstrained by civic or craft regulation." Rosser, *Medieval Westminster*, p. 122, and "London," pp. 50–51. For a discussion of the competition company members faced from suburban artisans and traders in the later sixteenth century, see I. Archer, *Pursuit*, p. 132.

6. Beier, "Engines of Manufacture," pp. 144, 157, 160. Beier based his argument on parish registers rather than on livery company records. Michael Power's analysis of seventeenth-century suburban Shadwell made no mention of any role for London's livery companies, though he found that more than 23 percent of Shadwell's population worked as craftsmen in shipbuilding and other trades; Power, "Shadwell," pp. 29–46, esp. p. 36. In his study of early-seventeenth-century Southwark, Jeremy Boulton used a sample of wills to argue that membership in livery companies was widespread among wealthier groups of residents of the Boroughside, a district south of the Thames and yet legally within the lord mayor's jurisdiction; Boulton, *Neighbourhood*, pp. 152–54. In this instance, Boulton was responding to suggestions of the lack of company influence in Southwark; see Johnson, p. 313; and Reddaway, "Livery Companies," p. 297.

7. Agnew, pp. 54–55.

8. This point is demonstrated in I. Archer, *Pursuit*, esp. pp. 139–40.

9. Pearl, "Change and Stability," pp. 12–13. Her estimate may be too high, since it apparently included a "Porters' Co." (n. 24), and as the next chapter will discuss, the Society of Tacklehouse and Ticket Porters was not a livery company. The description of the limited quantity of guild records is based on a study of the catalog of the Guildhall Library.

10. J. Archer, p. 148. After 1674, all aldermen were expected to live in the City; CLRO Rep. 80, fols. 17v–18r, 133v–34v, and Jor. 48, fols. 90v–91r, 122r.

11. Boulton, *Neighbourhood*, p. 167; Smuts, pp. 125–27.

12. On the jurisdictional complexities of the area known loosely as "Southwark" in the early modern period, see Johnson, pp. 93–329; and Boulton, *Neighbourhood*, pp. 1–12, 262–88.

13. GL MS 11571/6. The list for 1566–68 included "Ludgate, Fleet Street, and Westminster, etc.," that of 1568–70 contained "Ludgate, Fleet Street, and Temple Bar" as one section and "extra vagant" as another, that of 1570–72 included "Westminster and extra vagant," that of 1571–72 contained "Westminster and elsewhere," and that of 1572–78 listed "Westminster and elsewhere out of London." The presence of members of the Grocers' Company in Westminster is important because of the aristocratic clientele there, although other City companies seemed to have more difficulty establishing themselves in Westminster; see Rosser, "London," p. 49; and I. Archer, *Pursuit*, p. 132.

14. In a sample of wills proved between 1622 and 1646, Jeremy Boulton

found that most of the will-makers in the Boroughside of Southwark—an area outside the wall but within the bars of the City—who described themselves as grocers were members of the company, including several who served as wardens; Boulton, *Neighbourhood*, p. 153. The quarterage records also say little about those grocers whose commercial activities brought them into suburban areas. Several leading grocers were officers in the East India Company, which conducted considerable business with shipbuilders and other suppliers in eastern suburbs such as Deptford, Ratcliffe, Lymehouse, and Wapping. On grocer involvement in the East India Company, see Chapter 5 below. On East India Company business in suburban London, see Stevens, ed., pp. 13, 154, 208, 233.

15. GL MS 11571/6. In 1559, John Best returned to London after a long absence, and the court decided that he "shall be taken and reputed a brother of this company" and ordered him to pay his overdue quarterage "as a freeman ought to do." GL MS 11588/1, fol. 35r.

16. GL MS 11588/1, fols. 192v, 244v, 413r.

17. Ibid., fols. 65r, 86r, 117r, 210r.

18. GL MS 11638, p. 40. In 1523, an act of Parliament granted all of London's livery companies the right to inspect economic activity up to two miles away from the City; see Rappaport, pp. 45–46.

19. GL MS 11588/3, pp. 234, 554. The company had also hired searchers of street vendors in 1586 and 1611; see GL MSS 11588/1, fol. 383r, and /2, pp. 672–73.

20. The Grocers' Company was one of London's wealthiest retailing guilds, but the Waxchandlers' Company was one of its poorest. This evaluation of the relative wealth of companies is based on a corn assessment of 1632 which listed the Grocers' Company as contributing 900 quarters, the Vintners' Company 500 quarters, and the Waxchandlers' Company 25 quarters; see GL MS 5196, fol. 23r.

21. GL MS 9496, fol. 5r–v.

22. Although search books are extant for the period 1574–1664, the entries after 1604 are sporadic and do not give locations; although the Elizabethan records seldom mention the location of a shop, they are more consistent, and so they have been the basis of this discussion. The examples were found at GL MS 9493, fols. 13r, 15r, 21r, 105r.

23. GL MS 9491, fols. 87v–93r.

24. GL MS 15190, p. 34. In addition to its charter, a statute from the reign of Edward VI and letters patent from Queen Elizabeth in 1575 gave the company the right to license taverns in the City of London, its suburbs and liberties, and all areas within three miles of the City, though it exempted company members from the need to purchase licenses. This was a right that the company defended against the encroachment of a series of Crown concessionaires such as the Earl of Middlesex under James I, Lord Goring under Charles I, and the Duke of York under Charles II; GL MSS 15201/2, p. 393; /3, p. 30; /4, pp. 231–34; /5, fol. 44r.

25. GL MSS 15201/1, fols. 7r, 11v, 43r, 67v–68r, and /2, p. 28. For a dis-

cussion of controversies within the trade that may have influenced the enforcement of the company's regulations, see Crawford, pp. 104–33.

26. This analysis is based on Dale, ed., "List." Because none of the company's other membership lists have survived, there is no way to determine whether the poll tax list included all the company's members. However, even if the poll tax list is no more than a sample of vintners, there is no reason to believe that it was an atypical one.

27. The location analysis relies on *A to Z of Elizabethan* and *A to Z of Georgian*. Among the suburban taverns were those listed for places such as Westminster, Charing Cross, Covent Garden, and Wapping. Distinctions were occasionally obscured by reference to vague locations like Southwark—which was in this analysis considered between the walls and the bars—and Holborn, which was considered suburban, unlike Holborn Conduit or Holborn against Shoe Lane, which were between the walls and the bars. The court book added precision in the case of the Castle without Cripplegate, which the poll tax placed "near Cripplegate"; see GL MS 15201/3, p. 139.

28. GL MS 15201/4, pp. 36, 62. Also, in July 1639, a vintner sought the company's license to open a tavern in Blackfriars; 15201/4, p. 14. The company's court records indicated that members who lived as far away as Cambridge and York paid fines in order to avoid serving in company offices; see GL MSS 15201/1, p. 75, and /2, p. 322.

29. PRO E112/98/926. There is no answer attached to the brewers' bill.

30. GL MS 5458, fols. 62r–68r; GL MS 5452/1. All divisions were assessed, but fees were not collected from all of them that year. However, fees were collected from all divisions in subsequent years. A list of company members in 1628 contains addresses for some members, suggesting that the metropolitan nature of brewing was already established; GL MS 5445/15.

31. Because the quarterage list usually gives only the surname, comparisons with the livery list cannot be precise. Examples of suburban liverymen include William Fuller and Joseph Truman of Spitalfields and Shoreditch, Leonard Martin of Westminster, and Slackey Mayo of Whitechapel; see GL MS 5458, fols. 68v–72r.

32. GL MS 5625/1–2. A statute, 23 Henry VIII cap. 4, confirmed the company's authority to regulate coopers in the City of London and in the suburbs up to two miles from the City.

33. CLRO Letter Book HH, fol. 176r. For more on the feltmakers' attempts to form their own company, see I. Archer, *History*, pp. 63–70.

34. CLRO Letter Book HH, fol. 177v; J. Archer, p. 64.

35. PRO SP 14/127/21. On the activities of the Lord-Lieutenant of Surrey in the affairs of Southwark after it had been incorporated into the City, see Johnson, pp. 154–55.

36. GL MS 5385, fol. 31r. There are examples of the officers' enforcement activities throughout this volume, with other instances of suburban activities at fols. 15v, 101r.

37. For examples from the early seventeenth century, see GL MSS 2881/1, p. 148; /2, p. 31; /3, p. 138; and for the later part of the century, see, for example, /8, fols. 8r, 72r, and /9, fols. 25r, 28v.

38. GL MSS 2881/2, p. 39; /4, p. 17; /6, p. 29.

39. GL MS 2881/9, fol. 34r.

40. GL MS 2881/5, p. 117, compared with Dale, ed., "Members."

41. GL MS 4655/1, fol. 61r.

42. Ibid., fols. 50v, 51r, 65r, 68v, 83v, 90r, 95r.

43. GL MSS 4655/4, fol. 81v; /5, fol. 47v; /6, fol. 57v.

44. GL MS 4655/1B, fols. 20r, 22r, 43v.

45. For example, see GL MS 4655/8, fol. 17r, but subsequent entries contain additional evidence of weavers from suburban areas joining the company.

46. GL MSS 4655/5, fol. 47v, and /6, fol. 52r. The Ironmongers' Company also took a metropolitan approach to almsgiving. A pensioners list from 1686 indicated that the company distributed relief to people throughout the suburbs, including Clerkenwell, Holborn, Whitechapel, and Shadwell; see GL MS 17082.

47. On the importance of mobility to early modern building craftsmen and laborers more generally, see D. Woodward, esp. pp. 119–22.

48. GL MSS 7784/6, p. 25, and /8, p. 70. The reference to the Globe theater clearly challenges Agnew's assertion—cited earlier in this chapter—about economic license there. Jacobean letters patent confirmed the company's authority to regulate carpenters who worked in the City of London and in all suburbs and liberties up to two miles from the City. GL MS 7784/4, p. 12.

49. GL MS 7784/6, p. 61; other examples of company officers inspecting work sites in liberties are at GL MSS 7784/6, p. 57; /8, pp. 43, 66, 69; and /9, p. 29.

50. GL MS 7784/14, p. 32.

51. GL MS 4318, p. 72.

52. GL MSS 3047/1 and 3051/1, neither is paginated. In April 1615, a bricklayer named Marshall was fined for poor workmanship near Winchester House in Southwark, which may have been in one of the Bankside liberties. Also, in April 1616, the company fined a lime merchant at his shop in the Clink by St. Mary Overy's Priory.

53. GL MS 4318, p. 71.

54. The examples listed were from GL MS 3047/1, dated 4 December 1606 (Hertfordshire, Kent, and Bridewell); January 1606 (Havering). The Havering search included Romford and also, possibly, "Hornchurch in collier row"; see Powell, ed., p. 12, for a map of Havering. For more on the evolution of the economy of Havering and its connections to London, see McIntosh, *Community*, esp. pp. 92–175.

55. GL MS 4318, pp. 53–69. Although the precise state of the brick- and tile-making industry is impossible to evaluate historically, the claim that the Tylers and Bricklayers' Company had been inadequately supervising

production is belied by records indicating that more than a third of the new company's members had appeared on the older company's search roll in the early 1630s. Variant spellings preclude precise estimates.

56. GL MS 4318, pp. 113–14; the Tylers and Bricklayers' Company claimed that the new company raised prices "at the least 2s or 3s upon every thousand."

57. GL MS 4318, pp. 122–25.

58. Ibid., pp. 105, 106, 108. The records do not mention any outcome for this dispute. See Introduction above.

59. GL MS 4318, p. 101; CLRO Rep. 52, fols. 12v–13r. The companies were the Carpenters, Painter-Stainers, Masons, Plumbers, Tylers and Bricklayers, Blacksmiths, Joiners, Plasterers, Glaziers, and Paviors.

60. GL MS 3054/2. In September 1637, the officers of the Plumbers' Company decided that their company would bear the costs of defending any company member restrained by the New Corporation; GL MS 2208/1, fol. 98r. In May 1640, the lord mayor and aldermen supervised the distribution of the costs associated with one phase of the builders' case against the New Corporation. The Tylers and Bricklayers' and the Plasterers' companies shared the initial outlay of £39, and they then received contributions from the other companies mentioned in the preceding note; CLRO Rep. 54, fols. 172v–73v.

61. On the slow demise of the New Corporation, see Pearl, *London*, p. 37; and Ashton, p. 167.

62. GL MS 4329/6, 10 February and 5 March 1669.

63. For a different interpretation of this evidence, see Alford and Barker, pp. 84–87.

64. GL MS 4329/6, 21 April and 2 June 1670; CLRO Rep. 73, fol. 123v; Rep. 74, fol. 310r–v; Rep. 75, fols. 117v, 127r, 212r, 227r, 295v; Rep. 76, fols. 5v, 29v, 31v, 45r, 59r–v, 73r, 95v–96r, 98r, 101r, 164v–65r, 189v, 195v, 212r–v, 219r, 222r–v, 231v–32r, 262r, 286v–87r; Rep. 77, fols. 22v, 162v, 208v; Rep. 78, fols. 20r, 103r, 115v, 208v; Rep. 79, fols. 4v, 71v–72r, 97v, 119r, 133v, 142r, 256r, 343v, 384v, 422v; Rep. 80, fols. 50r–v, 124v–25r, 164r–v, 221r. In 1672, the officers of the Joiners' Company accused members of the Carpenters' Company of intermeddling in their craft contrary to an order of the Court of Aldermen of 1632, but the governors of the two companies cooperated in subsequent years in an effort to defend their members' rights to hire foreign sawyers as laborers; CLRO Reps. 77, fol. 208v; 93, fol. 58v; 98, p. 90; 103, pp. 163–64.

65. GL MS 3047/2–4. These records are not paginated and are not always in chronological order.

66. CLRO Rep. 74, fols. 214v–16v. In 1669, the officers of the Painter-Stainers' Company compelled Edward Johnson, a stranger, to pay quarterage and bind his apprentices at the company's hall; GL MS 5667/2, p. 103.

67. BL LMSS 160, fols. 95r–96r, 97r, and 169, fols. 131r–32r.

68. Foreigners had been active in petitioning the Elizabethan government

to enhance their economic interests in London; see I. Archer, *Pursuit*, p. 138.

69. BL LMS 169, fol. 130r.
70. On the careers of City magistrates, see Benbow, "Index."
71. Ian Archer found that, sporadically throughout the Elizabethan period, aliens were unjustly blamed for crises, thereby absolving London's elite of responsibility; see *Pursuit*, p. 140.
72. The standard interpretation of the City magistrates' opposition to the incorporation of the suburbs stresses their concern about the loss of their influence in those areas and the creation of a potential political rival in the shape of the New Corporation; see Pearl, *London*, pp. 33–37; and Ashton, p. 165.
73. GL MS 5196, fols. 50v–51v.
74. Ibid., fol. 7r–v.
75. Ibid., fols. 20r–21r, 24r–28v. For controversies surrounding the Elizabethan assize—including evidence of company members who charged excessive prices—see Benbow, "Court of Aldermen."
76. GL MS 5196, fol. 48v. This text is undated, but internal evidence suggests that it was from the early seventeenth century and probably was contemporary to the controversy over the price of bread during the 1630s.
77. GL MS 5197, not paginated. For the disputes that accompanied the charter, see Thrupp, pp. 119–31.
78. GL MS 5186, the volume is not paginated. This source contains several other cases such as Whitehorne's, which suggest that the threat of prosecution was often sufficient for the company to achieve its aims.
79. 1 James I. c. 22/xviii.
80. CHA Court Minutes 1665–83, p. 405.
81. PRO SP 14/127/12, 15.

Chapter 3

1. On the "custom," see Unwin, *Gilds*, p. 262.
2. This was an economic incentive for company membership that often goes overlooked in the historiography; see, for example, Reddaway, "Livery Companies," p. 297; and Schwarz, pp. 210–16.
3. On the vicissitudes of the business cycle and their influence on the employment and financial condition of merchants and artisans in early modern England, see Stone, "Social Mobility"; Sacks, *Widening Gate*, pp. 19–84; Berger; Rappaport, pp. 117–22; Grassby; Seaver, "Artisanal World"; Brenner; Earle, *Making*; Borsay, pp. 208–11; Mui and Mui; Linebaugh; and Schwarz.
4. Dekker, *Shoemaker's Holiday*, scenes 7–17. In his "Introduction" to the text (p. xi), Parr suggests that Dekker's source for the story of Eyre's deception was Deloney. On the social context of the play, see Seaver, "Artisanal World"; and Bevington.

5. Dekker, *Shoemaker's Holiday*, scene 3, line 4, and scene 21, lines 10–11.

6. H. King, pp. 3–5. On the general problem of deceit—and particularly in its relationship to religious matters—in the early modern period, see Zagorin.

7. Denison, sig. A3 and p. 19.

8. BL LMS 169, fol. 130r.

9. Seaver, *Wallington's World*, pp. 125–27.

10. GL MS 7784/4, p. 15. The records do not indicate whether Jerram was a freeman or a foreigner.

11. GL MS 7784/5, p. 93. The records do not indicate whether Blyth was a freeman or a foreigner.

12. GL MS 4318, p. 85.

13. GL MS 8334.

14. GL MS 7784/7, pp. 12–13. On the general movement away from the flexibility of the "custom of London," see Unwin, *Gilds*, pp. 261–66.

15. Hand was freed in 1592 and had bound an apprentice to the company in 1609; Copeland had been a member of the company since 1601 and had bound an apprentice in 1606. GL MSS 7784/5, p. 57; /6, pp. 79–80; and 4326/6, fols. 4r, 114r, 275r.

16. GL MS 3047/1 1605–6, 1615–16; these records are not paginated; see also the Quarterage Books 1588–1616. Among those fined in January 1606 was Thomas Borne, who was described as being "free of the pewterers."

17. GL MS 3047/1; I. Archer, *Pursuit*, p. 125.

18. GL MS 3047/1. The company's court book is fragmentary for those years, so there are no indications that any special action was taken against Iffe for his continued incompetence.

19. GL MS 3047/1, p. 92.

20. GL MS 3047/2. These records are not paginated consistently.

21. GL MS 7784/8, p. 18. The Court of Aldermen had considered a similar, anonymous complaint in 1612, which mentioned that the Sunday gatherings of day laborers, sawyers, and carpenters at Christ's Hospital were like those at Soper Lane on the other days of the week; CLRO Rep. 30, fol. 340r.

22. GL MS 7784/11, p. 9.

23. GL MS 7784/14, p. 14. The aldermen granted the company's request, establishing a meeting place for unemployed citizen carpenters and sawyers between 5 and 7 A.M. on working days at Cheapside between the Standard and the Cross, and ordered that carpenters no longer gather "at Christ Church to be hired as formerly"; CLRO Rep. 42, fol. 299v.

24. CLRO Rep. 80, fols. 29r, 40v–41r. Reddaway's failure to recognize the pre-Fire antecedents of the carpenters' actions caused him to overestimate the deleterious influence of the Fire Acts on the opportunities for journeymen; see his *Rebuilding*, pp. 120–21.

25. GL MS 7784/7, p. 38. The continued relationship of the Carpenters' Company with the Crown's work has been underestimated; see Schwarz, p.

213 n. 13, citing Alford and Barker, pp. 42–44. Members of the Tylers and Bricklayers' Company were also pressed into the royal service on occasion; see CLRO Rep. 29, fol. 132v.

26. GL MS 7784/7, pp. 32, 38.

27. GL MS 15201/2, p. 84.

28. GL MS 15201/4, p. 259. The precise costs of the project are not clear from the subsequent records; see ibid., pp. 264, 273.

29. GL MS 11588/3, p. 362. Similarly, in 1641, they awarded Mary Knight the "usual allowance for her pains as was formerly given to her late husband" for polishing the company's pewter; ibid., /4, p. 39. In 1610, the officers allowed Alice Hobbe to succeed to her deceased husband's place as company plumber, but in that case they assumed that her servants would be carrying out the work; ibid., /2, p. 633.

30. GL MS 11588/4, p. 427. The City government followed a similar course in allowing some staff positions to be inherited; CLRO Reps. 34, fol. 199r, and 44, fol. 320r.

31. SHA D1/1/1, fol. 31v.

32. GL MS 7784/6, p. 33.

33. CLRO, Rep. 65, fols. 11r, 22r. For another case involving two haberdashers who used the same shop signs, see CLRO, Reps. 66, fol. 338r, and 67, fol. 19v.

34. CLRO Rep. 67, fols. 43v, 48r, 67r.

35. On the office of City garbellor, see Pearl, *London*, p. 337.

36. GL MS 11588/1, fols. 308r, 310v. This episode did not halt his political career as a common councillor and a governor of Bridewell and St. Bartholomew's hospitals; see Benbow, "Index."

37. The company's officers also removed one of Palmer's apprentices. GL MSS 11588/1, fols. 320r–v, 328v, and 11571/7, fol. 30r.

38. GL MSS 11588/1, fol. 238r, and 11571/7, fol. 214v.

39. GL MSS 11588/1, fol. 435r, and /2, fol. 4; 11571/7, fol. 343v.

40. GL MS 11588/2, p. 677.

41. GL MS 11588/3, p. 27. The repercussions of this episode will be discussed further in Chapter 5.

42. GL MSS 11588/3, pp. 211–13, and 11571/10, fol. 463v.

43. GL MS 11588/3, pp. 371–72, 373–74, 383.

44. GL MS 15201/2, pp. 9, 22, 28, 29.

45. GL MS 15201/3, pp. 174–76.

46. GL MS 15201/4, pp. 248, 255.

47. GL MS 15201/1, fol. 50v; Prideaux, 1: 56, 67.

48. GL MS 15201/2, pp. 29–31. Webb was elected a warden of the Haberdashers' Company on 23 November 1611; GL MS 15842/1, fol. 176r; I. Archer, *History*, p. 238.

49. GL MS 15201/2, p. 164.

50. Ibid., pp. 478, 481.

51. GL MS 15201/1, fol. 51v–52r. The vehemence of the company's offi-

cers in this case may have been related to their desire to maintain the general reputation of taverns as having a "respectable character"; see Clark, pp. 11–15.

52. GL MS 11588/2, pp. 553–54.

53. GL MS 15201/1, p. 73A. This page was placed in the Court Minutes out of order, presumably because the court ordered the company clerk "to conceal this matter." For evidence of the illicit activity by officers of the Bakers' Company, see Benbow, "Court of Aldermen"; and Chapter 2 above.

54. On company disciplinary practices, see Rappaport, pp. 201–14. On the subject of magisterial rule and discretion more generally, see Wrightson, pp. 149–82; and Herrup.

55. For a discussion of the use of the term *decayed* in this context, see I. Archer, *Pursuit*, p. 122.

56. Grassby, pp. 82–98.

57. CLRO Rep. 45, fol. 77r.

58. CLRO Rep. 74, fol. 215r–v.

59. Pullan; Rubin, pp. 1–53; Wrightson and Levine; McIntosh, "Local Responses," and *Community*, pp. 276–87; Houston; Beier, *Masterless Men*, pp. 3–13; Jordan, pp. 177–80; Pearl, "Puritans"; I. Archer, *Pursuit*, pp. 182–83. Rappaport argued that in the sixteenth century, companies were important sources of charity for their members, but "it would be foolish to exaggerate the scope of their poor relief" because collectively each year they could support only a few hundred households (p. 200).

60. For a discussion of the problems involved in classifying different types of labor and their importance for the survival of poor families, see A. Smith, "Labourers," pts. 1–2; and Snell.

61. GL MSS 11588/2, pp. 93, 94, 114, and /3, pp. 275, 287, 311, 314; CLRO Reps. 40, fols. 91v–92r, and 42, fols. 145r–46v.

62. GL MS 913, fols. 1r–25v; CLRO Rep. 29, fols. 41r–42r.

63. GL MS 913, fol. 24r. On employment schemes, see McIntosh, "Local Responses," pp. 210, 232–34; P. Sharpe; Jordan, pp. 177–80; and I. Archer, *Pursuit*, pp. 56, 154.

64. GL MS 913, p. 76.

65. GL MS 4655/2, p. 171. This example further illustrates that there was no company of porters as such, but that porters were members of livery companies. This distinction undercuts Pearl's estimation of the number of freemen in seventeenth-century London because in her calculations she included members of a nonexistent "Porters' Company," thereby counting them twice; Pearl, "Change and Stability," pp. 30–31.

66. GL MS 11588/1, fol. 345v.

67. GL MSS 11588/1, fol. 393r, and /2, p. 55. For other examples of the company's exercising influence in appointments, see GL MSS 11588/2, p. 634, and /3, p. 264.

68. GL MS 11588/3, pp. 543–44.

69. CHA Court Minutes 1558–81, fol. 157v; SkHA Court Book III, fol. 120Br.

Notes to Pages 59–66   163

70. GL MS 15201/4, pp. 190, 309–10.
71. DHA Court Minutes 1594–1603, fol. 262r, and 1603–40, fol. 332r.
72. GL MSS 11588/1, fol. 3v, and /3, p. 584.
73. SkHA Court Book III, fols. 23v–24r.
74. GL MS 11588/1, fol. 234r.
75. GL MS 11588/4, pp. 389, 416, 412.
76. DHA Court Minutes 1603–40, fol. 332r; CHA Court Minutes 1558–81, fol. 157v.
77. For a different interpretation of the relationship between porters and livery companies, see Stern, pp. 1–21.
78. GL MS 11588/1, fols. 205v, 319v.
79. GL MSS 15201/1, fol. 5v, and /2, p. 63.
80. GL MSS 11588/1, fol. 234v, and /2, p. 289.
81. GL MSS 11588/2, p. 491, and /4, p. 383.
82. CHA Court Minutes 1665–83, p. 9.
83. SkHA Court Book III, fol. 210v.
84. GL MS 11588/3, p. 292.
85. GL MS 15201/1, fol. 62v.
86. GL MSS 11588/1, fols. 146v, 281r, and /2, p. 59.
87. GL MS 15201/4, p. 180.
88. GL MS 11588/4, p. 423.
89. GL MS 15201/2, pp. 12–14, 20, 44, 61–62.
90. GL MS 11588/4, pp. 437–39.   91. GL MS 11588/1, fol. 183r.
92. Ibid., fols. 8v, 20r.   93. GL MS 11588/3, p. 342.
94. GL MS 15201/4, pp. 55, 176, 396, 452.
95. SkHA Court Book IV, fol. 21v; GL MS 15201/2, p. 285.
96. GL MS 11588/1, fols. 229v, 344v, 46v.
97. GL MS 15201/5, fol. 220r.
98. GL MS 11588/1, fol. 65v. The company's clerk and beadle also had to be reappointed yearly.
99. GL MS 11588/3, p. 561.
100. GL MSS 11588/1, p. 321, and /2, p. 558.
101. GL MS 11588/2, pp. 232, 247, 249–50, 275, 278.
102. GL MSS 15201/2, p. 240, and /5, fols. 86v, 87v.
103. GHA Court Minute Book U, fol. 52v.
104. CHA Court Minutes 1558–81, fol. 40v; 1605–23, fol. 143v; 1639–49, fol. 74v; 1665–83, p. 592.
105. R. Sharpe, ed., pt. 2, p. 676 n. 4; GL MS 11588/1, fol. 34r.
106. GL MS 11588/1, fols. 95r, 148r, 202r, 212v, 245v, 246v, 250r, 251r, 253r.
107. Ibid., fol. 280v.   108. Ibid., fols. 346v, 375v, 382v.
109. Ibid., fol. 397r.   110. GL MS 11588/4, pp. 330, 447.
111. GL MS 11588/1, fols. 39v, 138r, 210v.
112. Ibid., fols. 211r, 234v, 267v, 299r, 345v.
113. GL MS 11588/2, pp. 61, 156.
114. Ibid., pp. 552, 561, 666, 677.

115. GL MS 11588/3, pp. 241, 521, 537.
116. Ibid., pp. 521, 522.   117. GL MS 11588/2, p. 567.
118. GL MS 11588/3, p. 365.   119. GL MSS 7784/4–11.
120. For examples, see GL MSS 7784/5/38, 58–59, 71; and 4326/6, fols. 355r–56v. On the risks associated with early modern building trades more generally, see D. Woodward, esp. chs. 3 and 5. On the economic prospects for widows in London, see Brodsky; and Boulton, "London Widowhood."
121. GL MSS 11588/3, p. 409, and /4, p. 526.
122. GL MS 7784/2/71.
123. GL MS 15201/4, p. 247.
124. GL MS 11588/4, pp. 293, 335.
125. SHA D1/1/1, fols. 160r, 160v–61v, 177v.
126. Ibid., fol. 139r.
127. Ibid., fols. 48r, 116r.
128. Ibid., fols. 67v, 114r, 135r. These examples, and the one referred to in the previous note, were from the late 1620s and early 1630s. The Salters' court books are not extant for earlier periods.
129. GL MS 11588/2, pp. 147, 156.   130. SHA D1/1/1, fol. 160v.
131. GL MS 15201/5, fol. 173r.   132. SHA D1/1/1, fols. 40r, 166v.
133. GL MS 11588/4, p. 373. For more on this sort of employment for poor women, see Willen.
134. GL MS 11588/4, pp. 421, 439.
135. GL MS 11588/3, pp. 468, 502, 567, 570, 598, 643. Bright also had a lengthy career in the company's service. He became a sanderbeater and pensioner in 1625, a servant porter at the waterside in 1628, and a master porter in 1633. His marriage in 1635 benefited from a dowry fund for maidservants of company members. His row with liveryman Harsenett in 1635 was discussed above. It is not clear why the records after 1628 continued to refer to him as "sanderbeater." In 1633, he was referred to as "George Bright junior," but the other evidence all points to there being only one "George Bright" in the company's service; see GL MS 11588/3, pp. 308, 397, 522, 549.
136. GL MS 11588/4, pp. 39, 98, 282, 464, 466, 572, 601.
137. SHA D1/1/1, fols. 117v, 131r.
138. Ibid., fols. 178v, 187v. His large donation to his company underscores the point made earlier that some porterships could be quite lucrative.
139. GL MSS 11588/2, pp. 663, 684, 752, 871, and /3, p. 28, 66, 173, 280.

Chapter 4

1. Barry, pp. 24–30; and Tittler, pp. 98–128. The nature of guild politics in London resembled that of English towns much more than that of Continental cities, which generally had more firmly established patriciates; see Strauss, pp. 57–115; Diefendorf; Amelang; and Nussdorfer, *Civic Politics*.
2. Unwin, *Industrial Organization*, and *Gilds*, pp. 217–42; Rappaport, esp. pp. 215–73; I. Archer, *Pursuit* esp. pp. 102–24.

3. Nussdorfer, "Writing," pp. 103–18.
4. Rappaport, pp. 298–301; I. Archer, *Pursuit*, p. 102; Davis, *Fiction*.
5. Gutteridge; Cressy, "Levels of Illiteracy"; and Earle, *Making*, and *City*, pp. 86–90. There are no court minutes extant for the Scriveners' Company.
6. GL MS 4647, p. 84. Ordinance 41 stated that the company clerk would make a pair of indentures for each apprentice bound in the company. Each master was to pay the clerk 2s for that process, or be subject to a fine of 3s 4d for making the indentures elsewhere.
7. GL MS 4647, pp. 158–59.
8. GL MSS 4655/1, fol. 24v, and 4647, p. 224.
9. GL MSS 4655/4, fol. 8v, and 4647, p. 31. Ordinance 12 called for a fine of 6s 8d to be levied against violators, and the extant Court Minute Books suggest that the regulation was enforced. Weavers' employment of women will be discussed at greater length in Chapter 6 below.
10. GL MS 4655/2, p. 134. In 1694, the company's assistants found that a renter bailiff's recordkeeping "might prove very prejudicial and would be of great loss to this company"; see GL MS 4655/10, fols. 47v–48v.
11. GL MS 7784/2/46, 52.
12. On the politics of complaining generally, see K. Sharpe, pp. 706–8.
13. GL MS 15201/3, pp. 108–9.
14. GL MS 4655/9, fols. 22v–25r. This was part of the more general *Quo Warranto* challenge to corporations.
15. GL MS 7784/5/43.
16. GL MS 7784/6/90, 89.
17. Ibid., 85.
18. GL MS 7784/8/17.
19. A case that apparently began in the company Court of Assistants and was then referred to the City chamberlain involved the dispute between William Copeland and his apprentice Richard Hughes; see GL MS 7784/6/78–80.
20. For the theme of tense apprentice/master relations, see S. Smith.
21. GL MS 7784/6/21.
22. According to Steve Rappaport, those who sought company alms would "file into the [company] hall on court days to plead for charity" (p. 197).
23. For the location of these texts, see the discussion in Chapter 3 above.
24. For the role of livery companies in poor relief, see Jordan, esp. pp. 85–165.
25. GL MSS 7784/7/18, and /10/33, 47.
26. GL MSS 7784/6/15, 20, and /10/46. Another possible explanation for their repetitiveness may be some similarity to standardized oral folktales whose form allowed improvisation while enabling them to be easily remembered and transmitted among the illiterate; see Burke, ch. 5. Also, W. K. Jordan noted that when Henry Smith, salter, endowed charities in six Surrey towns, he instructed the executors of his estate to post the provisions of his bequest in writing in each town so that the poor would be aware of them (p. 119).

27. GL MS 15842/1, fol. 171v; I. Archer, *History*, pp. 72, 75.

28. GL MS 11588/2, p. 579. There may have been other administrative concerns as well; for example, in 1647, the assistants of the Vintners' Company required widow Mary Taylor to bring "a certificate of her civil demeanor" before they would award her a room in an almshouse; see GL MS 15201/4, p. 252.

29. GL MS 7784/5/55. Because she asked for the continuance of her deceased husband's apprentice, her petition is not grouped among the alms-seekers.

30. GL MS 11588/3, p. 184.

31. GL MS 15201/4, p. 258.

32. For more on these matters, see Rappaport, pp. 215–73; and I. Archer, *Pursuit*, pp. 102–24.

33. For examples of the variety of courts, see the Weavers' Company's records for the early eighteenth century, which specify when a "full court" was held, as distinct from the business of committees; see GL MS 4655/11.

34. These quotations were from the standard formula used by wardens of the Grocers' Company in their exhortations to the company upon their taking office; see, for example, GL MS 11588/3, p. 48.

35. For the posting of the table, see GL MS 11571/12, fol. 407r–v, which is an inventory of the company hall in 1640. The quotation is from 1657, at which time the assistants ordered that "the livery table be perfected & made up (only leaving blank spaces for the names of those that have not paid their monies)"; see GL MS 11588/4, p. 404.

36. GL MS 11588/3, pp. 45, 422.

37. GL MS 11588/2, p. 777. Similarly, in 1620, Israel Owen claimed that although he had been willing and able to serve in company office, he had been passed over for promotion into the assistants' ranks "in his turn." The assistants accepted him for a fine of £50, placing him ahead of those who had served in junior wardenships; see GL MS 11588/3, pp. 153, 165.

38. The aldermen ordered the liverymen elevated to the Court of Assistants; see CLRO Rep. 67, fol. 325v. The Apothecaries' officers subsequently claimed that because there were no openings on their Court of Assistants, they would postpone implementing the aldermen's order to elevate the three liverymen; see GL MS 8200/2, fols. 66v–67v.

39. CLRO Reps. 109, pp. 126–27, 195, 219–20, 246–47, 371, 377, and 110, fol. 136v. Despite the ruling by the lord mayor and aldermen that promotion to a company's assistants ought to be based on seniority, the case of the two liverymen in question—William Naylor and Michael Tesmond—ultimately was dismissed for unspecified reasons; see CLRO Reps. 110, fols. 167v–68r, and 111, pp. 97, 152, 171. The Saddlers' Company court minutes are not extant for this period.

40. GL MS 11588/3, pp. 208, 215.

41. GL MS 15201/1, fol. 40v.

42. GL MS 11588/3, p. 222.

43. GL MS 11588/2, p. 138. Similarly, in 1603, grocer Thomas Middleton joined the assistants after he became an alderman; see ibid., p. 304.
44. GL MS 11588/3, pp. 53, 642, 645.
45. GHA Court Minute Book P, part I, fol. 49r.
46. For a discussion of office-avoidance in London, see Wunderli, "Evasion," pp. 3–18. On the costs and risks of early modern officeholding generally, see Grassby, pp. 99–106.
47. GL MSS 11588/3, p. 184, and /2, pp. 409–10.
48. GL MS 11588/3, pp. 256–57. These were typical excuses. Some members also avoided joining the livery. For example, in 1618, Henry Steele and Raphael Cleyton, "two ancient and free brothers" of the Grocers' Company, refused to join the company's livery and apparently avoided a fine; see GL MS 11588/3, p. 68.
49. GL MS 2881/8, fol. 165r. The City aldermen sometimes would deal with freemen who refused to serve in office or pay fines; see CLRO Rep. 68, fol. 139v.
50. DHA Court Minutes 1603–40, fol. 67r.
51. GL MSS 15201/2, p. 149, and /4, p. 501.
52. GL MS 2881/9, fols. 80r, 82v, 83v–85r. The beadle had been disciplined by the company's wardens on at least two earlier occasions; see GL MS 2881/9, fols. 53r–v, 78v.
53. SkHA Court Books I, fols. 57v, 75v, and V, p. 387.
54. SkHA Court Book I, fol. 18r; GL MSS 15201/1, fol. 73v, and /3, fol. 138. The case of this renter warden was discussed in detail in the preceding chapter.
55. GL MS 15201/4, p. 257.
56. GL MSS 11588/1, fol. 286v, and /3, pp. 22–23.
57. For example, in 1625, the Grocers' Company gave Thomas Coventry, the Lord Keeper of the Great Seal, twenty sugar loaves and other spices worth £20 "as a free and loving gratuity," and they made him a freeman of their company two years later; see GL MS 11588/3, pp. 310, 344. See also I. Archer, "London Lobbies."
58. GL MSS 11588/4, p. 159, /1, fol. 293r, and /3, p. 505.
59. GL MS 15201/3, p. 60.
60. GL MS 2208/1, p. 25, April 1640.
61. GL MS 15201/4, p. 256. They also sent a committee to search Child's study to recover any books or writings that involved the company's business; it is not clear whether the study in question was in the company's hall. The clerk of the Blacksmiths' Company built an office for "his clerks" in the company hall; see GL MS 2881/9, fol. 57v.
62. GL MS 15201/4, p. 450.
63. SHA D1/1/1, fol. 136r.
64. GL MS 11588/4, p. 94. They granted the reversion to Harris despite having denied reversions to Thomas Henshaw—an attorney of the Court of Common Pleas who had the recommendations of Sir Thomas Middleton

and Sir Arthur Haselrig—and to liveryman Robert Handson earlier during the court meeting because of their "long-standing order against reversions."

65. GL MS 11588/4, p. 253.

66. GL MS 4655/9, fol. 6r–v.

67. Occasionally, the officers would be warned to be more diligent in their posts; GL MSS 11588/1, fol. 423r, and /2, p. 127.

68. GL MS 11588/1, fol. 361r. See below, for the garden and tower.

69. GL MS 8046/3, not paginated; the decision cited here occurred on 7 May 1700.

70. GL MSS 11588/3, pp. 194, 266, 474, and /4, p. 523.

71. GL MSS 2881/6, p. 306, and /9, fol. 61v.

72. GL MS 15201/4, p. 322. In similar fashion, in 1613, William Ballard, who was identified as a "gent," offered to discover lands that belonged to the Grocers' Company as a result of expired entails, asking that he receive one-fourth of any proceeds. He made the offer in a handwritten note which the clerk presented to the assistants; see GL MS 11588/2, p. 786.

73. GL MSS 11588/2, pp. 675–77, 750, and /3, pp. 17–18, 440–41, 501–2. This was not the first time Bunbury had leased property from his employers: in 1624, he rented the company's weighhouse for three years at £40 per year; GL MS 11588/3, p. 287.

74. GL MS 15201/4, p. 21.

75. GL MS 15201/1, fol. 39v.

76. GL MS 15201/2, p. 162. This record is ambiguous, and "kitchen" may refer to the kitchen of the company hall.

77. GL MS 4655/10, fols. 43v, 46r.

78. GL MS 11588/3, p. 68.

79. GL MS 11588/4, p. 82.

80. GL MS 4647, p. 252. The record contains no indication of the outcome of this charge.

81. GL MS 11588/3, pp. 191–92.

82. GL MS 8046/3, not paginated. The action described here took place on 4 March 1700.

83. GL MS 11588/1, fol. 356v. Southaik had announced his resignation earlier in the meeting, claiming that he was no longer "able to discharge that room and service."

84. GL MS 11588/3, pp. 11–12; SHA D1/1/1, fols. 55v, 66v.

85. SHA D1/1/1, fols. 127v, 154v, 168v.

86. See GL MS 2881/8, fol. 34r, for an example of cheating during voting.

87. GL MS 11588/3, pp. 230–32.

88. Ibid., pp. 232–33. For an example of royal interference in the selection of a company officer during Queen Elizabeth's reign, see Doolittle, p. 12.

89. GL MS 11588/3, pp. 277, 300, 410, 415, 430, 434, 448, 451, 465, 474.

90. GL MS 11588/2, pp. 681, 684. In a similar move in 1610, the City's aldermen admitted that they had failed to comply with an order their predecessors made in 1597 limiting the number of reversions that a lord mayor

could grant to city offices in one year because "now of late years the Court not being informed or remembered of the said order"; CLRO Reps. 24, fols. 138r–39v, and 30, fols. 36r–38r.

91. GL MSS 11588/2, p. 781, /3, pp. 14, 60, and /4, p. 227.

92. GL MS 8046/3, not paginated. The action described here took place on 10 May 1704.

93. SHA D1/1/1, fol. 142v.

94. At a subsequent meeting, the assistants summoned William Gidley and Michael Fell "for their refusal of the contribution and animating of others"; see GL MS 15201/3, pp. 83–84.

95. GL MS 15201/3, pp. 108, 126.   96. GL MS 11588/3, p. 165.
97. GL MS 15201/2, p. 154.   98. SHA D1/1/1, fol. 32r.
99. GL MS 11588/3, p. 328.   100. GL MS 2881/9, fol. 6v.
101. SHA D1/1/1, fol. 95r.
102. GL MSS 15201/2, p. 309, and /3, p. 74.
103. GL MSS 15201/4, pp. 144, 185, and /2, p. 326.
104. GL MS 4655/11, fol. 26v.   105. GL MS 4647, pp. 200–203.
106. Ibid., p. 205.   107. CLRO Rep. 43, fols. 202v–4v.
108. GL MS 3043/2, not paginated; 10 August 1629.

Chapter 5

1. GL MS 11588/1, fol. 255r–v.
2. Brigden, *London*, pp. 35–36, 411–13; Sommerville, p. 78.
3. On the persistence of traditional beliefs and practices after the Reformation, see Scarisbrick; Watt; and Duffy.
4. On the problem of civic unity in early modern towns, see Scribner; Konnert; I. Archer, *Pursuit*, esp. pp. 18–57; and McClendon.
5. GL MS 11588/3, p. 97.
6. GL MSS 11654, pp. 6–7, and 11570, fol. 59v. For the early history of the company, see Nightingale.
7. GL MSS 11616, fols. 30r, 74r–82r, and 11571/3, fols. 91r–93r.
8. Hennessey, p. 77.
9. Brigden, *London*, pp. 113–14, 128, 161. Brigden suggested (p. 113) that Forman's "known reforming sympathies" may explain why he was "chosen for the City cure by its patrons, the Grocers, because there were in that company already some who favored the new doctrines."
10. GL MS 9531/10, fol. 10v. The presentment was in the name of "Thomas" Forman.
11. Brigden, *London*, p. 178; and idem, "Thomas Cromwell," p. 44. Brigden incorrectly identifies Petit as a warden in 1525. The wardens are identified in the Wardens' Accounts, GL MSS 11571/3, fol. 272r (1519–20: John Rest, Nicholas Lambert, John Petit), and /4, fol. 118r (1524–25: William Campion, Thomas Stevens, Edward Murrell).
12. PRO PCC PROB 11/24, fol. 84v. On the difficulty of using wills to de-

termine the religious views of testators, see Alsop; Marsh; and Burgess. In what follows, the emphasis is on the bequests for spiritual uses rather than the wills' preambles, which were their most problematic features. For an example of this approach to wills, see B. Harris, esp. pp. 103–5.

13. PRO PCC PROB 11/27, fol. 97v.

14. CLRO Husting Roll 240/54. The unnamed witnesses included William Butler, and the chantry was to benefit the souls of Sir Thomas Lovell and his wife, Isabell.

15. CLRO Husting Roll 240/55. The chantry was to benefit the souls of the family of Henry Adye and all Christians.

16. CLRO Husting Roll 241/35; GL MS 11571/5, fol. 332r.

17. Brigden, *London*, pp. 201, 209, 242.

18. Ibid., pp. 114–15, 235, 265, 311–22.

19. Ibid., p. 387.

20. GL MS 11571/5, fol. 310r–v; Kitching, ed., pp. 88–89.

21. Brigden, *London*, p. 411; Foxe, *Acts*, 5: 225–26.

22. Brigden names grocers John Petit, Geoffrey Lome, and John Blage as "leading evangelicals," but see GL MS 11571/5, fols. 114v, 118v. Both Blage and his former apprentice Richard Grafton were significant figures in the importing and distributing of translated Bibles at mid-century; Brigden, *London*, pp. 411n, 412, 419.

23. Mullins, section on Thomas Becon; Bailey, pp. 54–57; Brigden, *London*, p. 458.

24. GL MS 11588/1, fols. 6r, 10v.

25. CLRO Husting Roll 249/18. The will was proved in November 1557. The Court of Assistants discussed Laxton's estate "sundry times" before agreeing to accept it "with thanksgiving." Richard Grafton was among those appointed to oversee its undertaking; GLMS 11588/1, fol. 6v. Brigden makes no mention of Laxton, but by her reckoning, he must have been among the last Londoners to provide for beadsmen in his will; Brigden, *London*, p. 581. Although there is no way to attribute the authorship of the will to Laxton, the preamble was fairly traditional, leaving his will to "almighty god and to my maker and redeemer Jesus Christ his only son and to all the holy company of heaven."

26. GL MS 11588/1, fols. 115v, 116v. On the importance to Puritans of preaching, see Hill, *Society*, pp. 31–77; Seaver, *Puritan Lectureships*, pp. 15–54; and Collinson, "Lectures."

27. GL MS 11588/1, fols. 376v, 378v, 411v, 421v, 423r. The lord mayor was grocer John Hart.

28. GL MS 11588/1, fols. 185v, 187v. For more on Campion's career, see Pollen.

29. For examples of Whitgift's recommendations, see GL MS 11588/1, fols. 151r, 205r, 261r.

30. Brigden, *London*, pp. 286–87; GL MS 11588/1, fols. 100v–101r.

31. Hennessey, p. 386; GL MS 11588/1, fols. 109v, 141v. This court

record suggests that the recommendations of four divines were required as a condition of the donor's bequest that gave the advowson to the company. In that year Coverdale also advanced the nominations of Thomas Cartwright and William Power to be the first two recipients of the company's fellowships for divinity students at Cambridge and Oxford; their fortunes were better than Sheriff's; see GL MS 11588/1, fol. 117r-v.

32. Hennessey, p. 386; GL MS 11588/1, fols. 76v, 83v, 87v. In 1573, the successful candidacy of Thomas Cooke for the rectorship of All Hallows was advanced by two assistants' testimony that he was "an honest man"; see GL MS 11588/1, fol. 246r-v.

33. GL MSS 11588/2, pp. 253, 255; 594/1 pp. 46, 48; and 11588/2, pp. 245, 258. The popularity of Fenton's preaching among company members continued through his tenure at St. Stephen's. In 1615, the company paid to publish a sermon that Fenton delivered "for the public good that may grow in others who were not hearers thereof and are desirous to learn godly and divine instructions by reading the same"; see GL MS 11588/2, p. 862.

34. GL MS 11588/3, p. 307.

35. Ibid., p. 541. The three nominees were "Mr Lechford, Mr Molines, and Mr Saxby."

36. GL MS 11588/3, pp. 546-47.

37. Ibid., p. 547. In 1636, the assistants appointed Saxby to the rectory at Norhill in Bedfordshire, an advowson they administered through Lady Slany's estate; see ibid., p. 568.

38. GL MS 11588/3, pp. 559, 596.

39. GL MS 11588/4, p. 19. See also Liu, p. 60; for a discussion of efforts by members of other London parishes to participate in the appointment of pastors, see Brenner, pp. 412-15.

40. GL MS 11588/4, pp. 26-27.   41. Ibid., pp. 35, 36.
42. Ibid., pp. 36-39.   43. Ibid., pp. 41, 46-47, 61, 91.
44. Ibid., p. 103.   45. Ibid., pp. 172, 169, 173.
46. Brigden, London, p. 565.   47. GL MS 11588/1, fols. 64r-65r.
48. For examples, see GL MS 11588/1, fols. 322r, 333v, 345v.
49. GL MS 11588/1, fols. 10v-12r.
50. For the changing conduct and meaning of funerals, see Gittings; and Beaver.

51. GL MSS 11571/3-8; PRO PCC PROB 11/27, fol. 97v, 11/39, fol. 280r, 11/41, fol. 90r.

52. Machyn, Diary, pp. 111-12, 232; GL MS 11588/3, p. 10.

53. GL MS 11588/1, fols. 129r, 243v, 264r, 270r.

54. GL MS 11570, fol. 59r. The saint's name is spelled in a variety of ways in the company's early modern records; Nightingale, pp. 35-41, argues that "Antonin" is the correct spelling and that the feast day was 18 May.

55. GL MS 11571/3, fol. 286v.

56. Cressy, Bonfires, pp. 5-7; Hutton, pp. 123-30.

57. GL MS 11588/1, fols. 86v, 87v.

58. GL MSS 11588/1, fol. 274v, and /2, pp. 807, 912. According to the standard interpretation of late medieval and early modern urban ceremony, the year had two halves, one ritualistic and the other secular; the grocers' decision to leave their commemoration dinner in the ritualistic half of the year, which stretched from Christmas to midsummer, suggests their unwillingness to push change too far; see Phythian-Adams, p. 73; and Berlin, p. 24. On the changing meaning of ritual in community more generally, see Sacks, "Demise."

59. CLRO Husting Roll 249/18. For more on Laxton and his school, see Walker.

60. GL MSS 11588/2, p. 39, and /3, p. 601. Similarly, in 1642, the company's inspectors visited the almspeople and "exhorted them to pray for their benefactors"; see GL MS 11588/4, p. 53.

61. GL MS 11588/4, p. 242.

62. GL MSS 11616, fols. 250r, 205v; and 11588/2, fol. 807.

63. GL MSS 11588/1, fol. 179r, /3, p. 57, and /2, p. 733.

64. See, for example, DHA Court Minute Book 1603-40, fol. 138r; GHA Court Minute Book P, part I, fol. 125r, and Court Book Y, fol. 94r; and MHA Acts of Court 1560-95, fols. 99r, 151v, and 1595-1629, fols. 132v, 259r-v.

65. GL MS 11588/4, p. 370.

66. Ibid., pp. 439-40.

67. Ibid., pp. 74, 84.

68. GL MSS 11570, fol. 60v, and 11654, p. 103.

69. Roberts, p. 39.

70. Ibid., p. 50; and Cook.

71. GL MSS 11588/1, fols. 147, 46r, 89r, 279r, and 11571/7, fol. 267v.

72. GL MSS 11588/1, fols. 50r, 366r-v, 391r, and 11571/5, fol. 305r.

73. GL MSS 11588/1, fol. 122r, and /2, fols. 356r, 360r.

74. GL MS 11588/1, fols. 81r, 397r, 405r, 406r; Roberts, p. 175.

75. GL MSS 11588/1, fol. 433v, and /2, p. 9.

76. GL MS 11588/2, p. 436.

77. Ibid., pp. 587-88.

78. Ibid., pp. 812-14.

79. Ibid., pp. 816, 819.

80. GL MS 11588/3, pp. 27, 97, 124.

81. Roberts, pp. 208-24; CLRO Rep. 41, fol. 362r-v.

82. GL MS 11588/3, pp. 138-39, 327.

83. Ibid., pp. 420-21. The departure of the apothecaries was the major internal economic problem for the company during the early seventeenth century, but the assistants had to deal with other problems. In 1636, the assistants protested a plan sponsored by a group of confectioners to start their own company, and in 1640, a committee of assistants was empowered to petition Parliament regarding the overturning of patents on the sale of tobacco and other commodities that had previously been sold by company members; see GL MSS 11588/3, p. 560, and /4, p. 1.

84. Brenner, pp. 1-196.

85. Andrew Bayning and Paul Bayning were among members of the Levant Company, and they joined Oliver Stile, Nicholas Stile, John Dorrington,

Gyles Parslowe, and Robert Payne as charter members of the Spanish Company in 1605; see Carr, pp. 30–32; Epstein; Croft, pp. 96–97; and GL MSS 11588/3-4. Several leading grocers—including John Langham, Daniel Harvey, and George Clark—were active in the trade with the East Indies in the period, and the Grocers' Company itself invested heavily in the East India Company; OIL EICCB 11, fol. 103r; Brenner, pp. 78n, 361; GL MS 11588/3, pp. 68, 133, 155, 181. At the same time, other members of the Grocers' Company—such as Richard Quiney, John Sadler, John Warner, and Samuel Warner—invested in the emerging trade with the Americas; see Brenner, pp. 134, 147.

86. PRO SP 105/148/46 and /52; Brenner, p. 88.

87. GL MS 11588/3, p. 469; Brenner, pp. 145–48.

88. GL MSS 11592a; 11588/2, pp. 788, 876, and /3, pp. 356, 642, 648; Pearl, *London*, pp. 325–27; Brenner, pp. 134, 310, 326, 371, 397.

89. GL MSS 11592a, and 11580/3, pp. 3, 109, 145, 218, 333.

90. PRO SP 16/91/66i–iii.

91. OIL EICCB 10, fols. 105r, 132v, 168v, 169r–v, 170v–71r, and 11, fols. 72r, 79v, 117r–v; Brenner, p. 134; Pearl, *London*, appendix; *APC*, 1627–28, pp. 220–21; *CSPD*, 1627–28, 27 January.

92. GL MS 11588/3, pp. 471, 479; Brenner, p. 147. Samuel Warner claimed that he could not hold company office because his brother and partner, John Warner, was already a liveryman and thus their business would suffer because of the time they spent on company affairs. Warner also cited the example of "two of his neighbors" whom the company had allowed to avoid offices for a fine, a likely reference to Sadler and Quiney, who had appeared before the assistants only one meeting earlier; see GL MS 11588/3, p. 469.

93. Warner was joined on that occasion by William Underwood, who, like Warner, would later serve Parliament in London during the Civil War; see Brenner, pp. 520, 551.

94. GL MSS 11588/3, p. 459, and /4, p. 180; Pearl, *London*, pp. 191–92; Brenner, pp. 379–80; GL MS 11588/4, pp. 38, 55, 169, 513. Two of Northey's auditor colleagues also removed themselves from company business for extended periods at this time. Assistant John Wardell was allowed to fine out of the wardenship from France; GL MS 11588/4, p. 8.

95. GL MSS 11588/3, p. 316, and /4, pp. 8, 79–80, 356; Brenner, p. 430. Elsewhere, Brenner identified Waring as a colonial trader and political independent during the Civil War and Interregnum; see Brenner, pp. 327n, 373, 404, 407n, 430n, 431, 636.

96. GL MS 11588/4, pp. 601, 613.

Chapter 6

1. This position is developed most clearly in Dunn, p. 13.
2. Gwynn; Scouloudi, ed.; and Cottret.

3. Unwin, *Gilds*, pp. 246–51; Plummer, pp. 146, 302.

4. Gwynn, pp. 62–63.

5. Manning, pp. 187–219; I. Archer, *Pursuit*, p. 154. Concerns about tensions between native and alien weavers in 1595 may be seen in the Court of Aldermen's actions against a printer who published a pamphlet in the name of the yeoman weavers against strangers who wove silk; see CLRO Rep. 23, fol. 406v.

6. The quotations in this paragraph are from GL MS 4647, pp. 125–34.

7. GL MSS 4655/1, fols. 25v–26r, and 4647, pp. 211–18. Internal evidence indicates that the latter document—a petition from "the commonality of the Company of Weavers of London" to the lord mayor—dates from July 1627 at the earliest, but it described conditions going back to the mid-1590s.

8. GL MS 4647, pp. 139–41. The date of this document is derived from the mayoralty of Sir Thomas Cambell, the addressee; see Beaven, 1: 110. It is not clear that a copy of this petition was delivered to the lord mayor. In this period the company's officers were cooperating with the City governors to bring thirty foreigners—who were born in England—into the company through redemption, thereby addressing some of the petitioners' concerns about competition from nonmembers; see CLRO Rep. 30, fols. 78r–v, 110v, 162v; and Jor. 28, fol. 240r.

9. GL MS 4655/1, fol. 25v.

10. GL MS 4647, pp. 144–48. The date and authorship of this text are uncertain.

11. GL MS 4647, pp. 157–59. For more on the new looms, see Dunn, p. 14.

12. GL MS 4647, pp. 31, 158.

13. GL MS 4655/1, fol. 16r; Plummer, p. 17; GL MS 4655/1, fols. 22v, 48r, 90r.

14. For examples of this and similar constructions, see GL MS 4655/1, fols. 5v–6r, 30v.

15. GL MS 4655/1, fols. 4r, 7r, 20v, 21r, 22r, 22v, 24v, 43r, 48r, 52r, 64v, 71r, 76r, 80v, 87r, 90r, 91r.

16. The quotations in this paragraph are from PRO SP 14/81/56.

17. GL MS 4647, pp. 324–29.

18. PRO SP 14/127/12; Prideaux, 1: 133–34.

19. GL MS 4647, pp. 296–98.

20. Ibid., pp. 188–92.

21. Ibid., pp. 193–99. The yeomen presented some of these complaints to the lord mayor and aldermen; see CLRO Rep. 41, fols. 148r, 287v–89r. In August 1627, the Weavers' officers complained to the lord mayor and aldermen about a member of the Waxchandlers' Company who was found weaving, and the aldermen confirmed the weavers' right to demand that the waxchandler bind his apprentices at Weavers' Hall; see CLRO Rep. 41, fol. 314v.

22. GL MS 4647, pp. 200–205; CLRO Rep. 44, fols. 364v–65r.

23. GL MS 4647, pp. 220–27; CLRO Rep. 45, fols. 74v–79v. The aldermen

were not entirely convinced by the officers' arguments, finding spurious their claim that one Richard Fletcher could practice weaving because his wife was a weaver's daughter.

24. GL MS 4647, pp. 262–68. The two yeomen in question were William Counley and Samuel Seaton, both of whom were among the yeomen who appeared before the lord mayor following the meeting at the pub; see ibid., pp. 200–204.

25. GL MS 4647, pp. 253–56.

26. Ibid., pp. 300–312 (quotation on p. 305).

27. Ibid., pp. 340–48. 388–400, 408–26, 457–63. In their defense, the company's officers claimed that the company's ordinances empowered them to collect a silver spoon and 3s 4d from each new freeman; see ibid., pp. 399–400. Nevertheless, Ordinance 27 apparently gave apprentices the option of paying with a silver spoon instead of providing a breakfast for the officers because that custom had become "somewhat chargeable unto young men"; see ibid., pp. 57–58; and CLRO Rep. 51, fols. 286v–87v.

28. CLRO Rep. 49, fol. 31r.

29. GL MS 4647, pp. 480–88.

30. Ibid., pp. 215–16. According to the petitioners, Pell claimed that the company's officers allowed him to engage in these practices. The lord mayor and aldermen considered a similar complaint against Pell and weavers' assistant John Renshall on 17 March 1634; see CLRO Rep. 49, fol. 133v.

31. GL MS 4647, pp. 439–44. The lord mayor and aldermen readmitted Pell to the City's freedom in the following July, after he paid a fine of £5; see CLRO Rep. 52, fol. 214r.

32. CLRO Reps. 53, fol. 209v, and 54, fols. 147r–50v.

33. For the disciplining of a French weaver and the prosecution of a freeman of the Girdlers' Company, see GL MS 4655/1A, fols. 3r, 4v; examples of freeing apprentices—who were charged 3s 4d and a silver spoon—may also be found there.

34. GL MS 4655/1A, fols. 2r, 6r.

35. *Case of the commonalty*; Plummer, pp. 33, 49–50; GL MS 4655/1A, fols. 8v, 9v, 10r, 13r.

36. For examples, see GL MS 4655/1A, fols. 21v, 45v, 49r, 51r.

37. GL MSS 4655/1B, fols. 8v, 10r, 11r, and /2, pp. 3, 24–25.

38. GL MS 4655/3, fols. 14r–v, 19r, 28r, 28v–32v, 64r.

39. GL MSS 4655/4, fols. 9r, 13r, 97r–v, and /6, fol. 64r.

40. GL MS 4655/4, fol. 58v. The records contain many other examples of weavers certifying their membership in the French and Dutch churches.

41. GL MS 4655/4, fol. 110v.

42. GL MS 4655/5, fol. 13v. For examples of some who were admitted under these criteria, see ibid., fols. 16r, 18v, 24r.

43. GL MS 4655/5, fols. 25r, 49v, 55r.

44. GL MSS 4655/6, fol. 50v; /7, fol. 64r; /8, fol. 23v; and /6, fols. 27v, 30r, 38r.

45. GL MSS 4655/3, fol. 159v, and /4, fol. 40r.
46. GL MSS 4655/3-11, and 4660; Plummer, pp. 61-64. For more on women's work in this period, see Earle, "Female Labour Market."
47. Dunn, pp. 17-19, 21.
48. Jeaffreson, ed., pp. 60-65.
49. T. Harris, pp. 192-96.
50. Dunn, p. 22.
51. GL MS 4655/8, fol. 55v.
52. T. Harris, p. 196.
53. GL MS 4655/8, fols. 66v, 67r, 72r, 81v.
54. Ibid., fol. 69r. A similar case arose in August 1676, when Godfrey Kiesett agreed to pay a 40s fine for employing several weavers who had not been admitted to the company; see ibid., fol. 99r.
55. GL MSS 4655/8, fols. 81r, 112v, and /9, fols. 13r, 14v, 29r-v.
56. GL MS 4655/9, fols. 61v-62r.
57. Ibid., fol. 12r.
58. Ibid., fol. 37v.
59. Cottret, pp. 185-229.
60. *Corporation of Weavers; Complaint.* As a further indication of the tense relations between freemen and aliens in this period, in 1693 the Court of Aldermen prohibited any alien or alien's son from becoming free of the City except for extraordinary reasons. The aldermen renewed the prohibition in 1707; see CLRO Reps. 98, pp. 119-20, and 112, p. 63. For the continued agitation of London weavers, see de Kray, pp. 57-58.
61. GL MS 4655/11, pp. 21-22.
62. Ibid., fol. 22r-v.
63. Ibid., fols. 3v-4r, 5r, 6r, 15r, 19r.
64. Ibid., fol. 23r. The plaintiffs were identified in June as "such of the livery and other members of this company as have brought their bill in the high court of Chancery in the name of her majesty's attorney general against this court"; see ibid., fol. 23v.
65. GL MSS 11588/11, fol. 23v, and 4655/11, fols. 24v-25r.
66. GL MS 4655/11, fol. 25v; CLRO Reps. 109, pp. 501-2, and 110, fols. 21v-22r.
67. GL MS 4655/11, fol. 29r-v. The court records do not indicate whether the livery who drafted the new charter were involved in the Chancery suit.
68. GL MS 4655/11, fols. 30r, 32v-34v. The new charter confirmed the role of the livery in company elections, allowed the assistants to admit into the company anyone who had legally served an apprenticeship in the trade, and maintained the prohibition on women weaving; see GL MS 4641.
69. CLRO Reps. 112, pp. 336, 362, 376-77, 399, 415, 430, 475; and 113, pp. 228, 254.

Bibliography

Manuscript Sources

BRITISH LIBRARY
Lansdowne Manuscripts 20, 74, 160, 169

CLOTHWORKERS' HALL ARCHIVE
Court Minute Book 1558–1581
Court Minute Book 1605–1623
Court Minute Book 1639–1649
Court Minute Book 1665–1683

CORPORATION OF LONDON RECORD OFFICE
Repertories of the Court of Aldermen 23–24, 29–30, 34, 40–45, 49, 51–54, 65–68, 73–80, 82, 93, 98, 103–4, 109–13
Journals of the Court of Common Council 28, 40, 48
Husting Rolls 240, 241, 249
Letter Book HH

DRAPERS' HALL ARCHIVE
Court Minute Book 1594–1603
Court Minute Book 1603–1640

GOLDSMITHS' HALL ARCHIVE
Court Minute Book U
Court Minute Book P, part I
Court Book Y

GUILDHALL LIBRARY, LONDON

Livery Company Collections

Bakers' Company

5186 Prosecutions of non-freemen, 1631–1635
5196 Memoranda Books
5197 Ordinances and Memoranda Books

Blacksmiths' Company

2881/1 Court Minutes 1605–1611
2881/2 Court Minutes 1611–1617
2881/3 Court Minutes 1626–1631
2881/4 Court Minutes 1631–1639
2881/5 Court Minutes 1639–1648
2881/6 Court Minutes 1648–1658
2881/7 Court Minutes 1658–1662
2881/8 Court Minutes 1686–1699
2881/9 Court Minutes 1699–1705

Brewers' Company

5445/15 Court Minutes 1628–1634
5452/1   Quarterage Books 1724–1737
5458   Memorandum Book 1723–1792

Carpenters' Company

4326/6   Wardens' Accounts 1592–1622
4329/6   Court Minutes 1656–1670
7784/2   Papers 1602–1603
7784/4   Papers 1609–1611
7784/5   Papers 1611–1612
7784/6   Papers 1613–1614
7784/7   Papers 1614–1615
7784/8   Papers 1615–1616
7784/9   Papers 1619–1620
7784/10 Papers 1620–1623
7784/11 Papers 1623–1624
7784/14 Papers 1628–1629
8334   Miscellaneous Papers on the Regulation of Trade

Coopers' Company

5625/1 Search Book 1701–1715
5625/2 Search Book 1716–1730

Grocers' Company

11570 Memorandum on the Foundation of the Pepperers' Fraternity

11571/3   Wardens' Accounts 1511–1521
11571/4   Wardens' Accounts 1521–1533
11571/5   Wardens' Accounts 1534–1555
11571/6   Wardens' Accounts 1555–1578
11571/7   Wardens' Accounts 1579–1592
11571/8   Wardens' Accounts 1592–1601
11571/10   Wardens' Accounts 1611–1622
11571/12   Wardens' Accounts 1632–1642
11588/1   Orders of the Court of Assistants 1556–1591
11588/2   Orders of the Court of Assistants 1591–1616
11588/3   Orders of the Court of Assistants 1616–1639
11588/4   Orders of the Court of Assistants 1640–1668
11592a   Freemen lists
11616   Register of Grants and Lands
11638   Charters
11654   Ordinances

Haberdashers' Company

15842/1   Court Minutes 1583–1652

Ironmongers' Company

17082   Memorandum Book

Joiners' Company

8046/3   Court Minutes 1698–1707

Painter-Stainers' Company

5667/2   Court Minute Book 1649–1793

Plumbers' Company

2208/1   Court Minutes 1621–1647

Saddlers' Company

5385   Court Minute Book 1605–1665

Tylers and Bricklayers' Company

3043/2   Court Minutes 1620–1663
3047/1   Search Books 1605–1650
3047/2   Search Books 1650–1680
3047/3   Search Books 1681–1707
3047/4   Search Books 1708–1723
3051/1   Quarterage Books 1588–1616
3054/2   Wardens' Accounts
4318   Memorandum Book

Vintners' Company

15190	Charters
15201/1	Court Minutes 1608–1610
15201/2	Court Minutes 1610–1629
15201/3	Court Minutes 1629–1638
15201/4	Court Minutes 1639–1659
15201/5	Court Minutes 1669–1682
15361	Steven Skidmore's Gift, receipts and tenders

Waxchandlers' Company

9491	Quarterage Lists
9493	Search Books
9496	Charters

Weavers' Company

4641	Laws and Ordinances 1708
4647	Ordinances and Memorandum Book, 1585–1641
4655/1	Court Minute Book 1610–1642
4655/1A	Court Minute Book 1648–1650/1
4655/1B	Court Minute Book 1651–1652
4655/2	Court Minute Book 1653–1654
4655/3	Court Minute Book 1661–1664
4655/4	Court Minute Book 1666–1668
4655/5	Court Minute Book 1668–1669
4655/6	Court Minute Book 1669–1671
4655/7	Court Minute Book 1672–1674
4655/8	Court Minute Book 1674–1677
4655/9	Court Minute Book 1683–1685
4655/10	Court Minute Book 1692–1694
4655/11	Court Minute Book 1700–1721
4660	Calendar of Apprentices 1665–1706

Other Manuscript Collections

Christ's Hospital

12818/1–2   Childrens' Registers

Diocese of London

9531/10   Presentments

Society of Apothecaries

8200/2   Court Minute Book 1651–1680

Society of Tacklehouse and Ticket Porters

913   Ordinances and Memoranda Book

St. Stephen Walbrook Parish
594/1   Vestry Minutes, 1587–1614

MERCERS' HALL ARCHIVE
Acts of Court 1560–1595
Acts of Court 1595–1629

ORIENTAL AND INDIA OFFICE LIBRARY
Court Books of the East India Company, 10–11

PUBLIC RECORD OFFICE
Chancery Proceedings C2
Exchequer Bills and Answers 112/98
Prerogative Court of Canterbury, PROB 11
Privy Council Registers 2
State Papers 14, 16, 105

SALTERS' HALL ARCHIVE
D1/1/1   Court Book 1627–1684

SKINNERS' HALL ARCHIVE
Court Book I
Court Book III
Court Book IV
Court Book V

Other Sources

Publishers are listed only for twentieth-century works.

The A to Z of Elizabethan London. Compiled by Adrian Prockter and Robert Taylor. Lympne Castle, Kent: Harry Margury, 1979.
The A to Z of Georgian London. Compiled by Adrian Prockter and Roger Cline. Lympne Castle, Kent: Harry Margury, 1981.
Acts of the Privy Council of England. New series. Ed. John Roche Dasent. London: H. M. Stationery Office, 1908–12.
Agnew, Jean-Christophe. *Worlds Apart: The Market and the Theater in Anglo-American Thought, 1550–1750*. Cambridge, Eng.: Cambridge University Press, 1986.
Alford, B. W. E., and T. C. Barker. *A History of the Carpenters' Company*. London: Allen and Unwin, 1968.
Alldridge, Nick. "Loyalty and Identity in Chester Parishes 1540–1640." In S. J. Wright, ed., *Parish, Church and People: Local Studies in Lay Religion 1350–1750*, pp. 85–124. London: Hutchinson, 1988.

Alsop, J. D. "Religious Preambles in Early Modern English Wills as Formulae." *Journal of Ecclesiastical History* 40 (1989): 19–27.

Amelang, James S. *Honored Citizens of Barcelona: Patrician Culture and Class Relations, 1490–1714.* Princeton: Princeton University Press, 1986.

Analytical index to the series of records known as the Remembrancia. Preserved among the archives of the City of London. London, 1878.

Anderson, Benedict. *Imagined Communities: Reflections on the Origin and Spread of Nationalism.* London: Verso, 1983.

Archer, Ian W. "The London Lobbies in the Later Sixteenth Century." *Historical Journal* 31 (1988): 17–44.

———. *The Pursuit of Stability: Social Relations in Elizabethan London.* Cambridge, Eng.: Cambridge University Press, 1991.

———. *The History of the Haberdashers' Company.* Chichester, Sussex, Eng.: Phillimore, 1991.

———. "The Nostalgia of John Stow." In David L. Smith, Richard Strier, and David Bevington, eds., *The Theatrical City: London's Culture, Theatre and Literature, 1576–1649,* pp. 17–34. Cambridge, Eng.: Cambridge University Press, 1995.

Archer, J. L. "The Industrial History of London 1603–1640." M.A. diss., University of London, 1934.

Ashton, Robert. *The City and the Court, 1603–1643.* Cambridge, Eng.: Cambridge University Press, 1979.

Bailey, Derrick S. *Thomas Becon and the Reformation of the Church of England.* Edinburgh: Oliver and Boyd, 1952.

Barnes, Thomas G. "The Prerogative and Environmental Control of London Building in the Early Seventeenth Century: The Lost Opportunity." *California Law Review* 58 (1970): 1332–63.

Barroll, Leeds. *Politics, Plague, and Shakespeare's Theater: The Stuart Years.* Ithaca, N.Y.: Cornell University Press, 1991.

Barry, Jonathan. "Introduction." In Jonathan Barry, ed., *The Tudor and Stuart Town: A Reader in English Urban History 1530–1688,* pp. 1–34. London: Longman, 1990.

Beaven, Alfred B. *The Aldermen of the City of London.* 2 vols. London: E. Fisher, 1908–13.

Beaver, Dan. "'Sown in dishonour, raised in glory': Death, Ritual and Social Organization in Northern Gloucestershire, 1590–1690." *Social History* 17 (1992): 389–419.

Beier, A. L. *Masterless Men: The Vagrancy Problem in England, 1560–1640.* London: Methuen, 1985.

———. "Engines of Manufacture: The Trades of London." In A. L. Beier and Roger Finlay, eds., *London 1500–1700: The Making of the Metropolis,* pp. 141–67. London: Longman, 1986.

Bell, Colin, and Howard Newby. *Community Studies: An Introduction to the Sociology of the Local Community.* New York: Praeger, 1971.

Benbow, R. Mark. "The Court of Aldermen and the Assizes: The Policy of

Price Control in Elizabethan London." *Guildhall Studies in London History* 4 (1980): 93–118.
———. "Index of London Citizens Involved in City Government, 1558–1603." Privately printed, 1989.
Berger, Ronald M. *The Most Necessary Luxuries: The Mercers' Company of Coventry, 1550–1680.* University Park: Pennsylvania State University Press, 1993.
Berlin, Michael. "Civic Ceremony in Early Modern London." *Urban History Yearbook* (1986): 15–27.
Bevington, David. "Theatre as Holiday." In David L. Smith, Richard Strier, and David Bevington, eds., *The Theatrical City: London's Culture, Theatre and Literature, 1576–1649,* pp. 101–16. Cambridge, Eng.: Cambridge University Press, 1995.
Birch, W. de G., ed. *The Historical Charters and Constitutional Documents of the City of London.* London, 1884.
Borsay, Peter. *The English Urban Renaissance: Culture and Society in the Provincial Town, 1660–1770.* Oxford: Oxford University Press, 1989.
Boulton, Jeremy. *Neighbourhood and Society: A London Suburb in the Seventeenth Century.* Cambridge, Eng.: Cambridge University Press, 1987.
———. "London Widowhood Revisited: The Decline of Female Remarriage in the Seventeenth and Eighteenth Centuries." *Continuity and Change* 5 (1990): 323–55.
Brenner, Robert. *Merchants and Revolution: Commercial Change, Political Conflict, and London's Overseas Traders, 1550–1653.* Princeton: Princeton University Press, 1993.
Brett-James, Norman G. *The Growth of Stuart London.* London: G. Allen and Unwin, 1935.
Brigden, Susan. "Thomas Cromwell and the 'brethren.'" In C. Cross, D. Loades, and J. J. Scarisbrick, eds., *Law and Government under the Tudors,* pp. 31–50. Cambridge, Eng.: Cambridge University Press, 1988.
———. *London and the Reformation.* Oxford: Oxford University Press, 1989.
Brodsky, Vivian. "Widows in Late Elizabethan London: Remarriage, Economic Opportunity and Family Orientations." In L. Bonfield, R. M. Smith, and K. Wrightson, eds., *The World We Have Gained: Histories of Population and Social Structure: Essays to Peter Laslett on His Seventieth Birthday,* pp. 122–54. Oxford: Blackwell, 1986.
Burgess, Clive. "Late Medieval Wills and Pious Convention: Testamentary Evidence Reconsidered." In Michael Hicks, ed., *Profit, Piety and the Professions in Later Medieval England,* pp. 14–33. Gloucester: A. Sutton, 1990.
Burke, Peter. *Popular Culture in Early Modern Europe.* New York: Harper and Row, 1978.
Burton, Henry. *A Divine Tragedy Lately Acted.* London, 1636.
Calendar of State Papers, Domestic. London, 1858–97.

Carr, Cecil T., ed. *Select Charters of Trading Companies A.D. 1530–1707.* Selden Society, vol. 28 (1913).

The Case of the commonalty of the Corporation of Weavers of London Truly Stated. London, 1648.

Clapham, Henoch. *An Epistle Discoursing upon the Pestilence.* London, 1603.

———. *H. Clapham, his Demaundes and Answeres Touching the Pestilence, etc.* London, 1604.

———. *Doctor Andros his Prosopopeia Answered.* London, 1605.

Clark, Peter. *The English Alehouse: A Social History, 1200–1830.* London: Longman, 1983.

Collier, J. P. *The History of English Dramatic Poetry to the Time of Shakespeare and the Annals of the Stage to the Reformation.* London, 1879.

Collinson, Patrick. "Lectures by Combination: Structures and Characteristics of Church Life in 17th-Century England." *Bulletin of the Institute of Historical Research* 48 (1975): 77–91. Reprinted in Patrick Collinson, *Godly People: Essays on English Protestantism and Puritanism,* pp. 467–98. London: Hambledon, 1983.

———. *The Birthpangs of Protestant England: Religious and Cultural Change in the Sixteenth and Seventeenth Centuries.* Basingstoke, Hampshire, Eng.: Macmillan, 1988.

The Complaint of Diverse Liege-master Weavers Against the Irregular Proceedings of the Bailiffs, Officers, and Assistants of the said Weavers' Company. London, 1690(?).

Cook, Harold J. "Good Advice and Little Medicine: The Professional Authority of Early Modern English Physicians." *Journal of British Studies* 33 (Jan. 1994): 1–31.

The Corporation of Weavers at London and Canterbury do Humbly offer to the Consideration of the Honourable House of Commons . . . London, 1689.

Cottret, Bernard. *The Huguenots in England: Immigration and Settlement c. 1550–1700.* Cambridge, Eng.: Cambridge University Press, 1991.

Crawford, Ann. *A History of the Vintners' Company.* London: Constable, 1977.

Cressy, David. "Levels of Illiteracy in England 1530–1730." *Historical Journal* 20 (1977): 1–23.

———. *Bonfires and Bells: National Memory and the Protestant Calendar in Elizabethan and Stuart England.* London: Weidenfeld and Nicolson, 1989.

———. "Foucault, Stone, Shakespeare and Social History." *English Literary Renaissance* 21 (1991): 121–33.

Croft, Pauline, ed. *The Spanish Company.* London Record Society, vol. 9 (1973).

Curry, Patrick. *Prophecy and Power: Astrology in Early Modern England.* Princeton: Princeton University Press, 1989.

Dale, T. C., ed. "A List of the Taverns in London and its Suburbs in 1641 held by Members of the Vintners' Company." Guildhall Library Typescript.
———. "Members of City Companies in 1641." Guildhall Library Typescript.
Davis, Natalie Zemon. "Boundaries of the Sense of Self in Sixteenth-Century France." In Thomas C. Heller, Morton Sosna, and David E. Wellbury, eds., *Reconstructing Individualism: Autonomy, Individuality, and the Self in Western Thought*, pp. 53–63. Stanford, Calif.: Stanford University Press, 1986.
———. *Fiction in the Archives: Pardon Tales and Their Tellers in Sixteenth-Century France*. Stanford, Calif.: Stanford University Press, 1987.
de Kray, Gary Stuart. *A Fractured Society: The Politics of London in the First Age of Party*. Oxford: Oxford University Press, 1985.
A Declaration and Motive of the Persons Trusted . . . for Contributing the Value of a Meal Weekly, towards the Forming of some Regiments of Volunteers. 1643.
Dekker, Thomas. *The Shoemaker's Holiday*. Ed. Anthony Parr. London: A & C Black, 1990 [1600].
———. *The Wonderful Year*. London, 1603.
Deloney, Thomas. *The Gentle Craft*. London, 1597.
Denison, Stephen. *The White Wolf*. London, 1627.
Diefendorf, Barbara B. *Paris City Councillors in the Sixteenth Century: The Politics of Patrimony*. Princeton: Princeton University Press, 1986.
Dollimore, Jonathan. *Radical Tragedy: Religion, Ideology and Power in the Drama of Shakespeare and his Contemporaries*. 2d ed. Brighton, Eng.: Harvester Wheatsheaf, 1989.
Doolittle, Ian. *The Mercers' Company 1579–1959*. London: The Mercers' Company, 1994.
Duffy, Eamon. *The Stripping of the Altars: Traditional Religion in England c. 1400–c. 1580*. New Haven: Yale University Press, 1992.
Dunn, Richard M. "The London Weavers' Riot of 1675." *Guildhall Studies in London History* 1 (1973): 13–23.
Dunton, John. *The Night-Walker: or, Evening Rambles in Search after Lewd Women*. London, 1696–97.
Earle, Peter. "The Female Labour Market in London in the Late Seventeenth and Early Eighteenth Centuries." *Economic History Review*, 2d ser., 42 (1989): 328–53.
———. *The Making of the English Middle Class: Business, Society and Family in London, 1660–1730*. Berkeley: University of California Press, 1989.
———. *A City Full of People: Men and Women of London, 1650–1750*. London: Methuen, 1994.
Elborough, Robert. *London's Calamity by Fire Bewailed and Improved*. London, 1666.

Epstein, M. *The Early History of the Levant Company*. London: G. Routledge, 1908.
Farr, James. *Hands of Honor: Artisans and Their World in Dijon, 1550–1650*. Ithaca, N.Y.: Cornell University Press, 1988.
Finlay, Roger. *Population and Metropolis: The Demography of London 1580–1650*. Cambridge, Eng.: Cambridge University Press, 1981.
Finlay, Roger, and Beatrice Shearer. "Population Growth and Suburban Expansion." In A. L. Beier and Roger Finlay, eds., *London 1500–1700: The Making of the Metropolis*, pp. 37–59. London: Longman, 1986.
Foxe, John. *Acts and Monuments*. Vol. 5. Ed. S. R. Cattley and G. Townsend. London, 1838.
Gadbury, John. *London's Deliverance Predicted*. London, 1665.
Gildersleeve, Virginia. *Government Regulation of the Elizabethan Drama*. New York: B. Franklin, 1961.
Gittings, Clare. *Death, Burial and the Individual in Early Modern England*. London: Croom Helm, 1984.
Gossen, Stephen. *The School of Abuse*. London, 1853 [1579].
Grassby, Richard. *The Business Community of Seventeenth-Century England*. Cambridge, Eng.: Cambridge University Press, 1995.
Greenblatt, Stephen. *Renaissance Self-Fashioning: From More to Shakespeare*. Chicago: University of Chicago Press, 1980.
Griffiths, Paul. "The Structure of Prostitution in Elizabethan London." *Continuity and Change* 8 (1993): 39–63.
Gutteridge, H. C. "The Origin and Historical Development of the Profession of Notaries Public in England." In *Cambridge Legal Essays Written in Honour of and Presented to Doctor Bond, Professor Buckland, and Professor Kenny*, pp. 123–37. Cambridge, Eng.: W. Heffer, 1926.
Gwynn, Robin D. *Huguenot Heritage: The History and Contribution of the Huguenots in Britain*. London: Routledge and Kegan Paul, 1985.
Halliwell-Phillipps, J. O. *Outlines of the Life of Shakespeare*. Vol. 1. London: Longmans, Green, 1907.
Harding, Vanessa. "The Population of London 1550–1700: A Review of the Published Evidence." *London Journal* 15 (1990): 111–28.
———. "New Types of Urbanism: Early Modern London 1550–1750." *Franco British Studies* 17 (1994): 85–93.
———. "Early Modern London 1550–1700." *London Journal* 20 (1995): 34–45.
Harris, Barbara J. "A New Look at the Reformation: Aristocratic Women and Nunneries, 1450–1540." *Journal of British Studies* 32 (Apr. 1993): 89–113.
Harris, Tim. *London Crowds in the Reign of Charles II: Propaganda and Politics from the Restoration to the Exclusion Crisis*. Cambridge, Eng.: Cambridge University Press, 1987.
Haynes, Jonathan. *The Social Relations of Jonson's Theater*. Cambridge, Eng.: Cambridge University Press, 1992.

Healy, Margaret. "Discourses of the Plague in Early Modern London." In J. A. I. Champion, ed., *Epidemic Disease in London*, pp. 19–34. Centre for Metropolitan History Working Papers series, no. 1. London: Institute of Historical Research, 1993.

Hennessey, George. *Novum Repertorium Ecclesiasticum Parochiale Londinense.* London, 1898.

Herrup, Cynthia B. *The Common Peace: Participation and the Criminal Law in Seventeenth-Century England.* Cambridge, Eng.: Cambridge University Press, 1987.

Hill, Christopher. *Economic Problems of the Church from Archbishop Whitgift to the Long Parliament.* Oxford: Oxford University Press, 1956.

———. *Society and Puritanism in Pre-Revolutionary England.* London: Secker and Warburg, 1964.

Houlbrooke, Ralph. *Church Courts and the People During the English Reformation.* Oxford: Oxford University Press, 1979.

Houston, Rab. "Vagrants and Society in Early Modern England." *Cambridge Anthropology* 6 (1980): 18–32.

Howard, Jean. *The Stage and Social Struggle in Early Modern England.* London: Routledge, 1994.

Hutson, Lorna. *Thomas Nashe in Context.* Oxford, 1989.

———. "The Displacement of the Market in Jacobean City Comedy." *London Journal* 14 (1989): 3–16.

Hutton, Ronald. *The Rise and Fall of Merry England: The Ritual Year 1400–1700.* Oxford: Oxford University Press, 1994.

Jeaffreson, John C., ed. *Middlesex County Records.* Vol. 4. London, 1892.

Johnson, David J. *Southwark and the City.* Oxford: Oxford University Press, 1969.

Jordan, W. K. *The Charities of London 1480–1660: The Aspirations and Achievements of the Urban Society.* New York: Russell Sage Foundation, 1960.

Kaplan, Steven Laurence, and Cynthia J. Koepp, eds. *Work in France: Representations, Meaning, Organization, and Practice.* Ithaca, N.Y.: Cornell University Press, 1986.

Keene, D. J. "Suburban Growth." In Richard Holt and Gervase Rosser, eds., *The English Medieval Town: A Reader in English Urban History 1200–1540*, pp. 97–119. London: Longman, 1990.

Kellett, J. R. "The Breakdown of Gild and Corporation Control over the Handicraft and Retail Trade in London." *Economic History Review*, 2d ser., 10 (1958): 381–94.

Kenyon, J. P. *The Stuart Constitution.* Cambridge, Eng.: Cambridge University Press, 1986.

King, Henry. *A Sermon Preached at Paul's Cross the 25th of November 1621.* London, 1621.

King, John. *A Sermon at Paul's Cross on Behalfe of Paules Church.* London, 1620.

Kitching, C. J., ed. *London and Middlesex Chantry Certificates, 1548.* London Record Society, vol. 16 (1980).
Konnert, Mark. "Urban Values Versus Religious Passion: Châlons-sur-Marne During the Wars of Religion." *Sixteenth Century Journal* 20 (1989): 387–405.
Larkin, James F., and Paul L. Hughes, eds. *Stuart Royal Proclamations.* 2 vols. Oxford: Oxford University Press, 1973–1983.
Laurence, Anne. *Women in England 1500–1760.* New York: St. Martin's Press, 1994.
Leinwand, Theodore B. *The City Staged: Jacobean Comedy, 1603–1613.* Madison: University of Wisconsin Press, 1986.
Levine, Laura. *Men in Women's Clothing: Anti-theatricality and Effeminization 1579–1642.* Cambridge, Eng.: Cambridge University Press, 1994.
Levy, Eleanor. "Moorfields, Finsbury and the City of London in the Sixteenth Century." *London Topographical Record* 26 (1990): 78–96.
Lindley, K. J. "Riot Prevention and Control in Early Stuart London." *Transactions of the Royal Historical Society,* 5th ser., 33 (1983): 109–26.
Linebaugh, Peter. *The London Hanged: Crime and Civil Society in Eighteenth-Century England.* London: Penguin, 1991.
Liu, Tai. *Puritan London: A Study of Religion and Society in the City Parishes.* Newark: University of Delaware Press, 1986.
Loftie, W. J. *A History of London.* 2 vols. London, 1884.
Londons Lamentation. Or a fit admonishment for City and Countrey. London, 1641.
Lyon, Larry. *The Community in Urban Society.* Philadelphia: Temple University Press, 1987.
Macfarlane, Alan. *The Origins of English Individualism: The Family, Property and Social Transition.* Cambridge, Eng.: Cambridge University Press, 1979.
Macfarlane, Alan, with Sarah Harrison and Charles Jardine. *Reconstructing Historical Communities.* Cambridge, Eng.: Cambridge University Press 1977.
Macfarlane, Stephen. "Social Policy and the Poor in the Later Seventeenth-Century." In A. L. Beier and Roger Finlay, eds., *London 1500–1700: The Making of the Metropolis,* pp. 252–77. London: Longman, 1986.
Machyn, Henry. *The Diary of Henry Machyn, Citizen and Merchant Taylor of London, 1550–1563.* Ed. J. G. Nichols. Camden Society, vol. 42 (1848).
Mackenney, Richard. *Tradesmen and Traders: The World of the Guilds in Venice and Europe, c. 1250–1650.* London: Croom Helm, 1987.
Maitland, William. *The History and Survey of London.* 2 vols. London, 1756.
Manley, Lawrence. *Literature and Culture in Early Modern London.* Cambridge, Eng.: Cambridge University Press, 1995.
———. "Of Sites and Rights." In David L. Smith, Richard Strier, and David

Bevington, eds., *The Theatrical City: London's Culture, Theatre and Literature, 1576–1649*, pp. 35–54. Cambridge, Eng.: Cambridge University Press, 1995.

Manning, Roger B. *Village Revolts: Social Protest and Popular Disturbance in England, 1509–1640*. Oxford: Oxford University Press, 1988.

Marsh, Christopher. "In the Name of God? Will-Making and Faith in Early Modern England." In G. H. Martin and Peter Spufford, eds., *The Records of the Nation*, pp. 215–49. Woodbridge, Suffolk: Boydell, 1990.

McClendon, Muriel C. "'Against God's Word': Government, Religion and the Crisis of Authority in Early Reformation Norwich." *Sixteenth Century Journal* 25 (1994): 353–70.

McIntosh, Marjorie Keniston. "Local Responses to the Poor in Late Medieval and Tudor England." *Continuity and Change* 3 (1988): 209–45.

———. *A Community Transformed: The Manor and Liberty of Havering, 1500–1620*. Cambridge, Eng.: Cambridge University Press, 1991.

Merriman, John M. *The Margins of City Life: Explorations on the French Urban Frontier, 1815–1851*. Oxford: Oxford University Press, 1991.

Milton, Richard. *Londoners their Entertainment in the Country*. London, 1604.

Mui, Hoh-cheung, and Lorna H. Mui. *Shops and Shopkeeping in Eighteenth-Century England*. Kingston, Ont.: McGill-Queen's University Press, 1989.

Mullaney, Steven. *The Place of the Stage: License, Play, and Power in Renaissance England*. Chicago: University of Chicago Press, 1988.

Mullins, E. L. C. "The Effects of the Marian and Elizabethan Religious Settlements upon the Clergy of London, 1553–1564." M.A. diss., University of London, 1948.

N., E. *London's plague-sore discovered*. London, 1665.

———. *London's sins reproved*. London, 1665.

Nashe, Thomas. *Christs Teares over Jerusalem*. London, 1593.

Nightingale, Pamela. *A Medieval Mercantile Community: The Grocers' Company and the Politics and Trade of London 1000–1485*. New Haven: Yale University Press, 1995.

Northbrooke, John. *A Treatise against Dicing, Dancing, Plays, and Interludes*. London, 1853 [1577].

Nussdorfer, Laurie. *Civic Politics in the Rome of Urban VIII*. Princeton: Princeton University Press, 1992.

———. "Writing and the Power of Speech: Notaries and Artisans in Baroque Rome." In Barbara B. Diefendorf and Carla Hesse, eds., *Culture and Identity in Early Modern Europe (1500–1800): Essays in Honor of Natalie Zemon Davis*, pp. 103–18. Ann Arbor: University of Michigan Press, 1993.

Pearl, Valerie. *London and the Outbreak of the Puritan Revolution: City Government and National Politics, 1625–1643*. Oxford: Oxford University Press, 1961.

———. "Puritans and Poor Relief: The London Workhouse, 1649–1660." In

D. Pennington and K. Thomas, eds., *Puritans and Revolutionaries: Essays in Seventeenth-Century History Presented to Christopher Hill*, pp. 206–32. Oxford: Oxford University Press, 1978.

———. "Change and Stability in Seventeenth-Century London." *London Journal* 5 (1979): 3–34.

Perlman, Janice E. *The Myth of Marginality: Urban Poverty and Politics in Rio de Janeiro*. Berkeley: University of California Press, 1976.

Phythian-Adams, Charles. "Ceremony and the Citizen: The Communal Year at Coventry 1450–1550." In Peter Clark and Paul Slack, eds., *Crisis and Order in English Towns 1500–1700*, pp. 57–85. Toronto: University of Toronto Press, 1972.

Plummer, Alfred. *The London Weavers' Company 1600–1970*. London: Routledge and Kegan Paul, 1972.

Pollen, J. H. *The English Catholics in the Reign of Queen Elizabeth*. London: Longmans, Green, 1920.

Powell, W. R., ed. *Victoria County History of Essex*. Vol. 7. Oxford: Oxford University Press, 1978.

Power, M. J. "Shadwell: The Development of a London Suburban Community in the Seventeenth Century." *London Journal* 4 (1978): 29–46.

———. "John Stow and His London." *Journal of Historical Geography* 11 (1985): 1–20.

———. "The Social Topography of Restoration London." In A. L. Beier and Roger Finlay, eds., *London 1500–1700: The Making of the Metropolis*, pp. 199–223. London: Longman, 1986.

Prideaux, Walter Sherburne. *Memorials of the Goldsmiths' Company*. Vol. 1. London, 1896.

Pullan, Brian. "Support and Redeem: Charity and Poor Relief in Italian Cities from the Fourteenth to the Seventeenth Century." *Continuity and Change* 3 (1988): 177–208.

Rappaport, Steve. *Worlds within Worlds: Structures of Life in Sixteenth-Century London*. Cambridge, Eng.: Cambridge University Press, 1989.

Reddaway, T. F. *The Rebuilding of London after the Great Fire*. London: Jonathan Cape, 1940.

———. "The Livery Companies of Tudor London." *History* 51 (1966): 287–99.

Roberts, Raymond S. "The London Apothecaries and Medical Practice in Tudor and Stuart England." Ph.D. diss., University of London, 1964.

Roper, Lyndal. *Oedipus and the Devil: Witchcraft, Sexuality and Religion in Early Modern Europe*. London: Routledge, 1994.

Rosser, Gervase. "London and Westminster: The Suburb in the Urban Economy in the later Middle Ages." In John A. F. Thomson, ed., *Towns and Townspeople in the Fifteenth Century*, pp. 45–61. Gloucester: A. Sutton, 1988.

———. *Medieval Westminster 1200–1540*. Oxford: Oxford University Press, 1989.

Rubin, Miri. *Charity and Community in Medieval Cambridge.* Cambridge, Eng.: Cambridge University Press, 1987.
Sacks, David Harris. "The Demise of the Martyrs: The Feasts of St Clement and St Katherine in Bristol, 1400–1600." *Social History* 11 (1986): 141–69.
———. *The Widening Gate: Bristol and the Atlantic Economy, 1450–1700.* Berkeley: University of California Press, 1991.
Safley, Thomas Max, and Leonard Rosenband, eds. *The Workplace before the Factory: Artisans and Proletarians, 1500–1800.* Ithaca, N.Y.: Cornell University Press, 1993.
Sandcroft, William. *Lex Ignia: or the School of Righteousness.* London, 1666.
Scarisbrick, J. J. *The Reformation and the English People.* Oxford: Blackwell, 1984.
Schwarz, L. D. *London in the Age of Industrialisation: Entrepreneurs, Labour Force and Living Conditions, 1700–1850.* Cambridge, Eng.: Cambridge University Press, 1992.
Scott, Tom. *Freiburg and the Breisgau: Town-Country Relations in the Age of Reformation and Peasants' War.* Oxford: Oxford University Press, 1986.
Scouloudi, Irene, ed. *Huguenots in Britain and Their French Background, 1550–1800.* Basingstoke, Hampshire, Eng.: Macmillan, 1987.
Scribner, R. W. "Civic Unity and the Reformation in Erfurt." *Past and Present* 66 (1975): 29–60.
Seaver, Paul S. *The Puritan Lectureships: The Politics of Religious Dissent 1560–1662.* Stanford, Calif.: Stanford University Press, 1970.
———. *Wallington's World: A Puritan Artisan in Seventeenth-Century London.* Stanford, Calif.: Stanford University Press, 1985.
———. "The Artisanal World." In David L. Smith, Richard Strier, and David Bevington, eds., *The Theatrical City: London's Culture, Theatre and Literature, 1576–1649,* pp. 87–100. Cambridge, Eng.: Cambridge University Press, 1995.
Sharpe, Kevin. *The Personal Rule of Charles I.* New Haven: Yale University Press, 1992.
Sharpe, Pamela. "Poor Children as Apprentices in Colyton, 1598–1830." *Continuity and Change* 6 (1991): 253–63.
Sharpe, Reginald R., ed. *Calendar of Wills Proved and Enrolled in the Court of Husting, London, A.D. 1258–A.D. 1688.* London, 1890.
Shoemaker, Robert. *Prosecution and Punishment: Petty Crime and the Law in London and Rural Middlesex, c. 1660–1725.* Cambridge, Eng.: Cambridge University Press, 1991.
———. "Reforming the City: The Reformation of Manners Campaign in London, 1690–1738." In Lee Davison, Tim Hitchcock, Tim Keirn, and Robert B. Shoemaker, eds., *Stilling the Grumbling Hive: The Response to Social and Economic Problems in England, 1689–1750,* pp. 99–120. New York: A. Sutton, 1992.
A Short-Title Catalogue of Books Printed in England, Scotland, and Ireland

and of English Books Printed Abroad. First compiled by A. W. Pollard and G. R. Redgrave. 2d ed., vol. 1. London: Bibliographic Society, 1986.

Slack, Paul. "Metropolitan Government in Crisis: The Response to Plague." In A. L. Beier and Roger Finlay, eds., *London 1500–1700: The Making of the Metropolis*, pp. 60–81. London: Longman, 1986.

Smith, A. Hassell. "Labourers in Late Sixteenth-Century England: A Case Study from North Norfolk [Part I]." *Continuity and Change* 4 (1989): 11–52.

———. "Labourers in Late Sixteenth-Century England: A Case Study from North Norfolk [Part II]." *Continuity and Change* 4 (1989): 367–94.

Smith, Steven R. "The London Apprentices as Seventeenth-Century Adolescents." *Past and Present* 61 (1973): 149–61.

Smuts, R. Malcolm. "The Court and Its Neighborhood: Royal Policy and Urban Growth in the Early Stuart West End." *Journal of British Studies* 30 (Apr. 1991): 117–49.

Snell, K. D. M. *Annals of the Labouring Poor: Social Change and Agrarian England, 1660–1900*. Cambridge, Eng.: Cambridge University Press, 1985.

Sommerville, C. John. *The Secularization of Early Modern England: From Religious Culture to Religious Faith*. Oxford: Oxford University Press, 1992.

Sortor, Marci. "Saint-Omer and Its Textile Trades in the Later Middle Ages: A Contribution to the Proto-Industrialization Debate." *American Historical Review* 98 (1993): 1475–99.

Squire, John. *A Thanksgiving for the Decreasing and Hope of Removing of the Plague*. London, 1637.

Stern, Walter M. *The Porters of London*. London: Longmans, 1960.

Stevens, Henry, ed. *The Dawn of British Trade to the East Indies as Recorded in the Court Minutes of the East India Company 1599–1603*. London, 1886.

Stone, Lawrence. "Social Mobility in England, 1500–1700." *Past and Present* 18 (1964): 41–80.

———. "The Residential Development of the West End of London in the Seventeenth Century." In Barbara C. Malament, ed., *After the Reformation: Essays in Honor of J. H. Hexter*, pp. 167–212. Manchester: Manchester University Press, 1980.

Stow, John. *A Survey of London*. 2 vols. Ed. C. L. Kingsford. Oxford: Oxford University Press, 1908 [1598].

Strauss, Gerald. *Nuremburg in the Sixteenth Century: City Politics and Life between Middle Ages and Modern Times*. Rev. ed. Bloomington: Indiana University Press, 1976.

Thompson, R. *Chronicle of London Bridge*. London, 1839.

Thrupp, Sylvia. *A Short History of the Worshipful Company of Bakers of London*. Croydon: Galleon, 1933.

Tittler, Robert. *Architecture and Power: The Town Hall and the English Urban Community c. 1500–1640*. Oxford: Oxford University Press, 1991.

Tönnies, Ferdinand. *Community & Society (Gemeinschaft und*

Gesellschaft). Trans. and ed. Charles P. Loomis. East Lansing: Michigan State University Press, 1957.
Unwin, George. *Industrial Organization in the Sixteenth and Seventeenth Centuries*. Oxford: Oxford University Press, 1904.
———. *The Gilds and Companies of London*. 4th ed. London: Frank Cass, 1963.
von Gierke, Otto. *Community in Historical Perspective: A Translation of Das deutsche Genossenschaftsrecht (The German Law of Fellowship)*. Trans. Mary Fischer, ed. Antony Black. Cambridge, Eng.: Cambridge University Press, 1991.
Walker, W. G. *A History of the Oundle Schools*. London: The Grocers' Company, 1956.
Watt, Tessa. *Cheap Print and Popular Piety, 1550–1640*. Cambridge, Eng.: Cambridge University Press, 1991.
Wells, Susan. "Jacobean City Comedy and the Ideology of the City." *ELH* 48 (1981): 37–60.
Whetstone, George. *A Mirour for Magistrates of Cities*. London, 1584.
White, Thomas. *A Sermon Preached at Paule's Crosse on Sunday the Thirde of November 1577*. London, 1578.
Willen, Diane. "Women in the Public Sphere in Early Modern England: The Case of the Urban Working Poor." *Sixteenth Century Journal* 19 (1988): 559–75.
Woodward, Donald. *Men at Work: Labourers and Building Craftsmen in the Towns of Northern England, 1450–1750*. Cambridge, Eng.: Cambridge University Press, 1995.
Woodward, Josiah. *An Account of the Rise and Progress of the Religious Societies in the City of London, &c., and of the Endeavors for the Reformation of Manners which have been made therein*. 2d ed. London, 1698.
Wrightson, Keith. *English Society, 1580–1680*. London: Hutchinson, 1982.
Wrightson, Keith, and David Levine. *Poverty and Piety in an English Village: Terling, 1525–1700*. New York: Academic Press, 1979.
Wunderli, Richard. *London Church Courts and Society on the Eve of the Reformation*. Cambridge, Mass.: Medieval Academy of America, 1981.
———. "Evasion of the Office of Alderman in London, 1523–1672." *London Journal* 15 (1990): 3–18.
Zagorin, Perez. *Ways of Lying: Dissimulation, Persecution, and Conformity in Early Modern Europe*. Cambridge, Mass.: Harvard University Press, 1990.
Zimmerman, Susan, and Ronald F. E. Weissman, eds. *Urban Life in the Renaissance*. Newark: University of Delaware Press, 1989.

Index

In this index an "f" after a number indicates a separate reference on the next page, and an "ff" indicates separate references on the next two pages. A continuous discussion over two or more pages is indicated by a span of page numbers, e.g., "57–59." *Passim* is used for a cluster of references in close but not consecutive sequence.

Abell, William, 64
Achilles, 90
Act of Six Articles, 103f
Acton, Francis, 92f
Adye, Henry, 170n15
Agnew, Jean-Christophe, 2, 7, 28, 157n48
Aliens, *see* Strangers
Allstone, Constantine (and his wife), 69
Angellsey, William, 65
Anne, queen of James I, 92
Antwerp, 129
Apothecaries' Company, 84, 101, 117–20, 145, 166n38
Apprentices, 78ff. *See also* Weavers' Company
Archer, Ian, 3, 74, 152n47, 159n71
Ashton, Robert, 27
Augustine, 1, 90

Bacon, Benjamin, 85
Bakers' Company, 40f, 145, 162n53
Baliol College, Oxford, 89

Ballard, William, 168n72
Banks, Bartholomew, 68
Banks, William, 54
Bartholomew, Andreas, 129
Barton, Abell, 49
Bate, William, 56
Batherst, Timothy, 56
Bayning, Andrew, 89, 172n85
Bayning, Paul, 89, 172n85
Beadsmen, 104f, 113, 170n25
Beaver, sign of, 51
Becon, Thomas, 104–6 *passim*
Bedfordshire, 103
Beier, A. L., 7, 28, 154n6
Benson, Elizabeth, 82
Best, John, 155n15
Beyd, John, 91
Bignall, Robert, 54
Billesdon, John, 102f
Bills of Mortality, 11
Black Boy tavern, 96
Blacksmiths' Company, 34f, 86, 89, 92, 95, 158n59, 167n61
Blage, John, 104, 170n22

Blyth, Edward, 48, 160n11
Board of Trade, 24
Boleyn, Anne, 102
Bonham, a vintner, 85
Bonner, William, 79
Borne, Thomas, 160n16
Boulton, Jeremy, 154n6, 154n14
Bourne, Rubin, 90
Bourneford, Humphrey, 65f
Bowyer, Thomas, 111
Box, Anthony, a Grocers' Company liveryman, 85
Box, Anthony, a sanderbeater, 69
Bread, assize of, 40
Brenner, Robert, 120, 173n95
Brewers' Company, 32f, 42
Bridger, William, 112
Brigden, Susan, 8, 100f, 169nn9,11, 170n25
Bright, George, 63, 69, 164n135
Bristol, merchant of, 52
Brockbanke, William, 52
Brothels, 10
Browne, James, 59, 63
Browne, a Salters' Company almsperson, 69
Browning, John, 63
Bucer, Martin, 90
Buckley, Edward, 52
Building, attempts to limit, 17f, 24f
Bunbury, John, 87–90 passim, 168n73
Burfield, Rowland, 69
Burroughs, Charles, 88
Burton, Henry, 13, 152n30
Busby, Raphael, 84, 91
Bush, symbol of a vintner, 55
Butler, William, 103, 170n14

Caesar, Sir Julius, 18, 32
Callings, professional, 4, 47, 56, 60, 65, 71
Calvert, Sir George, 92f
Cambell, Sir Thomas, 174n8
Cambridge, 60, 89, 105, 156n28
Campion, Edmund, 105
Campion, William, 102f, 169n11
Canterbury, 139
Carpenters' Company, 36, 47ff, 51, 66f, 77–82, 158nn59,64, 160n25
Cartwright, Thomas, 170n31

Carwarthen, Michael, 49
Chambers, Humphrey, 109
Chancery, Court of, 9, 140
Chantries, 101–4, 113–15 passim
Chantries Act, 100
Charles I, 53, 78, 87f, 94, 106f, 118, 130–32 passim, 155n24; and the suburban economy, 20f, 37, 40, 140
Charles II, 78, 139, 155n24
Child, John, 88, 167n61
Child, Josiah, 24
Children, 61
Cholmeley, George, 96
Christie, Thomas, 119f
Church, Richard, 62
Ciprian, 90
City, see London, City of
Civil War, 21, 25, 109, 121f, 173nn93,95
Clapham, Francis, 70
Clapham, Henoch, 13, 151n28
Clark, George, 172n85
Clark, Hugh, 64
Clerke, James, 62
Cleyton, Raphael, 167n48
Clockmakers' Company, 42
Cloker, Henry, 114
Clothworkers' Company, 42, 59f, 64, 141
Cocks, Robert, 56
Coke, Dr. John, 103
Cole, James, 88
College of Physicians, 115f
Collinson, Patrick, 8
Common Pleas, Court of, 87
Community, 1–8 passim, 26, 115, 123, 126, 143f, 150n11, 172n58
Confucius, 1
Constantine, George, 35
Cooke, Thomas, 171n32
Cooke, widow, 81
Coopers' Company, 33
Copeland, William, 48, 160n15, 165n19
Coping, Robert, 68
Counley, William, 175n24
Coventry, Thomas, 167n57
Coverdale, Miles, 105f, 170n31
Coxed, Oliver, 66
Crime, 10, 19, 25, 27, 65

Index

Crown, the (royal government), 2, 9f, 16, 20f, 24f, 152n39; and livery companies, 39, 41, 50, 73f, 87, 94–97 *passim*, 118–22 *passim*, 129, 134f, 138
Curriers Company, 42
Curson, Walter, 67

Daniell, Hugh, 133
Dannize, Joyce, 53
Darnell, Richard, 69
Darnelly, Daniel, 118
Davies, Nicholas, 80
Davis, Natalie, 75
Davis, Philip, 79f
De Marie, John, 129
DeBoard, Henry, 138
Dekker, Thomas, 12, 15, 46f, 159n4
Deloney, Thomas, 159n4
Denison, Stephen, 47
Diggs, "Mr," 141
Disease, 2, 11–16, 21, 25
Dollimore, Jonathan, 150n6
Dorrington, John, 172n85
Dorset, Earl of, 40
Doughty, Will, 88
Drapers' Company, 59f, 86
Drayton, John, 103
Drunkenness, 63f, 79
Duffield, Rachel, 53
Dunn, Richard, 137
Dunton, John, 24
Dyers' Company, 38, 57

Eason, Michael, 53
East India Company, 59, 120f, 154n14
Easterly, Francis, 82
Eaton, Marjorie, 81
Edict of Nantes, 125, 130, 139
Edward VI, 103f, 112, 155n24
Edwards, William, 69
Elborough, Robert, 15f
Elizabeth I, 8, 15–18, 40, 105f, 110, 112, 116, 126, 155n24, 158n68, 168n88
Ely, Robert, 68
E.N., 14
Engine looms, 128f, 135–37
Essex, 38
Ewstaius, Peter, 129

Exchequer, Court of, 121
Eyre, Simon, 46, 159n4

Faulk, Henry, 30
Fell, Michael, 169n94
Feltmakers' Company, 33f
Fenton, James, 54
Fenton, Roger, 106, 171n33
Field, Andrew, 86
Fire (and Great Fire of London), 14–17 *passim*, 24f, 38, 44, 160n24
Firmin, Thomas, 24
Flanders, 127
Fleet Prison, 53
Fleetwood, William, 12
Fletcher, Richard, 174n23
Foreigners, 2, 45, 71, 150n5, 158n68; the Blacksmiths' Company, 34; the Brewers' Company, 33; the Carpenters' Company, 50; the Dyers' Company, 38, 57; foreign tradesmen's proposal, 18ff, 39–44 *passim*; weighhouse for foreigners' goods, *see* London, City of, Places
Forman, Robert, 102f, 169n9
Fortifications, 21–24
Foxe, John, 104
France, 125–29 *passim*, 135, 173n94
Freeman, William, 80
Freemen, 2, 28, 45f, 56–72, 129, 144f
Freestone, John, 52
Fuller, William, 156n31
Funerals, 111, 114, 171n50
Fynch, Herbert, 87

Gadbury, John, 14
Gale, a vintner, 85
Gardiner, Isack, 61
Garrett, Thomas, 103
Geneva, 127
Gent, a vintner, 85
Germany, 127, 138
Gidley, William, 169n94
Girdlers' Company, 175n33
Glaziers' Company, 158n59
Globe Theatre, 36, 157n48
Goldham, George, 51
Goldsmiths' Company, 42, 54f, 64, 85, 130
Goodyear, Victor, 65

Goosey, John, 69
Goring, Lord, 155n24
Gossen, Stephen, 12
Grafton, Richard, 104f, 170nn22,25
Grant, John, 53
Greene, John, 61
Greene, Lawrence, 82, 85, 106
Gregory, Joan, 55
Grocers' Company, 5, 24, 145f, 155n20, 167nn48,57, 172n85; administration, 83, 95; and apothecaries, 115–20; and City garbellor, 66; company clerks, 84–94 passim, 99, 168n72; company cook, 92f; cornkeepers of, 66; deceitful practices, 52–56 passim; employment of builders, 51; goods under company jurisdiction, 31, 101, 115–20; Grocers' Hall, 110–15 passim; and the metropolitan economy, 29ff; and Parliament, 95, 108f, 116–19, 122, 172n83; and poor relief, 67–70, 82; porters of, 58–64; religion, 99–115, passim, 169n9; St. Antonin, 101, 112–15 passim, 171n54; sanderhouse (and sanderbeaters), 64ff, 69; seniority, 83–86
Grove, John, 89f
Grymes, William, 68
Guilds, see Livery companies
Guy Fawkes Day, 63
Gwynn, Roger, 91, 118

Haberdashers' Company, 55, 82, 161n48
Hand, John, 48, 160n15
Handford, Sir Humphrey, 92
Handson, Robert, 167n64
Hansley, a grocer, 111f
Harper, Robert, 136
Harris, Francis, 88, 167n64
Harsenett, Samuel, 63
Hart, Sir John, 170n27
Harvey, Daniel, 172n85
Haselrig, Sir Arthur, 167n64
Havering, 157n54
Hearse cloth, 112, 115
Heath, Sir Robert, 88
Henry VI, 101
Henry VII, 36, 58

Henry VIII, 32, 104, 112, 115
Henshaw, Thomas, 167n64
Herrick, Sir William, 85
Hertfordshire, 157n54
Hetherington, John, 47
Heyward, William, 68
Higgins, Herbert, 60
High Commission, Court of, 47
Hinton, Philip, 88
Hobbe, Alice, 161n29
Hobbie, Robert, 64
Hodgson, Martin, 67
Holland, 128
Hoor, Owen, 80
Horses, 61
Howard, Jean, 8
Howell, Thomas, 107
Hughes, George, 65
Hughes, Katherine, 81
Hughes, Richard, 165n19
Huguenots, 2, 125f, 130
Hulme, Peter, 114
Hus, Jan, 102

Ibbett, William, 68
Identity, construction of, 3f, 6
Iffe, Henry, 49, 160n18
Inns of Court and Chancery, 9, 12
Interregnum, 35, 114, 122, 134, 173n95
Ironmongers' Company, 157n46

Jackman, Alderman Edward, 105, 114
James I, 18ff, 31–34 passim, 42, 77, 92f, 101, 117f, 127, 130, 155n24
Jean, James, 61
Jelly, James, 54
Jennings, "Parson," 104
Jennings, Robert, 62
Jerram, John, 47, 160n10
Jerusalem, 14, 152n32
Jesuits, 105
Jesus, 102
Jewel, Bishop John, 112
Johnson, Edward, 158n66
Johnson, Robert, 54
Joiners' Company, 89, 94, 158nn59,64
Jonson, Ben, 7
Jordan, W. K., 151n18, 165n26
Journeymen, 57

Kellett, J. R., 27, 153n2
Kent, 38, 157n54
Kent, William, 63
Kiesett, Godfrey, 176n54
King, Flory, 59f
King, Henry, 47
King, John, Bishop of London, 10
King, Raphael, 96
Kirwin, William, 17f
Knight, Mary, 161n29

Lake, William, 86
Lambert, John, 104
Lambert, Nicholas, 103, 169n11
Langham, John, 85
Laxton, Sir William, 104, 111–14 passim, 170n25, 172n59
Lechford, a minister, 171n35
Lecompt, Lewes, 138
Lee, Leonard, 24
Leicester, Earl of, 87
LeMoyne, Peter, 138
Levant Company, 120–122 passim, 172n85
Lewars, John, 129
Leyfield, Richard, 106
Liberties, *see* London, suburbs and liberties of
Liège, 129
Lindley, Keith, 11
Livery companies, 2, 6, 28, 83–98, 150n10. *See also individual company listings*
Lome, Geoffrey, 170n22
London, bishop of, 102, 108
London, City of, 8–11, 24, 144, 149n3; Bartholomew Fair, 31; chamberlain, 80, 130–32 passim, 165n19; custom of, 45, 48, 51f, 128, 159n1, 160n14; garbellors, 52, 66; recorders, 12, 24, 78; sheriffs, 85, 122
—Court of Aldermen (and its members), 9, 32–40 passim, 50, 93, 154n10, 158nn60,64, 167n49, 168n90, 176n60; and the Apothecaries' Company, 84, 166n38; and the Grocers' Company, 52f, 105–14 passim; and porters, 59f; and the Saddlers' Company, 84, 166n39; and shop signs, 51f, 161n33; and suburban reform, 15–20, 24f; and the Tylers and Bricklayers' Company, 97; and unemployed workers, 160nn21,23; and the Vintners' Company, 55; and the Weavers' Company, 76, 132, 141, 174nn5,21,23, 175nn30,31
—Court of Common Council (and its members), 9, 18ff, 31, 40, 161n36
—Lords mayor, 27–40 passim, 46, 149n3, 158n60, 168n90; and the Carpenters' Company, 48; and the Grocers' Company, 52f, 94, 105, 111, 117; jurisdiction of, 9, 39, 42, 45; and porters, 58–60 passim; and the Saddlers' Company, 84, 166n39; and shop signs, 51f; and suburban reform, 12, 15–18, 24; and the Tylers and Bricklayers' Company, 97; and the Vintners' Company, 55; and the Weavers' Company, 76, 97, 127–32 passim, 137, 141, 174nn7,8,21, 175nn24,30,31
—Parishes: All Hallows Honey Lane, 101ff, 106, 171n32; St. Giles Cripplegate, 13; St. Katherine Coleman Street, 81; St. Peter Cornhill, 61; St. Stephen Walbrook, 101, 104–13 passim, 171n33; St. Swithen, 67
—Places: Billingsgate, 49; Bishopsgate, 31, 35; Boroughside, 154n6, 154n14; Bridewell, 37, 80, 85, 157n54; Bridewell Hospital, 161n36; Bridge Ward Without, 9; Chancery Lane, 36, 49; Cheapside, 50, 160n23; Christ Church, 49, 160n23; Christ's Hospital, 11, 51, 160n21; Cornhill, 58, 96; Duck Lane, 48; Dutch Church, 130, 175n40; Emperor's Head Lane, 61; Fleet Street, 9, 29, 154n13; French Church, 126, 130, 175n40; Golden Lane, 36; Guildhall, 55; Holborn Bridge, 31, 36; Little Britain, 31; London Bridge, 9, 14; Ludgate, 29, 154n13; Moorgate, 9; Old Bailey, 31; Petticoat Lane, 36, 133; Royal Exchange, 10; St. Bartholomew's Hospital, 161n36; St. Nicholas

Shambles, 48; St. Paul's Cathedral, 10; Shoe Lane, 31; Smithfield, 49; Smithfield Bars, 31; Soper Lane, 160n21; Southwark, 9, 29, 33–37 *passim*, 135–37 *passim*, 152n47, 156nn27,35; Temple Bar, 9, 31, 62; weighhouse for foreigners' goods, 58–62 *passim*, 102f
London, Diocese of, 10
London, livery companies of, *see* Livery companies
London, population of, 2, 17–21
London, suburbs and liberties of, 144; defined, 9f, 149n3; ecclesiastical authorities in, 10; legal authorities in, 9–11; and livery companies, 2ff, 20f, 27–44; New Corporation of the Suburbs, 20f, 25, 37ff, 44, 158nn60,61, 159n72; relative licentiousness of, 2ff, 7–26, 144
—Parishes: St. Andrew Holborn, 151n17; St. Giles Cripplegate, 13, 151n17; St. Giles in the Field, 34; St. James Clerkenwell, 151n17; St. Leonard Shoreditch, 13, 151n17; St. Margaret Westminster, 151n17
—Places: the Artillery Ground, 35; the Bankside, 35, 46, 157n52; Barking, 151n17; Barnesby Street, 34; Bermondsey, 11, 151n17; Blackfriars, 9, 36, 149n3, 156n27; Blue Anchor Alley, 35; Castle Yard, 49; Chancery Lane, 49; Charing Cross, 31, 35, 156n27; Clerkenwell, 11, 33, 151n17, 157n46; the Clink Liberty, 10, 32, 157n52; Covent Garden, 156n27; Cow Lane, 35, 49; Deptford, 154n14; Drury Lane, 34; East Smithfield, 34; Finsbury, 9; the Globe Theatre, 36; Gray's Inn Lane, 32, 49; Hackney, 35; Hampstead, 34; Havering, 37; Holborn, 31–34, 156n27, 157n46; Holywell Priory, 9; Holywell Street, 35, 49; Horsleydown, 54; Hosier Lane, 49; Islington, 33, 36, 41; Kentish Town, 37; Lambeth, 32–34 *passim*, 151n17; Lambeth Marsh, 31; Lewisham, 37; Lymehouse, 154n14; the Minories, 24, 32, 36, 136, 149n3; Moorfields, 9; Newington, 32; Paris Garden, 9, 32, 149n3; Ratcliffe, 154n14; Ratcliffe Highway, 31; St. Martin le Grand, 10, 24, 32; the Savoy, 32; Shadwell, 33, 154n6, 157n46; Shoreditch, 33–36 *passim*, 156n31; Spitalfields, 33, 35f, 137, 156n31; Staple's Inn, 36; Stepney, 35; the Strand, 32, 36; Uxbridge, 151n17; Wapping, 34f, 154n14, 156n27; Wentworth Street, 34; Westminster, 9, 24f, 29–39 *passim*, 43, 62, 151n17, 154n13, 156nn27,31; Whitechapel, 32f, 35f, 156n31, 157n46; Whitecross Street, 34; Whitefriars, 9, 32
Lovell, Isabell, 170n14
Lovell, Sir Thomas, 170n14
Luther, Martin, 102

Macfarlane, Stephen, 24
Machyn, Henry, 111
Malin, John, 63
Manley, Lawrence, 8
Manwaring, Randall, 122
Marchant, Robert, 97
Marshall, a bricklayer, 157n52
Martin, Leonard, 156n31
Mary I, 104, 116
Mary II, 24, 127
Masons' Company, 48, 158n59
Mayo, Slackey, 156n31
Melancthon, Philipp, 90
Merchant Adventurers, 120–22 *passim*
Middlesex, 9, 13, 35, 38, 85, 136, 141, 149n3; Justices of the Peace of, 18, 24, 32, 40
Middlesex, Earl of, 155n24
Middleton, Sir Thomas, 93f, 167nn43,64
Miller, Alice, 81f
Milton, Richard, 12f, 15
Molines, a minister, 171n35
Moore, Thomas, 34
Morer, Robert, 117f
Moses, 128
Mullaney, Steven, 2, 7f
Murrell, Edward, 102, 111, 169n11
Mynshall, John, 31

Index

Nashe, Thomas, 14
Naylor, William, 166n39
Nebuchadnezzar, 15
'Newcastle, Duke of, 141
Newcastle, vintner of, 54
Newton, Francis, 53
Nichols, William, 79f
Norringrost, William, 92f
Norrington, Vincent, 85
Northamptonshire, 89
Northbrooke, John, 11
Northey, Thomas, 122–24 *passim*, 173n94
Nower, Burrell, 70

Oakley, John, 76
Obits, 101–4 *passim*, 113ff
Occupational groups: apothecaries, 101, 115–20, 172n83; bakers, 40f; barber-surgeons, 116; brewers, 32f; brick and tile makers, 37, 43; bricklayers, 19, 157n52; carpenters, 19, 152n31, 157n48, 160nn21,23; clerks, 74, 83, 86; confectioners, 172n83; coopers, 156n32; feltmakers, 43, 156n33; grocers, 55; haberdashers, 161n33; joiners, 50; laborers, 57, 160n21; leatherdressers, 34; notaries, 74f; porters, 57f, 64, 162n65; salters, 61; sawyers, 160nn21,23; scriveners, 74ff, 81, 83. *See also individual livery company listings*; Society of Tacklehouse and Ticket Porters
Ormeshaw, William, 113
Osborne, Sir Edward, 12
Oundle, Northamptonshire, 69, 94, 104
Owen, Edward, 66
Owen, Israel, 166n37
Oxford, 152n31

Painter-Stainers' Company, 158nn59,66
Palmer, John, 52, 161n37
Parliament, 21, 24, 38, 42f, 48, 87, 120–22, 155n18, 173n93. *See also* Grocers' Company; Weavers' Company
Parr, Anthony, 159n4

Parslowe, Gyles, 172n85
Paul's Cross, 11, 13, 47
Paviors' Company, 158n59
Payne, Robert, 172n85
Pearl, Valerie, 2, 7, 27f, 150n5, 153n4, 162n65
Pell, Thomas, 132, 175nn30,31
Pennington, James, 59
Peshall, Edmund, 56
Peterborough, 69
Petit, John, 102, 169n11, 170n22
Pettit, Philip, 106
Pewterers' Company, 160n16
Phillips, Thomas, 60
Pilkington, Robert, 63
Pipes, Sir Richard, 12
Plasterers' Company, 158nn59,60
Plato, 1
Plumbers' Company, 88, 158n59
Plush, Roger, 130
Plymouth, 106
Poll Tax (1641), 32, 156n26
Pooley, Isabell, 67
Poverty (and poor relief), 2, 11, 19, 24, 57–72. *See also individual livery company listings*
Power, Michael, 154n6
Power, William, 170n31
Privy Council (and its members), 10, 16f, 37, 40, 87
Proby, Sir Peter, 92
Prynne, William, 152n30
Purgatory, 115
Puritanism, 105, 170n26
Pyndar, Ralph, 63
Pyndon, William, 82

Quick, William, 118
Quiney, Richard, 121, 172n85, 173n92

Rappaport, Steve, 2, 27, 73ff, 150n5, 154n5, 162n59, 165n22
Ratcliffe, Hugh, 51
Ratcliffe, John, 64
Rayners, John, 49f
Ravenhill, William, 24
Reddaway, T. F., 160n24
Redding, Jane, 82
Reformation, 8, 99–115 *passim*, 122

Renaissance drama, see Theater
Renshall, John, 175n30
Rest, John, 169n11
Restoration, 122, 134f
Rhenish wines, 55
Riots, 11
Robinson, Bernard, 105
Robinson, Francis, 64
Robson, William, 68
Rogers, Philip, 114
Rogers, Richard, 108
Romford, 157n54
Rose Theatre, 46
Rosser, Gervase, 154n5
Rothram, Richard, 91
Royal works, master of, 50, 160n25

Sabbath (and Sunday employments), 13ff, 49f, 160n21
Sacheveral, Henry, 54
Saddlers' Company, 34, 84, 166n39
Sadler, John, 121, 172n85, 173n92
St. Antonin, see Grocers' Company
St. Mary, 102
St. Paul's Cathedral, 10, 15, 102
Salters' Company, 51, 67–70, 88, 91f, 94f
Sandcroft, William, 15
Sanderhouse (and sanderbeaters), see Grocers' Company
Savage, Robert, 30
Saxby, Thomas, 107, 171n35
Scarlett, Richard, 66
Schwarz, L. D., 153n4
Sclater, Francis, 52
Scriveners' Company, 76, 165n5
Seaton, Samuel, 175n24
Seaver, Paul, 47
Serle, Richard, 65
Shanks, Thomas, 67
Sheriff, a minister, 105f, 170n31
Shewall, Case, 90
Ship Money, 122
Shippey, Thomas, 51
Shoemaker, Robert, 24
Skidmore, Steven, 11
Skinners' Company, 59–63 passim, 86f
Skott, Thomas, 61
Slickland, Jonas, 136

Smith, Henry, 165n26
Smith, Humphrey, 95, 119, 122
Smith, John, a haberdasher, 55
Smith, John, a porter, 58
Smithes, Alderman George, 85
Smuts, Malcolm, 18
Soame, Sir Stephen, 114
Soames, Thomas, 122
Societies for the reformation of manners, 24f
Society, definition of, 1, 3, 146
Society of Tacklehouse and Ticket Porters, 58, 154n9
Soda, Anthony, 84, 117f
Sodom, 11, 14
Sommerville, C. John, 100
Sone, Clement, 60
Southaik, George, 87, 91, 168n83
Spanish Company, 120, 172n85
Squire, John, 13
Stanley, Robert, 54
Star Chamber, court of, 53, 88
Statute of Artificers, 34, 43
Steele, Henry, 167n48
Stephenson, William, 58
Stevens, Thomas, 169n11
Stile, Nicholas, 85, 172n85
Stile, Oliver, 172n85
Stocks, used for punishing deceitful artisans, 55
Stow, John, 17, 152n44
Strangers, 2, 21, 34, 43, 45, 48, 56, 71, 144ff, 150n5. See also Huguenots; Weavers' Company
Strawley, a vintner, 64
Stretchly, Edward, 88
Strong, William, 107f
Stroud, Mary, 51
Suburbs, see London, suburbs and liberties of
Surrey, 9, 32–38 passim, 107, 114, 149n3, 156n35, 165n26
Sutton, Daniel, 67
Sutton, Valerius, 54

Tamberlain, 12
Tanner, Timothy, 55
Taylor, Mary, 166n28
Tempest, John, 52
Tesmond, Michael, 166n39

Tetlar, John, 61
Thames River, 9, 29, 34, 50, 58–66 passim, 154n6
Theater, 2f, 7–16 passim, 21, 25f, 28, 70, 151n23, 152n39
Thomas, Michael, 107f
Thornhill, Richard, 99, 122
Three Herrings, sign of, 52
Titus, 15
Tomlinson, Samuel, 109
Tönnies, Ferdinand, 1, 3
Trade guilds, see Livery companies
Tripp, Henry, 106
Troughton, Andrew, 83
Troughton, Anne, 66, 69
Troughton, Miles, 66
Trowle, John, 129
Truman, Joseph, 156n31
Turville, Edmund, 109
Tuttesham, Henry, 63
Tylers and Bricklayers' Company, 36ff, 48f, 97, 157n55, 158nn56,59,60, 160n25

Underwood, William, 108, 173n93
Unwin, George, 73f

Vintners' Company, 11, 31f, 42, 50–69 passim, 82–90 passim, 94–96, 155n24, 166n28
Virgin Mary, 101

Wallington, Nehemiah, 14, 47, 152n33
Wallis, John, 49
Wardell, John, 173n94
Waring, Richard, 122, 173n95
Warner, John, 121f, 172n85, 173n92
Warner, Samuel, 108f, 121f, 172n85, 173nn92,93
Warren, John, 59
Warren, Nicholas, 117
Warren, Thomas, 108f
Wassall, Luke, 78
Watson, a minister, 109
Waxchandlers' Company, 31, 155n20, 174n21

Weavers' Company, 5, 57f; 78, 88–91 passim, 145; apprentices, 76, 175nn27,33, 176n68; assistants, 125–42, 176n68; bailiffs, 131–40 passim; beadles, 132, 134, 138; foreigners, 174n8; journeymen, 140; liverymen, 96, 131–35 passim, 139–43; and the metropolitan economy, 35f, 157n45; and Parliament, 35, 133–39 passim; strangers, 125–43, 174n5, 175nn33,40; wardens, 131, 137, 140; Weavers' Hall, 35, 127, 135, 174n21; women, 128, 133, 136, 176n68; yeomen, 127–36 passim, 142, 174nn5,21, 175n24
Webb, William, 55, 161n48
Wells, Susan, 7
West, Francis the elder and Francis the younger, 84
Whetstone, George, 12
White, Thomas, 11
Whitehorn, John, 41
Whitely, Thomas, 118
Whitgift, John, Archbishop of Canterbury, 16, 105
Widows, 81f, 90, 96, 112, 136, 161n29, 164n120, 166n28; and livery company staffs, 51, 61, 64ff, 69
Wilkinson, a lecturer, 92
Wills, 75f, 102f, 111, 113
Wilson, Aaron, 106
Winchester, Diocese of, 10
Wingfield, Robert, 78
Woodcock, Andrew, 111
Woodward, John, 85
Woodward, Josiah, 25
Wunderli, Richard, 10
Wycliffe, John, 102

Xenophobia, 126f

Yeomen, 50, 126, 137, 145
York, 156n28
York, Duke of, 155n24
Young, William, 64f

Zwingli, Huldrych, 102

Library of Congress Cataloging-in-Publication Data
Ward, Joseph P.
　Metropolitan communities: trade guilds, identity,
and change in early modern London / Joseph P. Ward
　　p.　cm.
　Includes bibliographical references and index.
　ISBN 0-8047-2917-4 (cloth).
　1. Guilds—England—London Metropolitan Area—
History.　2. Urbanization—England—London Met-
ropolitan Area—History.　3. London Metropolitan
Area (England)—Social conditions.　4. London Met-
ropolitan Area (England)—Population.　5. London
Metropolitan Area (England)—Emigration and immi-
gration.　I. Title.
　HD6462.L72W37　1997
　338.6'32'09421—dc21　　　　　　　　　　96-52156
　　　　　　　　　　　　　　　　　　　　　　　　CIP

∞　This book is printed on acid-free, recycled paper.

Original printing 1997
Last figure below indicates year of this printing:
06　05　04　03　02　01　00　99　98　97